Travelling Man

TRAVELLING MAN

ON THE ROAD WITH THE SEARCHERS

Frank Allen

Aureus

First Published 1999

Cover photograph and inside front sleeve © 1999 Ron Long, Studio 60's, Tel/Fax: (01895) 230780; inside back sleeve from author's collection.

Printed in Great Britain by Creative Print and Design (Wales).

A catalogue record for this book is available from the British Library.

Aureus Publishing 24 Mafeking Road Cardiff CF23 5DQ.

ISBN 1 899750 29 0

Contents

The Searchers

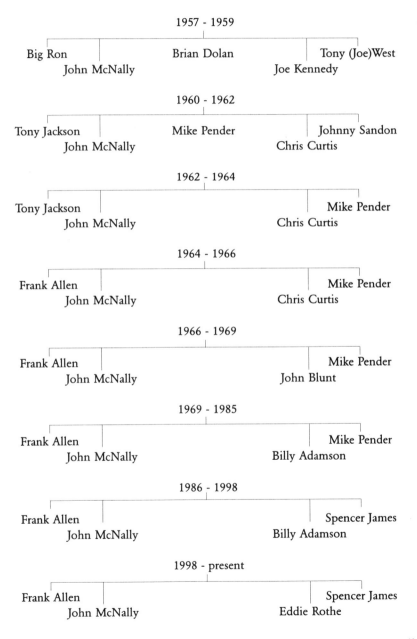

1957 - 1959

Big Ron	Brian Dolan	Tony (Joe)West
John McNally		Joe Kennedy

1960 - 1962

Tony Jackson	Mike Pender	Johnny Sandon
John McNally		Chris Curtis

1962 - 1964

Tony Jackson		Mike Pender
John McNally		Chris Curtis

1964 - 1966

Frank Allen		Mike Pender
John McNally		Chris Curtis

1966 - 1969

Frank Allen		Mike Pender
John McNally		John Blunt

1969 - 1985

Frank Allen		Mike Pender
John McNally		Billy Adamson

1986 - 1998

Frank Allen		Spencer James
John McNally		Billy Adamson

1998 - present

Frank Allen		Spencer James
John McNally		Eddie Rothe

The Searchers : Hits

Sweets For My Sweet
Sugar & Spice
Sweet Nuthins
Needles & Pins
Don't Throw Your Love Away
Love Potion Number Nine (US Single)
Someday We're Gonna Love Again
When You Walk In The Room
What Have They Done To The Rain?
Goodbye My Love
He's Got No Love
When I Get Home
Take Me For What I'm Worth
Take It Or Leave It
Have You Ever Loved Somebody

The Searchers : A Chronology

1963
John McNally (gtr/voc) - Mike Pender (gtr/voc)
Chris Curtis (drs/voc) - Tony Jackson (bass/voc)

1964
(August)
John McNally - Mike Pender - Chris Curtis - Frank Allen (bass/voc)

1966
(March)
John McNally - Mike Pender - Frank Allen - John Blunt (drs)

1969
(December)
John McNally - Mike Pender - Frank Allen - Billy Adamson (drs)

1986
(January)
John McNally - Frank Allen - Billy Adamson - Spencer James (gtr/voc)

1998
(November)
John McNally - Frank Allen - Spencer James - Eddie Rothe

Acknowledgements

In case I am never asked to write another book I had better take care of everyone.

For :
Susie Mathis and Lee Lowsley who were always there for me.
John McNally, my partner in musical crime.
Mary McNally who talked me through some difficult moments.
Matt Palmer who gave me a lot of fun and a lot of aggravation but always believed in my writing.
Alan and Kelly Field for their encouragement and who saw more in my work than I did myself.
Val Saddington for her expert tuition in computers.
Tim Viney & Sue West and all the members of the Searchers Appreciation Society who are not only fans but friends as well.
Wendy Burton for her help in the preparation.
David Wigg, Perry Press, Kenny Bell, Ed Bicknell & Jenny, Gary Goodchild, Des & Pat McMann, Mike & Sue Fraser, Andy & Maureen Cairns, my Godchild Phillippa Cairns and her sister Emily, Bruce Welch & Magda, Norman Newell, Lionel & Sue Blair, Mick Kirby, Stan & Sheila Hind, Sonia Beldom, Bobby Crush, Red Bond, Tom & Barbara Crossen, not forgetting Ray, Kristian and Mat, Kim Wassell, Paul Macbeth, Henry Marsh, Lisa & Steve Voice, Doug & Pat Humm, Helen Worth. All friends and important people in my life.

Foreword by Sir Cliff Richard OBE

I've been on the road. I've toured in a Transit van. The Shadows and I did concerts up and down the country, travelling in an sometimes having to spend the night at 'The Bedford'. Our Bedford coach was everything for us and, although it's tempting to say, 'Those were the days', we eventually graduated to trains and planes, and I'd be the first to admit there is nothing quite like being mollycoddled by British Airways in the first-class section of a Jumbo!

Travelling is a part of life now for almost all of us, but no-one does it more ferociously or more often than the pop musician. Yes, we see the world (from hotel windows); yes, we eat good food (always too late or too fast) - but, in spite of the drawbacks, few of us would exchange our lifestyles.

Being on the road has its moments of glory and its fair share of disappointments, and, in his years of touring with The Searchers, Frank Allen has had a taste of them all. I know you'll enjoy reading his version of what it's like to be a 'travelling man'.

Sir Cliff Richard OBE

Foreword by Mark Knopfler

The first time I went into a mental hospital was because of The Searchers. They were there to play a daytime charity show. The place was Leeds, the year 1969 or '70 and I was a local cub reporter. It was probably not the only time Frank Allen has played to an uncomprehending audience although I'm certain many of the patients, nursing staff and doctors felt the same thrill I always get when I hear Searchers songs.

Five or six years before then I can remember sitting with my first guitar trying to work out what happened during and after the middle-eight to 'Needles and Pins' and wishing I was in a beat group and a million miles from school.

Armed with a few hard-won chords and a fierce determination Frank made his escape from a colourless 50's childhood to prove that there can be life after Hayes, Middlesex. If you want to play music for a living you first need a sense of humour and then a lot of willpower. I think you'll realise this when you read Frank Allen's story, which is about a boy who saw a way out, took it, and has hung onto it ever since.

Mark Knopfler

Introduction

In June 1989 Cliff Richard gave me two of the best nights of my life. But before you go dashing off to the Sunday tabloids in an attempt to sully the name of the *stainless one* I have to tell you that the place was Wembley, the home of English football, and there were approximately 150,000 witnesses.

To celebrate a remarkable thirty success-crammed years in showbusiness Cliff, almost a mere mortal in those pre-knighthood days, had gambled slices of both his considerable fortune and even more considerable reputation by taking on the vast 75,000 capacity venue and we were guesting along with Gerry and The Pacemakers, The Shadows, The Kalin Twins, The Dallas Boys, Cathy McGowan, The Vernons Girls and Aswad. Cliff had always been one of the top dogs in pop with a pedigree that guaranteed sold out shows everywhere. But with one shrewd move he had catapulted himself into the midst of that elite band who could call themselves stadium rock acts.

The line-up of artistes appeared to be pretty sympathetically linked although I did consider the reggae outfit Aswad a bit of an odd choice. A bit like livening up a Pavarotti concert with half an hour of Rolf Harris, but ours was not to reason why. The first day had sold with an almost indecent haste and an option was taken up for a follow up show. The sun shone throughout the two days with an intensity and a brilliance that was rare for Britain, even in summer, but I did not keel over with shock. If Cliff didn't have influence then who did? Friends in high places indeed.

I stood and watched him on the first night as a hydraulic platform lifted him high above the crowd, looking like a junior messiah and bathed in spotlights which glinted on the spangles of his pure white suit. Surely the only rock star who could wear that colour with any degree of honesty. If he was indeed a rock and roll messiah then he was preaching to the converted, committed Clifftians every one.

Actually, I do believe there was a lady somewhere in the middle who came only to hear The Searchers and did not give two hoots about Cliff Richard. But she was quickly apprehended by men in white coats who speedily whisked her back to her maximum security twilight home with a minimum of fuss, where she will no doubt live out the rest of her days crafting pretty little macramé table mats while whistling the guitar riff to *Sugar And Spice*. To be honest, that little piece of self-deprecation was both unnecessary and untrue. A Cliff audience naturally gravitates towards the same heritage of melody and harmony that has always under-lined a style that is the hallmark of our own work. They took us to their hearts and made us feel good. The sound of nearly 80,000 people singing *When You Walk In The Room* is a humbling experience.

As I watched Cliff hold sway over that vast arena I remembered the pink-jacketed youth whose autograph I had queued up for at the stage door of the Chiswick Empire in the late fifties. Thirty years on he was looking, if anything, slimmer of hip and still young enough to be refused a drink at the backstage bar. It was all so unfair. At home I kept a por-trait in my attic which was growing younger every day.

His voice had altered through the years from an angry youthful growl to a silky smooth purity of tone that served the older performer well, and with a pitch that was as true as the gospels whose creed he adhered to. It occurred to me that if they were to release a live recording of this event there would be no need for any overdubs. Re-recording Cliff's voice would be like putting tits on a bull. An interesting cosmetics exer-cise but one which would serve no useful purpose whatsoever.

During our postage stamp of a slot in the proceedings we pounded our way through *Needles And Pins* and *When You Walk In The Room* look-ing immaculate in our dark suits and high buttoned collarless shirts. I was, however, hiding a secret. I might have looked like Doctor Kildare from where the crowd stood but from the rear I looked more like Worzel Gummidge. My jacket had recently undergone surgery and the scars were still showing.

A couple of nights before we had performed at the Rolls Royce Club at the factory in Crewe and somewhere between the end of our performance and the get-out by the roadies my suit had mysteriously acquired several haphazard slashes down the back. My jacket left the home of the elegant Rolls Royce motor car looking like the sartorial equivalent of a Wartburg. There was no time to repair or replace and the only solution I could come up with was to stick the ragged seams together from the inside with gaffer tape, the adhesive bonding whose standard form of use is to stick down the microphone leads to the stage. It did not look good. If anyone wondered why I never turned my back towards them that day, the truth is out.

If an audience of this magnitude was our shining hour I had also seen the other side of the coin. On the whole a bad night is a rare occurrence for us but I can still remember times when the approval was not so great. I have vivid memories of our performance at a social club in Middlesborough at the outset of the eighties. Our support act, a very, very blue comedian called Chubby Brown had appealed to their sense of the more than risqué and won tumultuous applause. His career and financial fortunes were soon to rocket into the stratosphere as the purveyor of material that pushed at the existing boundaries of decency before breaking through them with all the power of a stampeding herd of elephants. Chubby, as his name suggests, rather resembled a stampeding elephant himself. I think that maybe he had meant to go on the Rosemary Conley diet and had ended up on the Rosemary Clooney diet instead.

Our own show, as headliners, was very well received I recall, although maintaining the attention of the soup in a basket crowd was never easy at the best of times. Far too often they had come out simply for a chat and a pint with their mates and we were hardly more than an unwelcome interruption. I had a couple of friends tagging along with me that night and after the show one of them was mistaken by one of the audience for our lead singer.

'That was you up there on stage, wasn't it?' the guy asked. My friend decided to play along.

'Yes.' He answered and stood waiting for the inevitable compliment.

'Well, you were shite.' Gosh. What endearing cheeky chappies they are up there. They do not mince words in the north-east. *Why waste time wounding when you can maim?* is their motto. My chum was stuck for a suitable return. The slice of rapier wit that would crush this belligerent fellow refused to find its way onto his tongue.

'You were shite as well then.' It takes a rare talent to come up with a brilliant reply like that one, you have to agree. It was the verbal equivalent of a five year old sticking his tongue out.

'Aye, maybe. But at least I don't parade my shite,' came the final devastating put-down.

He had to admit he had a point, although the audience reaction had not been quite as negative as his opinion would indicate. In football terms it had been a nil-nil draw. But I was glad to have avoided the confrontation suffered on my behalf by my friend.

Life in a group, on the whole, has been a wonderful casserole of experiences, a variety of flavours and tastes to satisfy my hunger for experience. But I think I might be leading you slightly astray.

Both of the occasions I have chosen to include in this introduction took place on home soil and yet this is a book about travel, more often than not beyond the confines of Great Britain's shores. And lest I should further mislead you, neither is it a biography in any real sense, although certainly I have given thumbnail sketches of our origins and early days when good luck and circumstance paved the way for a modest degree of fame and an even more modest degree of fortune.

I have only managed to include a limited selection of our journeys around the globe and you won't find it running in any strict chronological order either. It jumps about like a kangaroo on a bed of coals. But that's the way my mind works now. I have to take my memory as I find it. Along the way I have slipped into tales of our trials and tribulations through the changes and break-ups without necessarily dwelling on the minutiae of details or the ferocity of the conflicts.

This book is meant to be a humorous, sometimes wry and certainly irreverent, but random look at a life of travel through the eyes of a sixties pop musician. If, having digested my explanation, you are still intrigued enough to continue through the pages of this my first, and possibly last, book, I hope you enjoy the fruits of my labours. If, on the other hand you now realise that it is not quite the work you were expecting, then why not buy it anyway and make an old musician happy.

1

Travelling Man

The terrain of The Falkland Islands is as barren and unwelcoming as a spinster's thighs. Chill winds from the Atlantic cut the air like an assassin's knife and the rugged landscape presents its most defiant countenance, as if to challenge the unwary newcomer to a gruelling and mind numbing initiative test before he is deemed hardy, or foolish enough to remain here on God's special place. God himself, quite sensibly, lives somewhere else. Barbados, I believe. Let's face it, you don't get to be God by being a complete dingbat.

Inside the somewhat warmer confines of a rabbit warren of tin huts that constitutes Mount Pleasant Airbase's operational and living quarters social activities are closing down for the night. The gymnasium has been cleared of its temporary seating and the makeshift stage dismembered by a bunch of rough tough 'volunteers' who never actually volunteered. The walls are still reverberating to the lingering strains of amplified guitars and drums that just a few hours earlier had fought, and lost, the battle for any reasonable quality of sound in a place to which any association with the words 'high' and 'fidelity' are pure fantasy.

But, cacophony or not, the evening had been a huge success and we were as happy as pigs in chiffon. A thousand khaki-clad kids of tender years to whom we were not exactly the first word in *cool* had roared their approval. No, strike that. This was not approval. This was ecstasy, in the most innocent sense of course, pill free and pure (I guess, though I may well be wrong about that). Just fresh from having their mothers wipe their arses and scrape away their vomit they were now young bucks straining at the leash, pulsating with adrenaline and testosterone, and with brand new musical gods of their own like James and M People to worship. Here they were, thousands of miles from home on a piece of land that had less appeal for them than the council tip back home and recreation facilities were, shall we say, restricted.

The impending show, hand chosen by men in gold braid twice their age and raised on the musical values of Val Doonican and The Carpenters, had not sent them into paroxysms of unrestrained delight. Who wants yesterday's heroes? The first words that sprang to mind when the impending arrival of those pop dinosaurs The Searchers was hurled at them with all the appeal of an exocet missile and without so much of a 'by your leave, squaddie' were 'farts' and old', not necessarily in that order. They had my sympathy.

We had dined well in the officers mess on a fine display of canapés and casseroles and the ubiquitous curry. No mess buffet is complete without a curry. It is, after all, the national British dish. My heart however was in the mess of the junior ranks where civility and ceremony were tossed aside and where they were no doubt by this time revelling in the joyfully abandoned throes of a good piss-up. The thought was very appealing but it was forbidden territory. The lads were considered by the hierarchy to be too rough for the namby pamby visiting luvvies.

Still, the wine here was acceptable and the conversation polite, if predictable. They were patronisingly civil to us and we replied in kind, strangers to each other's world and customs, feigning interest in matters that for the most part held little interest to most of us. But alcohol quickly loosens both the tongue and the inhibitions and the repartee could have been on the merits of pearl diving in Streatham and it would not have mattered a jot. We were in an understatedly drunken good humour.

The girl dancers, an essential item in a C.S.E touring show, had sloped off early for their beauty sleep, and not a moment too soon I thought. Casting any signs of misogyny aside, I have to admit that the girls have a tough time on these trips fending off the mostly unwanted attentions of a totty-starved contingent of rampant men whose requirement of a partner for the night is that it should be breathing and preferably, although not exclusively, female. We four musicians (Now that's a laugh. Tantamount to fraud, my mate reckons) were left with our two roadies and one of the supporting acts, a highly talented and off-the-wall ventriloquist by the name of Jimmy Tamley, a true party animal of thirty-something going on sixteen.

With a bunch of islands to be defended, planes to be flown and guns to be fired, the shutters were eventually pulled down on the bar. We realised we were going to get no more free ale and staggered off down the maze of corridors to where our luxury-denied accommodation awaited the returned of the conquering heroes. Thankfully a tiny bit of radar in the brain had remained active and we staggered off in more or less the right direction along the complicated trail of passages which took us past the cabins of the flight crews. We tried to be quiet. These lads need their rest. But we giggled like schoolgirls and, spotting the tiny self-made paper arrows on the doors which indicated 'Yes-I do want my room cleaning' or 'No-I don't want my room cleaning,' set about switching the direction of the pointers.

'My God,' said Tamley, 'You Searchers, you live life on the edge, don't you.' It was hysterical when you thought about it. Throughout pop history fables had been passed down about Led Zeppelin throwing television sets out of hotel windows. Wild man of pop Keith Moon of The Who had scandalised society by driving a Lincoln continental into his swimming pool. Even the adored-by-your-granny Beatles had the street-cred to get themselves into grapples with the law about drugs. And what were we naughty Searchers doing? Playing havoc with the sanitary arrangements of the Royal Airforce. Sex, drugs and Rock and Roll this was not. This was life in the bus lane.

The bus had first set out on its chaotic, meandering journey somewhere in the winter of 1958 when I was taken by my mother and father to purchase my first guitar from Youngs music shop in Lampton Road, Hounslow. It hung in the window and was priced at six pounds and ninepence. I stared at it in the moments before we entered the shop. I scrutinised every inch of its frame. The six gleaming steel strings running tautly down its neck. The lusciously curved body sprayed dark brown and stencilled in white on the lower bout with palm trees and the words *Palm Beach* beneath. I looked for what seemed a lifetime until I was convinced I had been right all along. It was a heap of dung.

But it was the only heap of dung I was going to get this Christmas. And it was the only heap of dung available at that price. I strummed the open strings. It made a horrible noise comparable to its price. Elsewhere in the establishment there were cool 'f' hole arch tops with sunburst shading and shiny white pick guards. Some even had cutaways that would enable me to make my horrible noises right up the top as well as down near the headstock.

3

Noises so high pitched that only wild animals could hear them clearly enough to object. There were no electric models here but I knew they existed somewhere in the world. Sadly, not in my world.

We trooped in and the appropriate amount was passed across the counter in exchange for that pathetic little apology for a flat top guitar. A further twelve shillings and sixpence had to be found for a brown canvas carrying case which twisted into a strange shape when being carried, making the instrument look as though it had come apart somewhere in the mid section. Even at that young age, just approaching fifteen, I knew this had no connection with style. Style was a guitar in a hard case not a paltry brown bag. Style had *Gibson* and *Epiphone* scripted in the headstock. At the very least it would have been *Höfner* or *Framus*. But it made me happy, for now. The salesman threw in a twenty page basic tutor free and we caught the bus home.

Over the coming months I managed to garner enough savvy to polish off a few standard chord shapes and eventually managed to stagger my fellow guitar enthusiasts at Spring Grove Grammar School with a rendition of the Chas McDevitt hit *Freight Train*. A friend had showed me the technique of picking the melody out with my pinkie whilst scratching out a rough rhythm with the remaining digits. They were dumbfounded at my prowess and before they had time to discover that this was the sum total of my both my talent and my repertoire I joined their group and refused to leave no matter how much they begged.

Chord by chord, song by song, I clawed, cajoled, bluffed and bullied my way in and out of other skiffle groups playing covers of songs that had charted by Lonnie Donegan and the Vipers. *Cumberland Gap* and *Pick A Bale Of Cotton* never sounded as bad as when they were endowed with the dubious benefits of my tortured vocals. As my expertise grew by the most infinite of degrees I sailed onwards and upwards into rock and roll outfits in imitation of my new heroes, Elvis Presley, Ricky Nelson, Buddy Holly and a string of others.

Here in England Tommy Steele had been hailed as the answer to Elvis. If that was the answer then someone had seriously misunderstood the question. He was in fact much more in the Bill Haley vein: smiling, bouncy and non-threatening. The first real home grown rival appeared in the shape of the smouldering, pouting Cliff Richard. His first record *Move It* throbbed its way deservedly up the charts to prove that just occasionally we could get it right here in Britain too. In the end Cliff was discovered to be as wholesome as apple pie but with those sultry features framing the well rehearsed sneer and in the absence of any further information he looked like the devil incarnate.

Frankie Laine and Johnny Ray gradually lost their importance rating in my musical hierarchy. I swivelled my hips precociously and screamed my lungs out in an attempt to get young girls in the audience to scream adoringly back at me in return. It was a fair exchange I reckoned. My philosophy was that you didn't have to be particularly good, although I really did think I was, but if you hung on in there long enough something would happen. And it did. I turned professional in 1961 with a highly respected band from West Drayton called Cliff Bennett and The Rebel Rousers. We never hit the heights while I was in the group but at least I had become a *bona fide* pro musician. It was not so much a case of 'local boy makes good' as 'local boy makes average'.

My chance meeting in Hamburg with The Searchers in 1962 proved to be the turning point. I was about to join a name that was already made. Number one with their very first hit *Sweets For My Sweet*, they repeated this chart glory with *Sugar And Spice, Don't Throw Your Love Away* and *Someday We're Gonna Love Again* before I made my debut singing and playing on arguably the group's strongest, if not biggest, hit *When You Walk In The Room*. Before our glory days subsided in 1966 we had also put out other discs with varying degrees of success. The lilting, folksy *What Have They Done To The Rain?* The hypnotically haunting *Goodbye My Love*. The not quite so memorable *He's Got No Love* and *Bumble Bee*. The underrated *Take Me For What I'm Worth* and the final chart entry *Have You Ever Loved Somebody* before real life and the need to survive against the odds took hold.

Music gave me the chance to work alongside many of my idols. We were there at the birth of Beatlemania and watched as they disintegrated under a melée of private problems, unlike us too rich to be blackmailed into staying together by the need for mere money. We mixed with the artistes from the legendary Motown stable when Martha and The Vandellas, The Temptations and The Supremes were merely support acts propping up the bill we headlined as the new young dudes from the U.K. We traversed Australia with The Rolling Stones, a combination as weird as teaming up Vlad The Impaler with Mother Theresa. We were lorded in Los Angeles and bombed in Bosnia. We shared stages with The Everly Brothers, Dusty Springfield, Tom Jones, Mark Knopfler and so many other icons of the genre. We played the vast Wembley Stadium with Cliff Richard in front of 160,000 people.

Along the way we also suffered humiliation at the hands of social club audiences who cared not a jot what horrendous journey you might have endured to present your puny entertainment before them, only that your gross fee was wildly out of proportion to the even punier wages for which they had probably toiled from sunrise to sunset. These people had 'proper jobs'. People like us were just taking the piss. Those audiences never ever recognised a net fee, the pathetic balance remaining after you had shelled out for your fuel, repairs, hotels, crew, commissions and a thousand other hidden expenses that kept you in the company of paupers. We saw our star descend and watched it rise again as the onset of rhythmic but repetitive and tuneless dance music in the eighties thankfully left our particular decade as the only melodic option open to them. All of life was a learning curve.

Simple three and four chord music had presented me, gratis and for nothing, with one of life's bonuses. I had seen the world with all its attendant sights, sounds and smells and been handsomely rewarded for it in the process. I never reached the ultimate heights and I never saw the depths that created casualties of so many others. On the whole I had been dealt a pretty good hand and my memory banks had been filled to overflowing with myriad reminiscences because of a career that has sent me round the world and back again. Which is precisely the point. I treasure memories now more than at any time in my life.

My mind tends to recall things in random spurts these days refusing to yield to the natural rules of chronology. It darts from the early tours to memorable trips undertaken in the more recent past and back again. It is hard sometimes to drag up the finite details of those early experiences. They say that the memory is the first to go. Or is it the eyes? I've forgotten. Which probably means that it is the memory. Or it would be were it not for the fact that I now have to don glasses to see the monitor. These days I walk into a room and the only name that springs to mind is Alzheimer, whom I immediately bump into, spilling the drink from his grasp.

Flying has changed a lot since I was a lad. Brought up in the neighbourhood of the fledgling Heathrow Airport of the fifties I remember gazing up in boyish envy at the dark blue Dragon Rapide bi-planes buzzing overhead like demented bluebottles, and wishing I could afford the ten bob (fifty pence in today's funny money) it cost to take to the skies for a fifteen minute pleasure ride. Heathrow in those times was little more than a shanty town at the side of the Bath Road with a bunch of prefabricated buildings making up the terminal and a control tower not much bigger than a modest detached house. Pretty soon the move was made to the central area and the beginnings of the 'gateway to the world' that we know today began.

Over the years I have flown Concorde and Caravelle, Trident and Tri-Star, Comet and Constellation and thankfully the thrill has never left me. I still feel privileged. I am, I confess, one of those sad anoraks who actually like airports. It excites me that here starts a journey to someone else's country. New sights and new sensations. The feeling of expectation always gives me a rush of adrenaline just as it did on my first ever flight back in the autumn of nineteen sixty two. I was Germany bound, an embryo pop musician headed for The Star Club in the heart of Hamburg's St Pauli district, just off the infamous Reeperbahn, and our carrier was a Viscount, the workhorse of B.E.A (British European Airways) which was later to join up with B.O.A.C (British Overseas Aircraft Corporation) and become the British Airways we know today. I remember it well.

As the white-knuckle ride began the huge plane lifted into the air while my stomach remained clamped to the ground. Scared? Not me. I was absolutely petrified. I did not understand, and still do not today, how anyone had the sheer arrogance to believe they could get an object that size up into the skies and make it stay there let alone get it back down again safely. Can you imagine the first person to do it? 'Well, it looks alright on paper. It should stay up. I think.' These days the fear has thankfully long since vanished and most times I am barely aware that we have taken off. By this time I am usually engrossed in a book or the in-flight magazine.

My parents, simple and untravelled Scottish folk, were impressed and awed by the adventure that lay ahead and imagined me returning with what they called my 'continental tan'. Neither they nor I realised then that Germany in September is pretty much the same as England in September with the same cloud and the same rain, a far cry from the seemingly ever baking skies of Mediterranean climes. But what none of us realised was that my maiden journey by air was to propel me not only to my first foreign land but also into the birth of arguably the most important decade of modern popular music. The Sixties.

The Beatles were already local heroes in Hamburg and had just scraped into the British top twenty with a song called *Love Me Do*. I was just one of an outfit called Cliff Bennett and The Rebel Rousers at that time and, like all the other flotsam of barely professional musicians who had traipsed over there in their rag-bag groups, I was jealous of their modest success. I was also shocked into open-mouthed amazement by the sounds and sights of the Reeperbahn where a smiling lady in a window seat did not necessarily indicate someone taking a welcome break from the household chores. But, as odd and unlikely as it might sound, the clubs of the Grosse Freiheit and surrounding streets had a charm about them not unlike London's Soho of the fifties. It was a gangsters' village with a camaraderie and a communal spirit of respect and self preservation that sucked you in and nurtured you once your face was deemed to fit. The Club owners knew the musicians, who were befriended by the bouncers, who guarded the 'working girls', who courted the musicians and vied for customers alongside the transvestites and pill-pushers of that infamous district. Later on I discovered another Hamburg, a thriving city centre with shops and store offering goods stacked with luxury and style to rival the best of Rome or Paris. The Deutschmark was on the rise.

Out of this environment came the style and music that was given the generic name of Merseybeat. Not a strictly correct term considering the melting pot of musical talent from the many parts of The British Isles. The Star Club was a slightly revamped cinema that presented artistes both unknown and legendary and the resident guitar idol, Tony Sheridan (nee-Daniel McGinnity), was from London via Norwich and Ireland. His backing group on a recording of *My Bonnie* was a pre-Ringo Beatles. A Scottish saxophone player by the name of Ricki Barnes came out of Bobby Patrick's Big Six to help him form the Star Club Combo. Alvin Lee led a trio from Nottingham called The Jaybirds. Ricki Barnes unfortunately rose to obscurity while a few years on Alvin and his group would knock 'em dead at Woodstock and achieve international fame under a new title, Ten Years After.

But certainly many of the favourites were indeed from that parallel world, the rough, tough seaport of Liverpool. The Big Three. Gerry And The Pacemakers. And The Searchers who, just one year later shot to number one in the charts with their very first single *Sweets For My Sweet* and shortly after acquired the services of one very grateful Southern domiciled bass player - me. I hung around with The Searchers mainly because teetotal, unworldly and boring old me had come across the only other quiet living, sober bunch of musos in that whole mad melee of teenage hormones let loose in a veritable den of iniquity. God, were we dull. But at least we survived with our sanity and our health intact. We all grew up very quickly in Hamburg. I was nineteen. I was in a foreign land. And my senses were being assaulted from all sides. It was thrilling.

The musical and social revolution that followed The Beatles meant that things would never the same again and intercontinental travel was for me now a way of life. American tours whisked me off to the places that I had only heard of in Chuck Berry songs and I learned the real names of the towns mispronounced by The Rolling Stones in *Route Sixty Six*. Australia in those days was thirty six hours away in a Comet. Few people could afford the fare then which meant that you could often grab a whole empty row of seats to get some much needed sleep. I wouldn't bet much on your chances now.

Liverpool may have provided much of the raw talent but in the sixties London was the 'swinging city', the place to be. The chicest of the new breed were to be seen either in a disco, behind the wheel of an E type Jaguar (definitely the roadster, not the hard top) or strutting like peacocks down the Kings Road in brocade Nehru jackets and ruffled shirts from Granny-Takes-A-Trip. My disco was The Cromwellian, my E-type a red soft top and a fair amount of my hard earned cash ended up in Granny's cash register.

America had been conquered by the Beatles and was ripe for invasion by armies of rock groups who simply reinvented their music and sold it back to them by the truckload. Over there we met our heroes on a level playing field at last. I remember the bill of the first show I ever played in The States as a Searcher but for the moment I'll keep you in suspense as to the identity of our American co-stars. The British contingent however con-sisted of ourselves, Dusty Springfield and Millie (*My Boy Lollipop*) and we jetted over on a Boeing 707. In-flight entertainment was in its infancy. There was one film, nothing more. I recall it was *Major Dundee* and was lis-tened to through earphones that resembled the pretend stethoscope from a very cheap doctor's play set. If you made it through to the end of the movie your ears were red and throbbing with pain.

We stayed in Manhattan but performed in the less than salubrious Brooklyn, at the Fox Theatre as a part Murray The K's Big Holiday Show. He was the motor-mouthed brash New York deejay who precociously, and unasked, dubbed himself 'the fifth Beatle' and presented extravaganzas which boasted a display of almost more stars than there are the heavens, as M.G.M studios were once wont to brag. Our poor little minds boggled almost to the point of self-destruct. Music and the aeroplane had made the world so much smaller and there was an awful lot more of it that this young man was going to see and much of it from a bird's eye view.

Not all of my air travel has been by civilian means. The forces need entertaining and a trip to The far flung Falkland Islands has to be made on an R.A.F. TriStar and even today takes eighteen hours with a short fuelling stop on The Ascension Islands. It used to be by Hercules, a hellish flight on canvas benches and no service of any kind. Nowadays an R.A.F steward brings round a trolley with a limited bar service and a boxed lunch consisting of a cheese sandwich, an apple, a carton of orange juice, some crisps and a sausage roll. Our drummer was a non-meat eater. 'Have you got any vegetarian meals?' the poor naïve lad cried.

'Certainly, mate,' came the answer, and the steward quickly reached out and removed the sausage roll.

I think that possibly the best thing about flying in these sophisticated times is that more people get to do it. I have flown in a jumbo jet where the bubble has been transformed into an elegant restaurant for the in-flight meal, a feast of gourmet delights and the finest of wines, but at heart I am still a tourist along with the rest of them and I just love the fact that it has become so affordable. Some of my happiest times have been on package holidays at knock down prices in the bars of the much maligned Benidorm and Magaluf. Lager louts may deserve their reputations. These excellent towns do not.

The package revolution has given people not only the opportunity of the experience to sail above the clouds but also the belief that it is their right to fly. And indeed it is, but I just hope that they never get too blasé. If I ever get to feel like that I shall simply shut my eyes and imagine myself, a little lad again gazing up at those tiny blue bi-planes way overhead in the skies above Heathrow Airport. Sheer magic. But I'm racing ahead of myself. Time flies as age progresses but I need to slow down a bit if I am to recall some of those memories.

Now where was I? Let's go back a bit. Right back.

2

It's A Small World

The journey of a thousand miles begins with a single step. What a load of absolute twaddle. Who said it? I have no idea. Probably the same guy who said 'He who laughs last has thought of a dirty meaning'. On reflection I would hazard a guess that it was probably dear old Confucius, bless him, though why we always look on anyone hailing from further East than Basildon dressed in a frock, a silly moustache and no socks as having the answer to the secrets of the universe is absolutely beyond my ken. He really should have been on Mastermind, subject (in the words of the great Basil Fawlty) the bleedin' obvious.

But when you are very tiny even one small step truly is a journey. I can just remember those infant days when an unsteady totter to the end of the garden was a great adventure to rival anything that would confront me later in life. Anything could happen. A great beast could leap out from behind the tomato plants and devour me. Maybe I would be slain by the giant killer rhubarb. I could get lost and maybe no one would bother to look for me. Or I could simply step in a dog turd. It's not easy being a tot in a world ruled by grown ups who possessed the power, had the maps and wrote the rules. For a new kid on the block there was danger in them thar hills.

From that point on everything was relative. As a child of the baby boom my world of travel was confined in the main to foot, bicycle or bus. Sometimes a train. Almost never a car. A motor car was then still a pretty rare sight to a kid in a working class suburb of West London whose age was still in single figures. There were a few in the surrounding streets and I actually got to ride in one. It was big, black and beautiful. The oval badge on the radiator grill announced Ford in elegant chrome script on a blue background and it had upholstery that could pass for leather.

It was a sort of faded moss green in colour and transported myself and a couple of my fellow Wolf Cubs to our church parade one Sunday morning but eventually became forbidden territory once it was leaked out that the owner and his wife were about to be divorced. That made them virtually untouchable in those ultra prurient post war years when what you were perceived to be was more important than what you actually were. People did not get divorced. At least not lightly. And once they had taken that awful decision, one which was almost too hideous to contemplate, we were kept well away lest the dreadful disease should somehow attack and taint us too.

Neither did free spirits have 'love children' in those innocent times. Sluts had bastards and the poor bearer of glad ridings was either rushed down the aisle for one of life's longer journeys with a miserable faced and regretful, if wiser, groom or hustled away to a place of refuge with sympathetic relatives to return a tad short of nine months later with or without the result of their ill-conceived labours. Back to face the music, the sniggers and the accusing glances from a glass-housed and judgmental society that was fifties Britain. A country still in the grip of post war austerity.

In fact most problems we did not want to confront were conveniently tucked out of sight. I can still recall a lad in our street arriving home like a prodigal son from a long period away working on a farm. I was impressed. It sounded like great fun and so glamorous. He was smoking a Craven A cigarette. I decided I too wanted to go and work on a farm and smoke Craven As. Later I discovered that the 'farm' was in fact borstal. To be truthful even that sounded like fun, but I never had the courage to voice that opinion. Shame was everywhere. But money was not and therefore neither was travel.

The first real honest-to-goodness journey I can recall must have taken place in nineteen fifty or thereabouts. William Byrd Primary School in Harlington on the West side of London stood at the edge of the Bath Road, barely a catapult's thrust away from the capital's main airport at Heathrow. They were attempting to teach me the rudiments of reading, writing and overcoming my natural timidity long enough to hold my hand up in class and get excused before crapping in my pants (oh yes, I did).

One day a great event was announced by way of a slip of paper handed to each of us and which we were entrusted to deliver home safely and reasonably crumple free. If we could inveigle the necessary funds out of our cash-strapped parents, twelve shillings and sixpence I believe was the princely sum, which is sixty two and a half pence in these decimalised days, we were to be transported far away to a week of adventure and excitement that was beyond our wildest imaginings. No parents. No classrooms. Just huge dormitories such as those we had read about in books about schools much posher than ours. Nature rambles where we would forage for rare flora and fauna and where we would keep our young eyes peeled for sightings of exotic birds and beasts. Camp fires and singsongs. Sausages cooked on wood fuelled fires. I had to be there. Whatever it took I really had to be there.

My father was an impecunious Scot whose appreciation of the value of money was definitely far in excess of its actual worth and who, having earned a bawbee or two by the sweat of his brow, had no intention of letting it escape from his very deep pockets. If I had been even slightly aware of the harsh realities of life I might have had a wee bit more sympathy for a hard working man who had struggled through the tough wartime years to keep his young family fed. But how was I to know about such practicalities? I was a kid. Food appeared like magic out of cupboards and frying pans and money was produced from purses upon request. It was an uphill task on the part of my mum convincing him that this vast expense would be a wise investment in my educational future, but somehow she did it.

Eventually the wondrous day came and the great, the good, and the tiny gathered in the playground. The great were our teachers, pillars of wisdom we could only aspire to emulate. The good were our parents. They were simple put-upon folk merely trying to survive in an era of deprivation from which they unselfishly shielded us. We were the tiny and if we were poor we never knew it. We had clothes, we ate food and we had fun, lots of it. On the whole life was pretty good. How do you know you are poor if every one else is as poor as you are?

Outside the stark and unremarkable brick building the charabanc stood in all its magnificence, a glorious monument to the coachbuilder's art, its sides adorned by bright swirls bordered in stainless steel. Colourful flourishes that surely rivalled anything the ceiling of the Sistine Chapel could offer. We ceremoniously boarded clutching our sandwiches and cakes wrapped in greaseproof paper which sometimes slipped from our grasp like a portion of Crackerjack's Double Or Drop. No one born after the mid sixties will remember Eammon Andrews' iconic television programme but it was a big part of my life. In a scene reminiscent of the one from Close Encounters, where the wide-eyed humans entrust themselves to the unknown as they innocently file onto the alien space craft which will transport them to goodness knows where, we breathlessly climbed the steps.

We were glad that Mrs Frame was not going but that Mr Staunton was. Mrs Frame was a small, ferocious woman whose walk was quick and strident and who did not so much look as glare. She had one of those faces you would never get tired of smacking. A Jewish girlfriend of mine had a word that would have fitted the bill perfectly. Verbissen. A withering glance that in an earlier time zone had turned the Medusa to stone. It was a mouth that looked as though it had spent a lifetime sucking lemons. A countenance of such malevolence and inconceivable age to my young eyes that I would shiver on the spot as she approached, goose-stepping like Atilla the Prune.

I have little doubt that I owe that poor misunderstood woman a grovelling apology now. Mister Edwards, the headmaster of that fine establishment, in those pre-P.C. days when we had head masters and not unisex head teachers, I remember as an equally terrifying character whose appearance would turn my legs to jelly. I met him again nearly five decades on down the line and I was faced with a charming elderly gentleman who was exactly as I remembered him except that his smile was as warm as an August day and his eyes radiated nothing but goodness. I imagine the frightening Mrs Frame in her twilight years metamorphosed into everyone's favourite granny.

Mister Staunton on the other hand was young and vibrant, ex R.A.F I believe, possessed an insatiable enthusiasm for seemingly every aspect of life and somehow managed to motivate the bunch of horrible smelly little warts to whom it was his unfortunate task to impart some degree of knowledge. He told us stories. Well no, he didn't so much tell them as weave those chilling tales of mystery and adventure. I have always been convinced that he knew as much, or as little, about the outcome of these masterpieces of suspense as his goggle-eyed, pint-sized audience. He was our idol.

The cakes and sandwiches were scoffed before we were out of sight of the school and ten of us lads squashed onto a back seat made for six and pulled faces at the smattering of motor cars that came up from behind before overtaking our plodding old war-horse of a bus. The journey, like those interminable infant days during the run up to Christmas, took an eternity but eventually we reached the end of our great crusade. Its grand title was The Battle of Britain House and near to the main structure there were a series of single story prefabricated dwellings set in an expanse of mostly uncultivated woodland. Here we spent seven days in an exhilarating world light years away from the one we had left behind.

We trekked, we foraged, we splashed in puddles and had pillow fights in the long, stark, multi-bedded huts where sleep, in our state of excitement, was hard to come by. We were lined up each morning and questioned as to whether or not we had 'done our motions' and a reply in the negative meant a walk to the ablutions block usually in a vain attempt to produce something that was not forthcoming. Red faced and breathless we were in greater danger from broken blood vessels than we ever were from constipation. On Sunday we attended the church service. Several decades later I was reminiscing with a companion who had shared this giant leap into the unknown and realised that we had actually gone to Ruislip. A journey of five miles. It must have taken all of twenty minutes.

That momentous journey to North Middlesex may have been one small step for man but it was one giant leap for kiddy-kind. I had broken free of the schoolyard gate. I had seen the big wide world without my mother looking over my shoulder checking to see that what I witnessed was both good and healthy for me. There was no responsible and strong hand ready to pluck me out of danger and into the safety of the corporate family bosom from whence only a few years before I had been taking my meals on draft. The apron strings lay in tattered shreds on the floor. I wanted more but how? Holidays were as rare as an off licence in Jeddah and consisted almost exclusively of the odd day trip to Bognor or Littlehampton courtesy of the Hillingdon British Legion. On such restrained adventures there was barely enough time to grab an ice cream cone and a couple of rides on the fairground, chaperoned by the womenfolk who still both knew and accepted their position in the family hierarchy while the men got pissed in the pub, before the whole ensemble was carted back to their little boxes in suburbia.

The only real vacation I can remember from my primary school years was a two week sojourn in Scotland during a summer break. My family had been evacuated during the war from Greenock, a smallish town thirty miles West of Glasgow which survived in the main on the profits from the shipbuilding yards of neighbouring Port Glasgow. Hitler had decided, quite reasonably, given the threat from the legendary British Navy, to give it a bit of a pasting and my Mum, Gran (on my mother's side) and brother Jackie were shipped out to the safety of England while my Dad did his bit for King and Country in the Argyle and Sutherland High-landers. God knows why they wanted him. He was about five foot nothing and couldn't have punched pussy with his paws up. At his height he would have had trouble spotting the enemy over even the smallest of hills. The greatest danger the Hun could expect from the diminutive private David McCormack Mc Neice was a swift kick in the shins or maybe a bite in the bollocks but I supposed in wartime it's a case of needs must when the Devil drives. I was not even a speck on the horizon at that point. That joyous prospect would be adjourned till one of those naughty nights of lust during a spot of leave. Alas, the first sassenach in the family was born in the family home of 33 Woodrow Avenue, Hayes, Middlesex on a chilly fourteenth of December, 1943. A joyous event for the whole of mankind I think.

I had never actually been to the beloved homeland so the prospect was quite exciting and I had enjoyed the coach trip to far off Ruislip. Scotland was even further and so in my poor deluded childish logic this ride would quite naturally be that much better. The more perceptive amongst you might have already spotted I was a bit of a thickhead as a kid.

In those pre-motorway days the A roads provided the main routes to the length and breadth of England and the mighty A1 accommodated the hardy traveller willing and able to endure the long trek north. Much of it was still single carriageway and meandered in that lazy, eccentric British manner that was typical of the times and of the national character. An American friend once passed comment at the narrowness of what I considered to be a fairly substantial thoroughfare. I suggested that surely they had something similar out there. He answered that they did but they called them driveways. Point taken but remember, size is not everything.

The flotsam and jetsam of fellow passengers too stingy to pay the extra cost of a comfortable and speedy rail journey boarded the coach at Victoria and settled down as best they could on the rigid, barely upholstered bum-battering benches that typified a conveyance of the age, single decked and years behind the luxury of today's contoured and reclining seats. But none of us were looking too far ahead in the flurry and excitement of the journey's commencement. Claims were staked and clothes were stowed amidst animated conversation. These were the days when people still talked to strangers before inhibitions and status redefined the social divides.

I very quickly made friends with a fat boy called Brian who was accompanied by his even fatter mother and oddly minuscule grandad, an old

Scottish soldier who had been decorated in the last war and was now badly in need of redecoration. They were going home to let the old fellah see the family before he shuffled off his mortal coil. I wasn't at all convinced he would make it in time. Fat Brian's mum lumbered down the aisle like a rogue elephant and wedged herself into the inadequate space between her seat and the one in front, her face red and getting redder by the second. I had visions of her eventually exploding and showering everyone with the contents of her insides that would certainly have the consistency and appearance of strawberry jam. Surely only a body filled with strawberry jam could make her that red. She looked as though she spent her days at Pies-R-Us. I liked Fat Brian's mum. She laughed a lot and didn't appear to look on kids as a nuisance to be either tolerated or belted. She also loaded the parcel shelf with a carrier bag stuffed with goodies of the edible kind. Definitely a person whose acquaintance was to be cultivated.

We set off at a stately pace and wound our way through the suburbs towards the speedier trunk roads which would allow us to pick up a bit of speed. Fat Brian and I played a game of spot the Austin but after an hour we hadn't even seen one and were beginning to go squinty eyed so we eventually settled for pulling faces at the overtaking traffic until we were deemed by my mum to be making a nuisance of ourselves and were made to sit still. Progress was excruciatingly slow but we figured Scotland could not be far. The driver pulled in to a transport café for a quick refreshment and toilet stop. I reckoned we must be about halfway. Fat Brian guessed we were a bit further along the route. We were actually at Baldock, still within spitting distance of the metropolis and still three hundred miles from our destination. Proportion is a sense that develops exceedingly slowly in children.

The rest of the trip passed with an exasperating slowness and I drifted in and out of consciousness. It was a rerun of an episode from a movie I'd seen in which the lone survivor of a shipwreck floats for days on a raft with hope of reaching civilisation fading fast. He opens his eyes to a blazing sun. He blacks out and when he comes round the sky is like coal. I was that castaway. I knew how he had felt. Houses gave way to landscapes of fields occasionally dotted with higgledy-piggledy stone built dwellings much cuter than the boring pebble-dashed council housing of my hometown but my boredom and severe discomfort stunted my appreciation of this splendid new vista. I relished the next pee stop, not because I had any need to empty my bladder but at least something happened on these occasions.

The men would troop out onto the grass verge and position themselves behind any available bushes or press themselves up against the side of the coach amidst much sniggering from those left inside the vehicle. Anything to do with the toilet area had good snigger value in those days. You never had to see anything. You rarely did. It was just the knowledge that the activity was based around the dangly bits of the body that were strictly taboo. It was always the men and almost never the ladies. They saved themselves for the legitimate cafés where they could take care of the necessaries with dignity and comfort.

I marvelled at them and their ability to be able to control their bladders for aeons. I decided that the fairer sex must surely be blessed with superior internal organs. Later in life I was to find out just how wrong I was and that all the ills in the world were encompassed in that mysterious generic term 'women's problems'. It was the discovery of 'women's problems' that helped me become the hopeless heathen I am today. On the basis of ladies' interiors I decided that there most definitely was no God. How on earth, or indeed in Heaven, could an almighty supreme being create his masterpiece with prehistoric plumbing? The whole world had gone digital and the female species was still saddled with an analogue sewage system. If the world had been a car factory God had created a Skoda.

Fat Brian and I ate our way through the major part of the journey, gorging ourselves on the bread pudding and fruit cake that his darling mum a few years before would have needed to plunder the ration books to make. It was nectar, and with the insensitivity that only a boy child can muster I ignored the fare that my own mother had lovingly prepared, jam sandwiches and banana butties, neither of which are good travellers. By the time you've gone any distance at all a once thick filling of jam soaks itself away into the absorbent bread leaving you with a soggy and almost tasteless pink mess that is totally bereft of the attraction it once had. It is an abomination to both the eyes and the palate.

Banana sandwiches are worse. I gave mine to Fat Brian with a feigned generosity and he scoffed them down. In fact he scoffed down anything he got his hands on. I love bananas, firm and fresh and sweet in the middle of two slices of lightly buttered (or margarined as it was in our skinflint household) bread. But the item has to be eaten quickly for it very soon turns to an ugly black overripe pulp that tastes as unpleasant as it looks. The only way an old banana butty can look any worse is when you eventually chuck up, as good old Brian did. He was brilliant. When he knew it was coming he tried to run up the aisle. God knows where he was going, but he never made it. His podgy frame just bounced from side to side off the seats like a human pinball as he tried to negotiate the narrow gangway. The poor chap a few seats along tried to dodge as Fat Brian approached. Brian instinctively held his hands up to his mouth but when he saw the ugly mess that was oozing from his blubbery lips he pulled them away in horror and let it pour over the horrified stranger. Shazam. Long live Brian The Magnificent. My hero. The coached stopped yet again for an unexpected combined clean up and pee break.

Brian slumped into a silent misery as he tried to sleep off the effects of his dramatic stomach eruption. The rest of us kids on board for a time became more even animated collapsing into fits of giggles as the deliciously dreadful pong wafted through the coach. The only smell that rates higher on a young boy's giggleometer is that of the passing of wind, preferably accompanied by an appropriate noise. But in the absence of a good loud fart the stench of foul smelling puke was a reasonable substitute until, like all smells, our noses became accustomed to it and we all drifted off into a limbo land somewhere between consciousness and the land of nod.

We eventually reached Scotland. Whether it was hours or days I did not know. In truth it felt like it had taken years and once we alighted in Glasgow we still had to catch a connection to Port Glasgow forty five minutes drive further up The Clyde. But that was mere bagatelle compared to the marathon we had just completed, and the journey was eased by the incredible sight of river traffic which was something new in my landlogged existence.

My relatives lived in an apartment at number four Keir Hardie Street, a stone's throw from the water and next to the railway lines. It was a warm and spacious flat one floor up in a thing called a tenement, and I liked it. But then I liked almost everything better than anything in my own mundane environment. That's what kids are like. It is the nature of the beast. Never appreciate. Never be thankful. Just want what you don't have and give your parents hell for not delivering a better life on a silver platter. What a rotten little bastard I must have been.

My Aunt Mattie and my Uncle Willie, my Dad's twin and an exact replica, were nice and welcoming. I had two cousins I was meeting for the first time, Tommy and Willie the younger. They were wild tearaways brought up on a diet of the Friday night fights at the Palladium dance hall in town where the Catholics tried to beat the shit out of the Protestants and vice versa. On the second day I went out to explore the hillside at the back of the estate and was approached by two local lads who spoke in accents as thick as an elephant sandwich. When I could decipher the jargon I realised to my absolute horror they were threatening to beat me up.

'I bet I could fight you', said one. I bet you could, I thought to myself and strained to keep my bowels under control. What on earth was happening? Hadrian had spent a hell of a lot of energy constructing a bloody great wall to keep these savages out of England and here I was on the wrong side of it, faced by a couple of juvenile delinquent Picts and about to suffer an attack of woad rage. I was well aware in the short time I had been there that religion was the main excuse for a good scrap but what they didn't know was that my own faith was neither 'Papist' nor 'Proddy'. I happened to be a devout coward, and before you could say come back you snivelling wretch I was off like a ferret up a trouser leg. I couldn't fight but I could run and within seconds I was back in the flat from which I refused to emerge for days.

Eventually I risked the outside world again and thankfully came to no great harm during the rest of my stay. In truth it was quite pleasant and a relaxing change to the relatively claustrophobic environs of Middlesex. I sailed on the paddle steamer that majestically glided down the Clyde with its cargo of tourists reflecting on a bygone age of a more tranquil nature. We crossed the water to Dunoon where the Highland Games were held each year though sadly not at the time when I was in residence. We rented a paddleboat at Largs and had afternoon tea in Inverkip. And I still had not seen anyone in a kilt.

I met relations I had no idea existed. Uncles John and Duncan and Auntie Jean. And Auntie Maisie, a rather masculine looking, heavy set woman who wore sensible brogues and was always in the company of a younger and prettier girl who went by the somewhat androgynous name of Ray. Curiously Auntie Maisie never did get married. I liked Ray and Maisie a lot. They fussed over me and called me their little chicken. I tried not to think of the long journey home and my memory of the return is hazy. I think I am still in denial in much the same way your mind might block out a murder or a terrible accident you have witnessed. When I returned to school my tales contained nothing negative. I recounted only stories of thrilling sights and sounds and wonderful adventures that stung them with a jealous rage. Tales that were much more thrilling than reality could testify to. Yes, I was already destined for the fairytale land of showbiz and I had learned a vital lesson. Never let the truth get in the way of a good story.

Scotland was the beginning and the end of formal holidays for me apart from the odd day trip to the seaside and a week in the Isle of Wight much later on in my teenage years with my schoolmates, the cost of which had to be borne by me. For that one my father had originally agreed to give me seven pounds spending money. I figured that it would be sensible to have a bit of spare cash and so I took a week's work alongside my brother, who had quit school by this time, in an airport canteen. The labour was hard. By the end of the sixth day my bones were aching and I was nauseous from the stench of the ever-simmering stockpot, but I had my wages which by coincidence happened to amount to seven pounds. On realising this, my dad figured I was okay for cash after all and neglected to forward his promised subsidy. I could tell then that the good things in life would depend on my own wits.

That vacation was undertaken by train, a rare treat indeed although I would sometimes catch the milk train to Brighton with the rest of my skiffle group to serenade the holidaymakers as they passed by our busking pitch under the arches next to the beach. We took the milk train because we couldn't afford the normal fare. This way lost you a night's sleep but saved you a good deal of money and by the end of the afternoon our washboard collection divvied up would reimburse our expenses and allow us the luxury of a fish and chip supper before returning home. Great fun, and something that can only be done with the energy that belongs to youth.

The rest of my teenage travel was mundane. I was normally to be found on a number eighty-one heading to Hounslow where I would switch to a trolley bus that would drop me outside Spring Grove Grammar School in Isleworth. Unless of course it was one of those awkward kind of eighty-one buses that stopped at Hounslow West, in which case my search for education, which I never really found by the way, necessitated three vehicles. Only a real fruitcake like me would choose a school six miles from home just because he thought the uniform looked cool. But the building itself was truly beautiful, a mansion that had once been owned and lived in by the Pears Soap family, complete with minstrel-galleried music room, a mosaic-lined art room and its own private chapel in the rolling grounds. Don't bother to look for it. The house is still there, just. But it is now surrounded by a travesty of sixties architecture. Soulless cubes of glass and plastic erected for the benefit of the new Polytechnic unit that usurped the land when we were moved to a purpose built school towards the end of my educational years. By whatever insane reasoning the authorities decided that our mansion, like Jason's sirens, was too beautiful to be gazed upon by mere mortals.

My input in class was minimal and the results reflected the fact. I was lousy at most subjects. The physical exertions of the sports field and the gymnasium were anathema and Latin was all Greek to me. Considering the part that travel was to play in my adult life Geography was foreign territory to my memory banks. Maths was merely an impossibility. A bunch of numbers in a hopeless tangle doing things to each other that I found extremely difficult to forecast. I departed that place of learning with just three O levels. English Language, French and Woodwork. Just about the only thing I was qualified to become was a furniture maker in Quebec.

There I was, a teenager in the first throes of feeling some sort of disturbing movement in the trouser region and I had already caught the travel bug, but I soon realised that here in the twentieth century and hurtling towards manhood at an alarming pace that to travel in the true sense of the word there was only one solution. I had to leave the ground.

3

Heil Hamburg

Heathrow airport was left far behind in the worst covering of snow and ice in decades and our fragile flying machine had somehow managed to skid its way into the skies after several hours delay and the threat of a total shutdown till morning. I was still feeling very shaky. Memories of Munich were still fresh in the mind and I was not yet ready for that most radical though undoubtedly most effective of all career moves. A quick plummet downwards. Besides which a struggling bunch of nere-do-well plank spankers and other assorted musicians falling out of the skies would not make quite the same splash in the news sheets as those beloved Busby Babes had done in that terrible tragedy of 1958. Football has almost always taken precedence over mere music. We might achieve glamour and fame. They had achieved immortality.

It was December the thirtieth nineteen sixty two and I was about to see in my first New Year away from home as an excitable eighteen year old Rebel Rouser. Under the guidance of our glorious leader Cliff Bennett, he of the chubby boyish face and the astonishingly soulful voice, for a white lad, we were headed over to the fatherland to undertake our second season at The Star Club. Barely six months previously I had experienced my first plane journey and if I was apprehensive on that occasion I was scared shit-less this time. It was still new to me. I sat looking out at the dark night sky and reflected on my recent past.

My teenage years had up to now been spent chugging up and down the

A and B roads of Great Britain of England in a series of minibuses, early versions of today's people carriers, such as the Bedford Dormobile and similar types constructed by Austin and Commer. Our conveyance of choice was the Ford Thames. This sad piece of machinery became known to us as the Ford Igloo due to the total inefficiency of the heating system which could not have managed to melt even the softest of Mister Whippy's ice creams and, in attempt to harness its puny power, we would construct a covering of coats to channel the warmth into the passenger compartments where our legs froze in the harsh British winter temperatures.

The man who designed that vehicle must have been a practical joker of some magnitude. Truly a prince among jesters. It had been given a windscreen wiper system that worked on a vacuum from the engine and the harder you pressed on the accelerator the slower the blades traversed the windscreen. In a heavy downpour driving was Russian Roulette on wheels as the blades crawled with a painful slowness from one side to the other. The inept perpetrator of that machinery truly deserved to perish in a Ford Thames negotiating a hairpin bend on a steep incline in a snowstorm. Physician heal thyself indeed.

The road was a place for pioneers and adventurers in those days. At one point in our embryonic years a moment of sheer madness caused us to decide to switch to an almost prehistoric London ambulance, a monstrous machine with a long old fashioned bonnet which displayed the almost mystical name of Daimler. We had somehow got it into our heads that the Daimler company constructed magical machines that simply did not break down. Like the legendary Rolls Royce they might occasionally 'fail to proceed' but we put our complete trust in that magnificent marque. Oh foolish youth. We painted it blue and white and announced our name to the world in an amateur cringe-worthy script in the little panel above the screen which had once proclaimed 'ambulance'. It broke down after only a couple of months popping its geriatric clogs outside Hull University after a tappet-knackering two hundred mile slog and refused to budge any further. We did manage to return a few days later and tow it back South (at least they did - I opted out due to a migraine or split ends or something) but it never again moved under its own power and once more the Thames Van ruled.

But I was now on one of fortune's upgrades and soaring through the ink-black skies for a triumphant return to the seedier side of life across the channel where I was about to perform for the natives in a cheery atmosphere of forgiveness, because God knows they were paying me enough to let them off their transgressions in the war. I was an unashamed mercenary whose conscience could easily be bought for a mess of pottage. Five hundred marks a week to be exact. In those days the pound demanded an exchange of eleven units of the vanquished's currency, making my wages for the month almost two hundred pounds. A veritable king's ransom. My only other occupation, eighteen months as a clerk at the publishers of Penguin books, rewarded forty hours of drudgery with six pounds ten shillings.

Our first season in Hamburg earlier that year had paid for my first car, a nifty little powder blue Ford Anglia, the model with the racy swept back rear window and currently languishing in a garage as a result of my sliding it into a traffic bollard three nights previously. The ice covered roads and my diabolical driving skills, or lack of them, had taken their toll. In case you are an ardent collector of trivia, a traffic bollard's replacement value in nineteen sixty two was twenty two pounds.

But for the moment I was out of danger from over aggressive traffic bollards and descending out of the dark skies into a vista of crispy white, speckled with the twinkling lights of a Germany that resembled an ill-formed but succulently enticing Christmas cake just waiting to be sliced into and devoured. The prospect of another month here filled me both with excitement and dread. The sights, sounds and smells of sin city had been a revelation to my young senses but my immaturity on the last trip had kept me in a state of unease and homesickness. It was the longest time I had spent away from home and the four weeks had felt like a year.

Still, for that kind of money I was more than willing to give it another go and suffer in silence if necessary. I stared out at the juddering wings as the Viscount lost height, skipping heartbeats with each change in the sound of the engines. I concentrated my vision at the point where these monstrous power pods gripped the flimsy wings and prayed an atheist's prayer. Rolls Royce, do not fail me now.

The aeroplane dipped from one side to the other as we neared the tarmac and my overactive brain exaggerated the angle to the point where a wing tip must surely scrape the ground before spinning this whole ridiculous machine, and we its contents, into a freezing oblivion. But it did not. We slid to a halt and taxied to the terminal building alive, healthy and grateful and the pounding in my heart subsided from the cacophony of a steam hammer to the bearable volume of a mere kettle drum

Immigration negotiated and baggage in hand we trooped into the arrivals hall to be met by Horst Fascher, ex-boxer, manager of The Star Club and one time jailbird, having spent time incarcerated on a manslaughter charge following one of his more unfortunate fights. Short and stocky and possessing one of those slight lisps that so many pugilists seem to have, he welcomed us in his bluff but jovial Germanic manner and led us out to the waiting white Cadillac coupé. We were suitably awed. We were still at that age when your car stood for more than your breeding or your brain power and we had never stood next to let alone ridden in a Cadillac.

We went straight to the club leaving the hotel check-in formalities till later, and by the time we arrived The Beatles were into their second set of the night. This was what we wanted to see. We had heard from the bar staff and the customers about this ragged looking long haired band of Scousers during our last trip and had watched them rise from a bunch of no marks to a number seventeen position in the British charts with *Love Me Do*. We were impressed by this. Cliff Bennett and The Rebel Rousers had been recording for almost three years and despite releasing half a dozen singles we had not even managed a sniff at the best selling lists. 'Only number seventeen?' I heard someone scoff much later. At that time I would have shown my arse in Debenhams' window for a number seventeen. Ironically the wheel turns full circle and the feeling is much the same nowadays. Debenhams, prepare yourself for my naked butt.

We stood and observed with a steely determination to remain dispassionate about these potential rivals. After all, we were the groups' group, the hard edged, brass-based outfit who sold soul to the ballrooms and were respected and admired by other musicians while the rest of the big jessies around the country ponced about the stage imitating Cliff and The Shadows, strumming along with thin guitars and lightweight bits of musical fluff they passed off for a rock and roll repertoire. We were here to witness the dismantling of a myth. But it was not to be.

They were good. Very good. Just guitars, bass and drums like the rest of the run of the mill outfits but tough and raunchy and with more edge than a broken piss pot. On top of which they had personalities that were as mature as a ripe old Camembert. We may have been all around the same age but we were boys while those four figures up there on the stage were men. They were a little more reserved than we had been led to expect but the Brian Epstein-imposed suits and the first glimpse of fame had maybe calmed them a little. That night they were in an assortment of black and white waistcoats, ties and shirts. They were well aware of what they had to do to make it and they exuded a natural power and charisma as they worked their way through their hour on the podium and contemplated the fortune that was ahead of them. Cliff Bennett, not a man to bestow a compliment carelessly, loved them. So did I.

As they played and sang they bantered with the crowd in pidgin English and pidgin German occasionally pleasing punters with the odd request. There were shouts for special songs from Bettina as she tended her bar towards the back of the converted cinema building. 'Ein wunsche for Betty' Lennon would yell and the more than buxom blonde would pout back, throwing a big air kiss in gratitude to her beloved John. Bettina was a large girl, imposing and hard to miss as she dispensed her drinks, looking for all the world like two women sewn together, with a vanilla coloured candy floss beehive hairdo and a bosom on which you could land a helicopter. I fancy that more than a few had already crash landed on those mighty orbs.

The following evening, New Year's Eve, I encountered John Lennon exiting the dressing room area as I was going in. I introduced myself and raised a hand in friendship. He shook it and listened as I told him how much I enjoyed their set and that I hoped they were going to have a great success with the new single, due out in January.

'Oh yeah, Frank', he replied with a guarded deliberation and a piercing gaze. 'I watched your show. Great. I've been talking to people in the club and it seems that next to Cliff you're the most popular member in the band'. He paused. 'I can't think why. Your harmonies are fucking ridiculous'. There was a second or two of deafening silence as I tried to assemble my thoughts. Had I heard right? I had never encountered this kind of instant frankness before. Obviously there was a joke there somewhere and I had missed it, but he wasn't laughing. Neither was I. Inside I was trembling. I was a nervous person at best and I was not at my best.

'Well anyway, I hope it all goes well for you', I continued, waffling like someone now on auto-pilot.

'Yeah great, all the best', he answered magnanimously. The ships passed in that German night and the next day they flew off to be legends and conquer the world. I merely wanted to conquer my embarrassment. I met no other Beatles that evening. I had no wish to. I was all Beatled out. I was not a complete pillock. I had no wish to repeat such an encounter until I had honed my skills in the thrust and parry of witty and sardonic conversation on the grindstone of experience and academia. I had severe doubts though that they would ever match those of Mister Lennon.

In later years I was to discover that it was this very evening that produced the infamous Star Club Tapes, a set of rough and ready recordings made on a domestic machine by Kingsize Taylor who was there to perform with his band The Dominoes. Kingsize by name, kingsize by nature. Born

Edward Taylor and known as Ted to his chums, this huge beast of a man was a butcher by trade and sang in a Fats Domino-esque manner whilst playing his big Höfner President guitar with a set of chipolata-shaped fingers that might well have been manufactured for sale in his own shop. In 1998, after an unsuccessful attempt in the seventies, the by now Lennon-less Beatles managed to halt the CD release of these awful, though certainly historic, recordings.

The next day I arose from where our entire group occupied a five-bed room in the Hotel Germania on Detlev-Bremer Strasse and wandered outside to refamiliarise myself with the area. A short distance in one direction was The Hotel Pacific on Neuer Pferdmarkt, the New Horse Market, a plain purpose built establishment where we would stay on future occasions. Our own lodgings were in a large converted German house, rock solid and immaculately clean as German establishments tend to be, putting our homeland equivalents to shame.

A left turn out of the hotel door took me down to The Reeperbahn, the wide thoroughfare that was the main artery of the St Pauli/Altona District. On this imposing street the elegant Café Keese, where the uptown slummers stop off for a snack and an aperitif before experiencing the smutty forbidden fruits of the red light district, and the Opera House on the other side stand in an incongruous juxtaposition to the downmarket trade that brings in the tourists and the money.

The porn movie houses and sex shows litter the surrounding side streets culminating in one short, narrow stretch which offers wall to wall sleaze, The Grosse Freiheit. The words stand for the street of the great free living. Liberal it may be. Free it is not. You could unload a month's wages in a night here with little or no effort. Maybe your teeth along with it if you state any objection to the extortionate bill presented to you at the end of your insanely drunken revels.

I wandered along to number thirty nine where the Star Club presented a less glamorous sight in the harsh light of the day, its decaying façade managing not at all to hide its former use. The only films shown here now were of the hard core sex kind in the room above the club. The one armed doorman stood outside in his military greatcoat and peaked cap and a cigar dangling from thick unsmiling lips, possibly a little old for what was once Schickelgruber's glorious SS but he could have played the part well.

Next door The Monika Bar was being cleaned ready for the evening's rush hour. Beautiful girls in heavy makeup and light clothing constantly wandered in and out. But these were girls with more than their fair share of nature's attributes. Many a sailor's wandering hands had groped between these thighs expecting to caress a mossy, smooth landscape only to encounter an altogether much rockier terrain in the form of one meat and two veg. Down there was a complete set of wedding tackle that only needed to be lashed to a toothbrush to perform that most manly of deeds. Young men grow up very fast in Hamburg.

Almost opposite was the building which was once the Kaiserkeller, the small basement club whose owner, Bruno Koshmeider, had first contracted The Beatles to play in Germany. And still further along, almost at the end and on the other side Koshmeider's other venue, the mightily run-down Indra, stood virtually neglected and no doubt pining for the place in history due to it for allowing the Fab four to tread its boards at the outset of their quest for fame.

I was in need of some sort of sustenance and headed down towards the waterside where a twenty minute stroll would lead me to the Seamen's Mission, a little British Oasis in a land of words incomprehensible. A late breakfast of cornflakes or a cheap plate of pork chop and chips was pretty much a routine for those aimless Hamburg days.

On the way I couldn't not resist a peek at the Herbertstrasse, the small closed off street which was the pivotal place for all of the city's sex on sale. I wanted to check that it had not been some figment of my over fertile imagination. On my first visit I had entered in wide-eyed wonderment at a sight that up to that point I never knew existed. Heavy green metal screens blanked it off from the curious gaze of corruptible youth. This was an X-rated adults only place. Paradoxically quaint and village-like with its shiny cobbled surface and flanked by what could have been a Disney version of a quaint old German hamlet, the large picture windows opened directly onto the street and behind them sat the ladies of both the night and day. Here the motto was 'open all hours'.

The goods on offer came in all shapes and sizes and all states of undress and without exception were shopsoiled. What coverings they had were in lace or leather, boots and basques feeding the lascivious appetites of their potential customers who strolled slowly by as if merely taking the air on a pleasant Sabbath afternoon. A svelt raven-haired amazon clad from head to toe in thonged leather, lolled with her legs crossed in an armchair casually puffing on a cigarette. A short scruffy man with a day's beard and a button-popping beer gut approached and she leaned forward to impart the price and the options available. Haggling done he entered and the curtains were drawn shut for an indecently short time.

29

In the adjacent window a veritable behemoth of a woman came into view from a back room and settled down to read a magazine. Her red corset bulged with an excess of flesh held up by a pair of legs that resembled two upturned Guinness bottles. She was a mountain of the female species. In a world of sex for sale she was a one woman supermarket. Sometimes it pays to buy in bulk.

My fellow window-shoppers affected an air of nonchalance which I tried in vain to copy. My observations were made from the corners of my extremely embarrassed eyes. Embarrassed for them and embarrassed for me. Yes, Hamburg was a twilight world which was to be my home for the first part of 1963. I was thrilled and I was appalled. I would have fun and I would be bored to the point of narcosis. During my time there I watched my heroes from the side of the stage. The Everly Brothers sang the sweetest harmonies ever to come out of Kentucky and looked like the teen gods they were in their tail coats and pin striped trousers. Joey Dee arrived with his Starliters and shattered everyone's preconceptions of them as a lightweight purveyors of gimmicky dance-inspired trivia. His late night sessions were exercises in the power of white soul.

I got to play bass in Bo Diddley's backing band and to experience the mind-numbing boredom of his insistent and repetitive Bo Diddley beat which went 'rum te tum tum-rum tum' for ever and a day and which was adapted with great success by performers like Buddy Holly. He confided to me that his outlandish stage costumes were made out of furnishing fabric. It was cheaper than regular suit material and these were still times when the great but hard up black performers were only just beginning to suss out just where they had been royally ripped off by the men in suits who were sharper, less principled and knew all the angles. People like Bo, born Elias McDaniel, were no longer slaves but were treated like slaves by some. Up there on the stage in his curtain suit he pounded his monotonous beat looking like something from the window display at Waring and Gillow.

I witnessed the onset of madness in the unpredictable Gene Vincent whose Be Bop A Lula had been an anthem of my youth. Obsessed with weaponry he would produce a gun or a knife at will and threaten anyone in the vicinity. He died young. In his forties. I am amazed he lived that long. The patch-eyed Johnny Kidd waved a cutlass and plied his 'theatre rock', leaving the club with a gift of a painted galleon backdrop that the club had commissioned especially for his season there while French-domiciled Vince Taylor swivelled his hips wildly enough to detract from his less than average voice.

And Bill Haley, the podgy country rocker from Michigan whose Rock Around The clock had started it all concentrated on salvaging whatever he could from the wreckage of a career that had been annihilated by the arrival of younger, sexier, thinner and more talented performers in the same over populated arena. He puffed his way around the stage in a parody of the enthusiastic clowning about that kids had once screamed for and with a sardonic look on his face and a kiss curl on his forehead he kissed the good times goodbye.

I revisited St Pauli in the mid seventies to find that the Star Club was no more. When the fashion of Merseybeat had become unfashionable and the boy wonders had achieved birthdays that put them past their sell by dates this shrine to teen beat was turned into an emporium more suited to its surroundings. It was renamed The Salambo. The fantasy sex of rock had been replaced by almost the real thing and naked couplings rocked mechanically back and forwards in an automated and contrived approximation of the copulative arts on the very stage where we had once sung our primitive songs. What had replaced us was also primitive but it lacked the heart that we in our exuberant youthfulness had possessed.

As the revolving stage swung round to reveal a new erotic tableau each time it was linked with the running gag of Napoleon with his pants down and a flaccid member dangling limply between his legs despite the attentions of a topless Josephine who was attempting to massage some life into it. I was mildly impressed. He was quite reasonably endowed and I could quite happily have dumped my paltry erect appendage for his altogether more spectacular limp one.

When finally the entertainment had run its course and the final tableau hove out of view Bonaparte came into the picture for one more battle, this time proudly displaying a stiffy like a flagpole on which you could have hung the Tricoleur as the Marseillaise blasted out triumphantly. Boney had finally achieved the success that had eluded him at Waterloo. It was all very amusing, but oh so sterile and sexless. In my heart I knew that the stage had oozed more eroticism when it was The Star club.

Altona had always thrived on an industry built on sleaze but woven into the fabric of that most bohemian of societies had once been a charm and a character that was now ripped out and replaced with a nothingness. A void that I feared would never be filled with anything worthy of comparison. The doormen looked older. The eyes were eyes of men waiting to die while their way of life was dying around them and there was nothing to look forward to. A further visit in the eighties found me standing in front of a gaping void. Number 39 Grosse Freiheit had disappeared completely, consumed by fire. Whether deliberate or accident I know not but it was surely a merciful release.

But all this was way off in the future. My present was in a time when naked rock and naked bodies coexisted in a unique and vibrant camaraderie. My experience would be widened and my sanity would be threatened but life was a learning curve and I was here on a crash course. John, Paul, George and Ringo by now had stepped back on British soil for a date with destiny. But I had my own date with destiny on the horizon. I was about to meet four other Liverpool lads plying their trade under the name of The Searchers.

4

*The Show's Not Over
(Till The Fat Man Twists)*

In a land of drunken slobs I had somehow encountered three models of sobriety, John McNally, Mike Pender and Chris Curtis. The fourth, Tony Jackson, was off getting completely ratted most of the time so there were virtually no encounters with him. As for me, I had not yet learned to imbibe alcohol. I was so pure and unspoilt I might as well have been the Singing Nun. It was not till my thirties, geriatric in rock and roll terms, that the demon drink gripped me and even then his grip was so light that I was never actually in danger of a successful abduction. Watch this space.

We hung about together avoiding the permanently-on-offer excesses that occupied virtually every spare moment of our musical brethren. In our moments of hunger we would put a temporary hold on our constant hoarding of take-home cash and pop into Alphonse and Gretel's to partake of an artery-clogging frikadelle that only cost a couple of marks. This original Hamburg version of the eponymously named meat patty was a hockey putt shaped mass of indeterminate meat mixed with goodness knows what else to give it an economic bulk. Musicians and dogs tend to eat the same things from time to time. There is no such thing as a free lunch and one's digestive system would belch a wicked revenge in an unrelenting acid attack for the rest of the day. But we still retained the major part of our wealth and we were young. We would, of course, live forever.

In a rash moment of free spending we might treat ourselves to a Chinese meal in the Chug Ooh, which Curtis wittily renamed 'The House Of The Little Train That Hurt'. Back in their bunks at the seedy block of flats where Weissleder placed most of his British employees Mike and John would settle down nightly to write back home long letters of loving thoughts to their future wives. Musicians of this nature were as rare as a turbocharger on a tortoise. The rest of the rock fraternity were out humping themselves stupid on top of the local frauleins who seemed ever ready to reply 'Ja' when back home they were used to getting a severe knock back at the merest brush of a hand against a tit.

The American helicopter carrier the USS Thetis Bay was in port and the Reeperbahn was awash with rampant hormones. Hordes of spotty young septics (septic tanks - Yanks) ran riot through the vice dens of Hamburg divesting themselves of their virginity at the earliest opportunity and many of them quickly found way through the doors of the Star Club. Some of their more troublesome number found their way out of the same club with an even greater velocity accelerated by the muscle power of the burley bar staff. Trouble there was dealt with speedily and with an unsurprising lack of consideration for the recipient's well being. Spilt blood caused no more concern than spilt beer.

The violence was not necessarily meted out to the customers alone. This was gangster city and its own peculiar codes of honour had to be maintained. We were on stage one evening pounding out yet another inevitable cover version of yet another inevitable American rocker when my attention was distracted by 'noises off' as they say in 'theatre-speak'. In the wings there was something happening to which the description 'kerfuffle' would have been hopelessly inadequate and murder would only by good fortune be proved an exaggeration. Horst Fascher's younger brother Freddie, I discovered later, had transgressed. He had, it seems, become involved with the girlfriend of one of the neighbourhood gangsters. I believe that the area of involvement, as is invariably the case, was the toilet region, a definite no-no in the most civilised parts and when you are dealing with people whose favoured pastime it is to hurt and maim this is the ultimate taboo. The safest option is always to put it away and zip it up or risk the possibility that you may be left with nothing to zip up.

From where I pounded on the strings of my little cherry red Gibson bass I caught sight of heavy blows reigning down relentlessly. Blood flowed. I could see it clearly. In my mind I could hear the crunching of broken bones. Of course I could not, but I had no doubt that bones were indeed being broken. The only good thing about this, I figured, was that these were not my bones. When the dirty deed was done and the due punishment had been meted out the severely damaged Freddy was dragged out through the auditorium in full view of the audience. Why waste the chance to give future troublemakers the benefit of an object lesson? Some people looked, but not for long. Such occurrences were not a novelty in the Grosse Freiheit.

Years later I was reminiscing about the incident to be told the appalling story that the young lady in question had not come off as lightly as Fascher the younger. It may be apocryphal, such tales tend to take on a life of their own, but my informant ventured that she had been asked to leave her hotel immediately - via the third floor window. Gosh, they were such loveable rogues those St Pauli residents. They had a naughty streak in them but they were always good to their old mums, bless 'em.

There were other characters around town equally as colourful and thankfully less violent. Adrian Barber, a skinny cerebral looking guitarist with a group from Liverpool called The Big Three, was a living demonstration of true eccentricity who may well have been the role model for Chris Curtis' later adopted persona. As orderly as his mind was in the field of audio electronics where he was considered to be a bit of a genius, in his day-to-day existence it shot off at a different angle entirely.

Deciding it was a touch lonely so far from home he deemed that a pet would ease the situation and he took to trailing a hair brush behind him as he went for his daily walk through the streets of St Pauli. To give them credit the St Pauli locals hardly offered a glance in his direction. They were quite used to the 'crazy English'. The Beatles had set fire to a cinema and pissed on nuns so there was nothing particularly impressive about some nutter dragging a hairbrush in his wake. This was fairly tame stuff.

Before long he contrived a pregnancy for his cherished chum and before long a small trail of toothbrushes followed on, attached by string to their 'mother'. Before too long Adrian acquired a real pet, a living, breathing being in the form of a pig that he had purchased from the local market. It was a short-lived domestic situation. It was not suitable for a man to live with a pig in the apartments supplied. Someone objected. It may have been the pig. Adrian eventually quit The Big Three to stay on at the club as its sound technician. He had found his spiritual home.

Late at night after we had finished and if I was still on too much of a high to head back to the Germania I could watch Tony Sheridan reach deep down inside himself to rip out the tortured emotions of someone who had at some time in his life might have suffered badly. In a blues ridden display of angst he would wail his *Nobody's Child* with an intensity that rarely come out from beneath skin that pale.

He was the 'nearly man', almost becoming one of Cliff Richard's Drifters, later to become The Shadows, at the birth of British rock and roll in the late fifties. He was away from the 2 Is the night Cliff's young manager, John Foster dropped in on a hiring mission. Sheridan's prowess and mature jazz/rock feel was legendary in Soho. His nimble fingers could dance a ballet over the strings of his blond Grimshaw electric guitar. But time was tight. Things had to move fast in a world of passing fads and transitory teenage trends and Cliff's first major tour was about to hit the road. Instead Foster picked out the young Hank Marvin who managed to row his fellow Geordie Bruce Welch into the rhythm guitar spot. The rest, for Bruce and Hank, was history. For Sheridan the rest was the footballer's equivalent of a first team place in the third division.

Disillusioned, he moved to Hamburg where a modest local fame proved an acceptable compromise and cut a record, with a group of young British punks providing the chunking backing track to a rocked up version of the traditional song *My Bonnie (Lies Over The Ocean)*. The Beatles very quickly proved that they were nobody's backing group and their fame was to sail effortlessly over every ocean. Sheridan was left to bask listlessly in yet another touch of reflected glory. Maybe the kind of bitterness that such events might have caused to fester in his bowels also endowed him to sing the blues with conviction.

When we ran into him further on down the line in the eighties he was a white haired, grizzled man, still in Germany and pounding out *Skinny Minnie* and *What'd I Say* with conviction and energy while somehow managing to maintain a sense of humour. He had become a follower of the Bagwan Shri Rajneesh and dressed in a musty shade of claret as dictated by the hairy guru whose picture he kept in a bulky wooden locket which hung around his neck.

Sceptical to the end, I tend to feel that such emotional props that are to be found in mystic cults usually arise from the desperation and emptiness that follows in the wake a personal crisis in one's life. True, that cannot always be right but I certainly had my doubts about a self-appointed prophet who allowed his followers to shower him with gifts of a dozen or more Rolls Royce motor cars, not to mention my contempt for this insane obsession spiritual leaders seem to have with foisting pointless and unflattering fashions on their disciples. But if it gets you through the day who am I to preach? But then, who are they to preach either?

While I was in Hamburg I got to know the three tame Searchers well and when, a year on, they were up there at number one in the charts with their first ever single *Sweets For My Sweet* I found I was by sheer accident and good fortune a friend of the stars. Surely a just reward for being an incredibly nice person I thought. Hit followed hit and the gap between Tony and the others widened to the point where it was a chasm impossible to bridge. Negotiating the Kwai would have been easier. Thus I was offered the opportunity of a lifetime which, being a complete nerd as I have already mentioned, I turned down. Why? Goodness knows.

I remember the moment well. I was dining with Chris Curtis in a Spanish restaurant called Antonios. It was in London's Long Acre just across the street from where The Hippodrome disco stands now and it featured flamenco music and dancing while you washed down your paella with a pleasant Riojah. Most of my life I have spent sitting on a fence to the point where the splinters in my bum do not hurt anymore. I did not want to make the decision. I mumbled some half hearted excuses. Cliff Bennett and The Rebel Rousers were about to be signed by Brian Epstein and I didn't want to rock the boat. That was what I told myself. In truth I was simply scared. We moved off the subject and concentrated on the clicking of heels and the clacking of castanets.

A month or so later, in the autumn of '64 I was walking down a street in a small Irish town, the name of which I do not remember or have any great wish to, mainly because the promoter welched on at least half the money due at the end of our short tour there. Such a loss is either a good reason to remember or a good reason to forget depending on your philosophy in life. Up to that point I had kept silent but on impulse I mentioned the offer to a fellow Rebel Rouser. He was Moss Groves and played one of our two saxophones, an instrument described a little unkindly by some wag as an ill wind that nobody blows good. On hearing of my remarkable decision he offered the advice, 'Don't be so bloody stupid. Ring them up, tell them you'll take the job, and ask them if they want a sax player as well'. I did. They still wanted me, but sadly for Moss they did not want a sax player. There was already quite enough ill wind in the air. Fortunately any good wind seemed to be blowing my way.

By that time chart success had re-routed The Searchers and the days of performing for Fascher and Weissleder had gone, but Germany was to figure greatly in our lives over the ensuing decades. They had graciously cast aside all memories of the hostilities of the war and had accepted and adopted the hard edged sounds of those early British outfits, staying with them when other nations had deserted the sinking ships like cowardly rodents. We Brits had graciously promised not to give them another good kicking as long as they behaved themselves and paid to listen to our music. After all, they were two-nil down. They'd have to be insane to start another barney.

When we had completed our three years of fully fledged fame and the instinct for survival forced us to get on with the real life business of touring under the lesser banner of has-beens or a nostalgia act we took took advantage of the prospects still open for us in the land of the Hun earning more than a few honest pfennigs touring the clubs and bars throughout that vast country and at last taking the opportunity to see what the towns and villages were like, from the onion-domed confections that housed the leder-hosed Bavarians to the bleak, mundane industrial horrors of Dortmund and Stuttgart.

Even in our reduced circumstances it was a fun time with an audience close enough to see the whites of your eyes and drunk enough not to notice the bum notes. Invariably the club owners were as pissed as the punters and as different to their British counterparts as chalk and typewriters. Our dressing room was more often than not the booze cupboard. When we vacated at the end of the night it would be well on the way to becoming the booze-less cupboard. What folly. Teenage musicians in business for money, sex and drink (there were few drugs around at this time). It was like setting Jack The Ripper loose in a street full of prostitutes and saying 'don't do anything naughty'.

Late nights were the norm, mainly because the favourite occupation of mine host was to get absolutely ratted with the musicians at the end of his working day. It was a running competition as to whether the proprietor would be too far gone to hand over the money at the end of the night or the band got too plastered to count it properly. Being boring and relatively sober little Searchers we always won that one and on the occasion where the marks were just not there to be coughed up we simply dismantled the sound system and took it away with us.

As the seventies faded into the eighties and the nostalgia graph began its curve upwards the venues in Germany became grander. Travelling was not quite the same because we now flew in for one or two nights only to play in stadiums holding any amount from two to thirty thousand people. We were no longer fallen idols. We had hung on in there and become living legends. No more the trips along the accident strewn autobahns from village to village, from club to club. Now it was Heathrow Airport to its equivalent in Germany, coach to hotel, bed for the afternoon, rise for coach to arena where the backstage catering would satisfy our stomachs without emptying our pockets, perform for maybe half an hour and back to the hotel bar for a general piss-up in the company of like-minded reprobates.

These visual memory feasts gathered habitually together former luminaries from Britain, the U.S.A. and the continent in astonishing numbers and combinations and we were meeting the idols of our youth and our compatriots in the charts on neutral ground. The Mamas And Papas, whose 'Mama Cass' replacement had been transformed into an eight stone anorexic version of her former glory for one of its line-ups. Well, what could you expect? She was long dead, poor thing. No amount of coaxing would get her back on stage again and fat female singers were thin on the ground.

Desmond Dekker, the reggae king whose life bears as much relation to reality as Lester Piggot's tax return. Showaddywaddy, the fifties send-up group who had aged from teddy boys into teddy men. Mud and Marmalade. Slade and Sweet. The Troggs and The Tremeloes. George McCrae, almost a modern act compared to some... And Little Eva, these days more recognisable as Positively Enormous Eva. They were all there and enjoying their second wind. Some were by now so out of shape they struggled to find their second wind. Dozens of survivors strutted the remains of their stuff on stage in various states of career decline and bodily decay. Some had worn well. Others were well worn. And on one such bill was a man whose name was and still is synonymous with the greatest revolution in dance since the Charleston, The King of The Twist, Chubby Checker. Or Was it?

Come on now, admit it. Have you ever seen Chubby Checker and Winnie Mandela in the same room? Have you ever seen them in the same photograph? Of course you haven't. And do you know why? Well, I have my own theory. They are one and the same person. It was back in the summer of '94, somewhere in the wilds of former East Germany. In the wake of the dissolution of the Communist bloc countries maybe it should have a symbol instead of a name, like Prince: 'The Country Formerly Known as East Germany'.

The Searchers had played a concert alongside a couple of German supports and were due to join up with a bunch of nostalgia acts for a huge open air festival in Bad Segeberg, a moderate sized town about an hour's drive from Hamburg. The roster included Smokie, Sailor, Hot Chocolate, The Manfreds, Barry Ryan and others including The Chubster himself. Be downstairs in the lobby at seven thirty a.m., we were told. The tour bus, with all the rest of the motley crew on board, would pick us up. We picked ourselves up from our comfortable beds at an unsociable hour to assemble in the lobby, bleary-eyed and breakfastless. Seven thirty came. And it went.

So did eight. Half an hour later a bunch of not very happy bunnies saw the tour bus draw up. John McNally was fuming. Steam hissed from his ears like a character from The Beano. There was danger in the air. Beware. This man does not take prisoners!

The door swung open and we cursed our way to our seats, passing what looked like a crumpled brown duvet, topped off by a red, black and green crocheted woolly beret. It was not at first obvious but it transpired that there was a person dwelling within this debris of rags. There was a vague resemblance to Edna, the inebriate woman, a role once played on television by the veteran actress Patricia Hayes but another name quickly entered my brain. Good heavens, it was Winnie Mandela, in the flesh. Or at least in a silly hat. But it could not be Winnie. She wasn't on the tour, and anyway it would be years before she would become a nostalgia act. She was surely back in South Africa washing Nelson's socks or playing centre half with her football team. A second glance told us that this was in fact the original Lord Of The Dance himself. King Twist. The man who launched a thousand injured spines.

Henry Marsh, one of the two keyboard players from the group Sailor, felt we were due some sort of explanation regarding the delay. 'They had trouble getting Chubby out of bed,' he whispered. I was not impressed. 'He's probably been up all night crocheting that fucking hat,' I suggested. 'Drive on.'

When we arrived at our destination we eschewed a pointless sound check for a sensible sleep. Call me Gekko if you like but sound checks are for wimps. We did one in 1964. Didn't like it. It invariably alters beyond all recognition between the check and the show and one man's bass is another man's boom. The forty winks did me a power of good and I felt refreshed when I finally made the venue later that night. I headed straight for catering.

Catering was teeming with hungry souls. It is the meeting place. The heart of any tour. Where folk gather to wait for their turn to go on stage or just to chew the fat with chums. Chewing the fat is often preferable to chewing the food. It is one of life's little lotteries. Sometimes good, sometimes bad and sometimes non-existent. A cauldron of soup was steaming in the corner and my bowl tasted good. It is bean soup. At last I had the chance to use that terrible old chestnut, 'What soup is it? It's bean soup. I know it's been soup, but what is it now?' Even the jokes are oldies and goldies on these shows.

As the tour continued I was to discover that the same soup would appear almost every night. It had its own itinerary and transport and a backstage pass for every venue. Like Frankenstein the caterers seemed to have no control over their monster. They were sadly deficient in the creative department. Or maybe the budget just wasn't that good. I had a forgiving spirit but my stomach, which seemed to have an existence of its own, was bearing its own grudge and I had an uneasy feeling that its vengeance would be against me and my digestive system rather than the soup's creators and their bank balance.

A roar went up from the crowd as Chubby danced on stage and I wandered over to check him out. His American band were cookin' and he was wowing the crowd. For a man of his not inconsiderable bulk he was surprisingly lithe and graceful as he demonstrated the dance cult that had become one with his name. A little way into his act he displayed his first sign of eccentricity and, believe me, he has a whole cupboard full back there on whatever planet he lives on. There was a song in his show in which he introduced his band. It was a good band. In fact, they were excellent when, like tonight, they were playing well. They had been with him a while, some musicians for a number of years.

'And on bass we have', he began. Slowly, as if time was grinding to a halt, he turned to his bass player and silently he mouthed, in very precise and exaggerated lip movements, 'What's your name?'

The bass player stared back in astonishment. 'What?'

'What's your name?', the King of Twist repeated.

The guy's face took on a very hurt expression - like a small boy who had been forgotten when the sweets were passed round or when they were choosing the sides for baseball. 'Jim', he answered, bewildered and cut to the quick at this slight. Chubby nodded. He turned to face the audience once more, and then as he started to speak, an action replay. In more time than it takes an elephant to gestate he traversed one hundred and eighty degrees to face the bassist again.

'Who?'

'Jim'.

The whole thing could only have taken a minute or two but it seemed like an eternity until, triumphantly, Ernest Evans, a.k.a. Chubby Checker, living legend, was able to tell the gathered hordes in a booming voice, 'Jim'. By this time most of them had forgotten what was supposed to be happening. Others had forgotten who the current chancellor was or which year they had left home for this concert. But they stoically gathered their communal wits about them in time to applaud the embarrassed, horrified and almost anonymous, musician. It was a nerve-racking spectacle. After our show I would be grateful for the comfort and ambience of the bar.

The most important thing on the first night is the hotel bar. First of all it has to be open. Secondly, it has to remain open. And thirdly, it has to be fully stocked with extremely strong alcohol. It sets the tone of the whole adventure. The major fun of these tours is not so much the shows - although it is preferable to have more good ones than bad - as the rare opportunity to be away with friends that have been absent for too long and to be alleviated of the usual restrictions that apply when there is a sober journey home to be undertaken after the performance. Nothing of the sort here. This is aprés ski without the ski but if there is no snow there are other slippery slopes to be negotiated and 'on the piste' takes on a different meaning entirely. No responsibilities. Just fun, fun, fun. Till your daddy takes your wine glass away.

There are certain customs that surround the use of such places. One choice is to pace yourself and sip lightly while indulging in an initially sensible conversation that leisurely turns to either incomprehensible gibberish or mawkish sentimentality as the hours pass by. If your light sipping has been light enough it is quite possible to proceed in time to your chamber none the worse for wear, more or less.

Alternatively you could join a 'round'. It goes something like this. You 'stand' a round. Another reveller reciprocates by standing the next round and so the ritual continues as one after the other your fellow drinkers stand their round. It is easy to realise when the standing has to cease because you proceed to fall down. From that position you somehow find your way to your room on the tenth floor. You have no idea how you managed it of course. You never do. This is part of the ritual and a skill that you do not learn. It simply comes with the territory.

Once inside your room, which takes a mean average of four and a half minutes from your first attempt at inserting an oversized key into a curiously shrunken lock, it is customary to recite the traditional prayer. In order to accomplish this you must first enter the *en suite* bathroom and talk to God on the great white porcelain telephone. More often than not a gift of food is offered up at this point. The prayer has a preordained structure. In this prayer it is usual to request of your maker that you be released from your mortal existence as swiftly and as painlessly as possible. Tradition dictates of course that your prayer is never answered. Now you are left only with the promise which, as all followers of the creed know, is 'never again'. Tradition also dictates that this solemn promise is never kept.

Having completed these important tasks you are now expected to complete the 'crawl of penance' to where your mattress is waiting in the main chamber. Particularly devout followers like me have been known to remain in this prone position by the side of the bed for several hours but such excessive devotion is only expected after exceptional acts of worship and is not demanded of novices. Once on your place of rest you can only hope that your bed, which by one of God's miracles is spinning furiously, will eventually spin you into a welcome oblivion.

Meanwhile, back in the real world the bar filled up as the acts finished and the shuttle buses returned from the hall. This particular night I had decided to pace myself. Just a couple of hours, then sleep. After all, there were a lot of shows and a lot of long journeys to come. I must be sensible and mature about this. The words 'plans' and 'best laid' sprang to mind. After pacing myself for some time, theoretically before retiring to my room, my room remained more than a few paces away. I was beginning to wobble and felt the onset of nausea. My addled thought waves detected a distant whisper calling from my place of rest, a promise from my bed that I would feel better if I was lying in it. When I got there I discovered that my bed was lying. I did not feel better. I felt distinctly worse and my brain did a re-enactment of the opening to The Time Tunnel, spinning ever downwards to sink unconscious in a sea of spritzers. Was it four a.m. or five? Who cared? This was pension rock. And after all, Scarlett, tomorrow is another day!

Chubs was definitely the 'character' of the tour. Some say they broke the mould when he was born. I just think they scraped the mould off the top and pretended nothing was wrong, just like you do with old cheese. On the bus the next day he was to be found in his usual seat at the front of the bus, darning his jeans with a circular needle, the kind you use for stitching canvas and the like. When he had finished, it wasn't the neatest job in the world, but at least he had completed the task. I had witnessed scenes like this during recreational therapy sessions at the twilight home where my poor old Pa was incarcerated in his fading years.

It was on this long drive that we showed our British eccentricity at its loopiest. I was chatting away to Henry Marsh when he nudged me and pointed towards the driver.

'I'm sure he's nodding off,' he said. I looked and had to admit that in the rear view mirror the eyelids did appear to be dangerously near to closing.

'What do you think we should do? I asked.

Henry shrugged. We pass the information to others nearby. Nobody

seemed willing to make any kind of definite move. It seemed a bit imper-
tinent to criticise an experienced coach driver. For ages we sat, humming
and haahing. Henry swore the bus had swerved towards the verge earlier.
Then the ridiculousness of the situation hit us. Our lives were in jeopardy
but we sat in embarrassed silence. How bloody British of us. Die if necessary, but for heaven's sake don't draw attention to yourself. Finally, Henry
took the bull by the horns and went to the front to engage the driver in
scintillating conversation. Face had been saved.

At a later point in the tour Chubby pulled another surprise from up his
sleeve. He decided to strangle his road manager. Not too unusual perhaps.
Surely it happens every day. The victim, a New Yorker in his mid-twenties
by the name of Rob, had decided to capture the fun atmosphere on camera and began to snap away. Unfortunately, Chubby decided to snap as
well. Or at least something in his head did. He wrestled Rob to the floor
and tightened his hands around his throat. He was joking, surely? But the
poor guy's face was turning blue. Someone eventually managed to prise
them apart. Rob was out of his mind with anger. Chubby was merely out
of his mind. He appeared oblivious. Maybe this was an everyday occurrence in the life of a twisting superstar.

Half an hour after departure time the next morning the bus was still two
Americans light. Chubby's drummer hadn't received an alarm call. He
managed to get himself together quickly and joined the rest of us. That
only left Rob the almost asphyxiated road manager. They called him on
the house 'phone and we waited. Fifteen minutes later and still no Rob.
Charlie the manager went up to the room. He returned after ten minutes,
grim faced. Apparently, Rob was still seething after his near demise at the
hands of the Philadelphia Strangler. Charlie retrieved money from his
briefcase at the back of the bus and got off again, followed closely by King
Twister. Five minutes later, Charlie and Chubby were back. 'Okay, let's go.'
So there it was. All of you who still work for Chubby Checker - two paces
forward. Not you, Rob.

If Chubby travelled through life by the scenic route then reggae legend
Desmond Dekker was negotiating a few side roads of his own. Conversation with him was not a simple task but I made one attempt. Once again
it was in the grim confines of the former East Germany which, no matter
how 'former' it is, will always remain East Germany. There is a pervading
gloom that seems to hover over this vast expanse, a grey fog of despair that
is intangible yet ever present. If countries were food then this was a boarding house porridge.

It was check out time at a tower block hotel that only knew of the families Hilton and Sheraton as rich and distant relations. Its foyer was furnished with stick furniture long since out of fashion but too young to be anywhere near becoming trendy again. I spied Desmond at the desk. Wearing his ever present black beret which led me to suspect that beneath might lie a follicle-free zone. As it appeared to be welded to his scalp I was unlikely ever to be privy to the secret.

The dark glasses were mandatory and below that he wore a black shirt and black leather jeans, another item of clothing I can't remember ever seeing him without. Someone suggested that they were not leather trousers at all and that he had simply polished his legs but I knew they were wrong as they flared out at the ankles and stopped in a straight line just above the feet.

I walked over clutching my prized Guinness Book of Hit Singles in which I had already acquired the signatures of an impressive number of artistes. I opened it at the appropriate page in readiness and politely asked him if he would write over his entry. He gazed in wide-eyed astonishment as if he could not quite take it in and indeed he could not.

'Whoa man, these are my records,' he said not quite believing what he was seeing. I nodded and confirmed that they certainly were.

'What is this book, man?' I was amazed. I had never encountered anyone, certainly not a performer who had never heard of the tome. I let him into this closely guarded secret. This book contained every hit single ever released in Great Britain. His state of astonishment refused to subside.

'I gotta have this book, man.' I pointed out that there was not a problem. You could get them in most booksellers.

'But I gotta have this one. This one got my records.' I carefully explained that every one of them had his records in. It was not just mine. At last he appeared to grasp it.

'Where can I get one?' he asked. I suggested a W. H. Smith would be the simplest solution.

'Is there one around here?' he wanted to know. I patiently suggested that East Germany was probably not the most convenient location and that it would be better if he waited till we got back to the U.K. He signed and I returned to my little group exhausted. I reasoned that if he and Chubby were touring Germany together in the future that perhaps the Chub would be gracious enough to give Desmond a lift home on the way to whichever galaxy he was currently a resident.

5

Go West Young Man

The huge Boeing 707 lurched uncomfortably as it hung precariously in the skies over New York awaiting its turn in the holding pattern for the chance to put down in the promised land. This was my personal Mecca, the birthplace of it all with rock and roll cemented in every brick of the skyscraping monoliths below. This had been the place of my dreams for years. Another jolt as it buffered against a cloud formation. My stomach did a forward roll and threatened to unload the meal we had been served a few hours ago. I was still new to this flying game.

As the plane buffeted my mind replayed a scene from the night before, a rather smart cocktail party in St John's Wood, the kind where the wine is older than the guests and the canapés are presented more for their artistic merit than their ability to satisfy the cravings of your stomach.

'What sign are you?' I was caught unawares by the question which had come out of the blue. The tiny cluster of guests had up to that point been discussing the merits or otherwise of the Beatles and the new music in general. Standard fare in the wake of the new hysteria. I turned my head to face the voice which belonged to a woman in her mid thirties I guessed, delicate in appearance and dressed in one of those smock-like creations of the period that were oh so fashionable. She stood there waiting like a badly made lampshade with teeth. A younger version of Miss Havisham and in a kind of soft focus as if she were covered from head to toe in a fine film of talcum powder ready to be wrapped in tissue and put away only to be brought out on special occasions.

46

'What?' I was still too young and uncouth to say pardon.

'What sign are you?' My hackles rose. I hated that star sign crap.

'No entry', I replied in a tone that might just have overstepped the line between mild impudence and biting sarcasm.

'Very funny. Come on, what's your sign?' politeness got the better of principles.

'Sagittarius'.

'I knew it'. Oh yeah, great. I'm impressed. If you knew it why did you need to ask? I wanted to say but didn't. She reached out and took my hand, turning it palm up. I winced inwardly but went with the flow. This mumbo jumbo stuff was loathsome and ridiculous to me. I had long since discarded religion and superstition, depending on logic and simple common sense to get me safely from the current stage of my life to its hopefully peaceful end and resented having to bear the slings and arrows of outrageous fortune-tellers.

'I don't believe in horoscopes and all that', I offered hoping she would bow to my cynicism and give up. She took no notice and traced her finger along my life line.

'You are going to travel', she said with an affected and self satisfied look of inscrutable wisdom. Brilliant. Who isn't? In fact I was indeed going to travel. The very next day in fact, to the United States of North America. This could not have been exactly a divine revelation to her as I had already been discussing the impending tour with every Tom, Dick and Henrietta in the place. I was the only pop star there, albeit a pretty new one and not very important in the pop star ratings due to my being drafted in rather than having been there from the outset. But in that particular room I was a fairly interesting catch.

'Be careful', she continued unabashed and undeterred by my impatience.

Be careful? What on earth was the woman on about? I was going on an aeroplane for God's sake. How can you be careful on an aeroplane? You either get on it or you don't and from then on it either crashes or it doesn't. Are there two Ls in bollocks? I desperately wanted to say but instead I simply withdrew my paw.

'Can't be doing with all that', I said nearly adding that the only tale the lines on my palm could tell that I helped my mum far too much with the washing up. I excused myself from her company and went off to mingle in more earthbound company.

I still thought it was pure drivel but I couldn't help reflecting wryly as the hairy descent got under way. If there truly was a God then he was apparently not too pissed off with me denying his existence because Pan American flight 101 from Heathrow touched down and rolled along the tarmac to a safe stop on that afternoon of September the 7th 1964. I had arrived.

We had travelled 'cattle class'. I was unaware then that teenage idols are supposed to be in First, Club at the very least. A council house lad like me was just grateful to be on anything with an inside toilet.

The reception inside the terminal building was not exactly at Beatle level but there were a lot of girls waiting and more than willing to scream at anything with long-ish hair and an English accent. They had been hyped up for weeks by Murray The K, the brash New York Jewish deejay who had cleverly attached his rising star to the coat tails of The Beatles and to the whole of the second British Invasion. We would need those loud screams at the shows because we weren't really all that good in musical terms, just very fashionable which is after all what pop stardom is essentially about.

We were hustled into a room for a press conference at which, being the new boy, I was little more than an observer. I tried to take it all in. The people looked different. I was glad of that. I wanted very much for it to be and to feel different. Even the smell of the place was different. I was Charity Hope Valentine ahead of her time. If my friends could see me now. We tried hard to respond to the questions of the press with the same quality of irreverent wit that the Beatles had delivered on their momentous visits but it didn't quite cut it. Still, a Dick Van Dyke accent and hair down to your ear lobes was all they required in the current wave of the love of all things British.

We were herded outside past grappling hands and high pitched yelling voices into the waiting limousine, an enormous black stretch Cadillac whose front was right before us but whose rear was still parked somewhere around the next block. The interior was red leather and the shade of the upholstery matched the deep pile carpeting. It was also bigger than our lounge at home. I wanted to move in right away. I could convert the ashtray into a bathroom.

We took in the sights as we headed out on the freeway towards Manhattan passing Shea Stadium with hardly a glance. It was just the home of a baseball team, The New York Yankees, but in a year's time it would be the setting for perhaps the most iconic of all The Beatles' U.S. concerts. It was at Shea that stadium rock was invented.

The buildings of the city that seemed merely huge on the skyline grew

48

to monstrous proportions as we neared them, like desperate arms stretching up to grab their own little piece of space and fresh air in the claustrophobia of that great metropolis. We were Lilliputians in the land of Brobdignag. It occurred to me that the skyscraper might just be the architect's equivalent of the red sports car. The penis extension.

Was the red E type I bought in '67 just such a thing with its long phallic bonnet complete with power bulge along the centre? The honest answer is probably yes, an answer to which I have no complaint. Heaven knows I would have been grateful for a tad extra. Not that I was either pauper or prince in that area you understand. It was, as one of my friends so directly put it, 'pleasant without being memorable'. Did architects brag to their girlfriends 'Have you seen the size of my building?' Answers on a postcard please to Architectural Digest.

We spilled out onto the pavement in front of The Americana Hotel on Broadway and checked into our rooms on the eleventh floor. As we went up in the elevator I saw that Phyllis Diller was appearing in cabaret here. I had no idea who Phyllis Diller was but she certainly was not first in line when good looks were being passed around. She had been landed with the kind of face like that wouldn't get a kick in a stampede. In time it would be revealed to me that her less than wonderful visage was her stock in trade and her raucous patter of self abuse had made her rich and famous. The fame however like some wines never did travel well and she remained virtually unknown to the Great British public.

My room seemed vast and luxurious. Hotel life for me was still in its infancy and carpets on the floor and furnishings that matched were symbolic of the finest materialism, delicious decadence to be savoured and enjoyed. A linoleum-free environment where curtains boasted more than one thickness of material. Nirvana indeed.

I switched on the bulky Zenith television, twice the size of any comparable device available in England, and waited for the magic of colour to appear. This truly was 'Tomorrowland'. We were still a few years away from this wonder of the modern age back home where we were stuck with a paltry two channels and hour upon hour of blank screen. As I stared at the beauty of it all a familiar image appeared on that small rectangle and a sound emitted that sent shivers down my spine. If I had believed in omens then this surely would have been one. Eddie Cochran was pumping his way through *Twenty Flight Rock* pushing his Gretsch 6120 hollow body back and forwards in a display of unbridled excitement and energy. This was *The Girl Can't Help It*, the greatest rock and roll film of them all and the song was the same one with which Paul McCartney has so impressed the virtually unimpressionable John Lennon in a word perfect rendition way back there at the birth of The Beatles.

I rushed into John McNally's room and switched his set on to the right channel. Cochran's Bigsby arm vibrated the final chord and it was a signal to move. I had to see something of New York. The others had already been there and done it when they flew over for The Ed Sullivan Show earlier that year. We settled on The Peppermint Lounge, the uptown club where the Twist had started out and the jumping off point to fame for Joey Dee And The Starliters with whom we had worked at The Star Club.

Joey and his cronies had long since departed his old stomping ground and as we entered there was no one on the small podium, just the sound of records coming from hidden speakers. We were asked for I.D. I had no idea what an I.D. was and was astonished that people were required to carry them. It felt like wartime or some kind of third world police state. Culture shock dealt a second blow when I discovered you had to be twenty-one in most American states to drink alcohol. At this point in my life I was completely teetotal anyway but back home you could bluff your way into a pub the minute you managed to scrape the bum fluff off your face.

At least New York was civilised enough to admit anyone eighteen or over and, after quizzing us on age and profession, the manager dispensed with the need for us to run back and fetch the proof that was in our passports, adding that being musicians we also avoided the cover charge. We entered, we sat and we observed the sparsely populated interior of a place that had roared through its fifteen minutes of fame and was heading out the other side fast. We exited even faster, our expectations vanquished like the passing craze that had once brought them in here by the hundreds. The club that had spawned The Twist was now experiencing its own twist of fate, dying on feet that were more tired than those of its dance weary customers.

Walking along Broadway was truer to the image I had of the city although 42nd Street had already begun its descent into the seedy twilight world of porn. If Busby Berkley had seen it in this condition he would no doubt have taken the elevator to the top of The Empire State Building and jumped off without a moment's hesitation. Accompanied of course by two dozen blondes in spangled gowns falling in perfect synchronisation alongside him and smiling all the way. Over on Times Square The Animals were appearing at The Paramount, the theatre where teen hysteria had been invented when bobbysoxers had been bribed to scream at a skinny Italian kid called Sinatra. Supporting them was Elkie Brooks, still years ago from any real degree of fame. America had embraced Britmania.

We were torn between cricking our necks to look upwards and marvel at the sheer magnificence of Man's achievement in the realms of construction and assimilating the astonishing variety of cultures and classes that made up the most cosmopolitan city in the world. 'Give me your tired and your hungry' the words went. A lot of the people around me looked very tired indeed. The hungry approached to ask for handouts and, being British, I stared ahead trying not to falter and pretending that it wasn't happening. The immaculately attired plutocracy strode purposely towards their next fortune jaded and unconcerned by the adjacent poverty. Here the law of the jungle applied. Kill or be killed. The survival of the fittest. There would have been no need for Charles Darwin to venture further than these environs to compile all the data necessary for his Origin of the Species.

Shops were open the whole time while back home we were still enslaved by archaic laws which forced you to starve or at the very least suffer severe discomfort if you had misjudged your timing when stocking the household. I checked out stores selling anything from gold plated cutlery guaranteed not to wear off, at least not until you got back to your own country the following week, to items of outrageous lingerie that was never meant to be worn merely in the pursuit of comfort and modesty.

I bought a hairdryer, as much for the illicit thrill of completing the transaction at midnight as the necessity of compensating for the 220 volt model I had packed and which threatened to douse the Americana in complete darkness at switch-on. It was extremely cheap and it worked perfectly. Just the once. Never again after that maiden voyage did it whirr into life. Recognising a sucker when I saw one in the mirror I did not take it back to the store from whence it came. I was too ashamed. I capitulated and replaced it later with a model which would perform with an efficiency and longevity in direct proportion to its price. After an hour or so of people gazing we quit the streets for the comfort of our beds and a fitful, jetlagged sleep.

At 10 a.m. the next morning we were assembled in the foyer and soon bundled into the limousine for the trip to Brooklyn, one of the five boroughs that constitute New York City. Over the big steel Brooklyn Bridge we drove, travelling through streets poorer than those we had left and where dishevelled bodies lounged in various states of drunkenness and every other kind of stupor along the sidewalk. Instead of ivy the walls of the buildings were adorned with winding and rusted metal fire escapes snaking their way past windows behind which every facet of desperate

America was trying their damnedest to survive. The city was still perspiringly hot that September. Back home the Autumn chill would have been setting in by now. It was all so very different. Here they spoke an English of sorts but there the similarity ended.

The Fox Theatre came into view, a monument to the glorious age of Deco when picture houses were palaces for the people. Places to forget their impoverishment and wallow in the make believe glamour purveyed by people whose own true glamour was being provided by that very same cash strapped poor. If the building was a feast for the eyes then the words above the entrance was truly a musical gourmand's heaven. Our name was there in bold, black letters among a galaxy of stellar names in the field of popular music.

Dusty Springfield. We knew she would be there as we shared the same office and agent back in London. Her to-die-for voice and dramatic pop-diva persona had captured the U.S. market with her perfectly executed recording of Burt Bacharach's *Wishing And Hoping*. She wasn't just one of the best singers in Great Britain. She was one of the best singers in the world. Also from the U.K. was Millie, the tiny reggae star (or Blue Beat as it was then known) whose song *My Boy Lollipop* had repeated its British success across the Atlantic.

The list of American acts was one to boggle a mind in a way that the mind could have no possible defence. Marvin Gaye, the jewel in the crown of Motown, lean, tall and handsome and possessing one of the sweetest and most soulful voices known to man. The Supremes, barely on the rise with *Where Did Our love Go* and about to consolidate the impression that had been made with their new release *Baby Love*. The Temptations who up to that point had been one of Motown's greatest success stories and The Contours whose *Do You Love Me?* had been covered and charted in Britain by Brian Poole And The Tremeloes. The sensual and sexy Ronettes *(Be My Baby)* featuring lead singer Ronnie who was still in the early days of her courtship by the legendary Phil Spector.

The list seemed endless. Martha And The Vandellas *(Dancing In The Streets)*, The Shangrilas *(Remember, Walking In The Sand)*, Smokey Robinson And The Miracles *(Mickey's Monkey)*, The Dovells *(The Bristol Stomp)*, Jay And The Americans *(Only In America)*, The Newbeats *(Bread And Butter)*, Little Anthony And The Imperials *(Tears On My Pillow)*. It was all too much. These were people we had revered and idolised throughout our musical apprenticeship. Here they were almost taken for granted by a large part of American record buyers despite the astonishing sum total of their hit recordings and yet held in the highest esteem by a British public who could only be granted their diet of soul via a sort of osmosis through the turntable.

Filling out any spare inch of space left in the theatre would be the musicians of the Earl Warren Orchestra who would be puffing, pounding and scraping away for almost the entire length of the non-stop extravaganza. In fact the only short break on the proceedings was to be the quick set-up for our entrance on stage during which we would have to get plugged in and dash our way through our three song set. Three songs was a veritable privilege and declaration of our extreme importance in the pecking order. Most of the acts were there to perform a single hit before sliding off to one side as the next slid on from the other.

Once inside the theatre we were given a run-down. The opening was to be a make-believe airport scene with the acts passing one by one through the terminal gate to be welcome by an over-the-top and hideously dressed Murray The K. His attempt at fashion consciousness promised to do as much good for that industry as Al Capone did for law and order. Murray was at that 'in between age'. His persona as a hip godfather to the kids was fighting a losing battle with his appearance, that of a dyed-in-the-wool Sinatra-influenced fogey. The appalling line in the kind of sweater that would embarrass even a golfer was only outdone in sheer awfulness by his 'ring-a-ding-ding' 'Fly Me To The Moon' vintage hat.

As if those crimes were not enough he perpetrated yet another by inventing his own teenage-speak called 'meazerry' (pronounced me-a-zerry) the rules of which are too complicated and stupid to enter into here and which made Bill and Ben sound positively intelligent. The idea was that you could have a conversation in front of strangers without them understanding what you were saying. The fact that these strangers could hear this and savvy that whatever you were saying was probably offensive at worst and downright rude at best put you in great danger of getting a severe smack in the face. In Islington or Bethnal Green you'd never get out alive.

The inside of the Fox was reminiscent of a third world sweatshop, every tiny dressing room crammed to bursting point with human flesh and with all the smells that go with it. Mingled with the human smells of course were the herbal smells that accompanied the more private pastimes of that melée of worldly-wise musicians. It was a hell hole that would have been enforceably closed by the health department had it been the workplace of any other profession than the music fraternity who, quite reasonably, deserved nothing better.

We were all secreted away in our minuscule cubby holes made even more minuscule by the number of bodies expected to occupy each, the Americans renting portable air conditioners to control the sweltering and

53

increasing heat. We declined and while the others crisped like salads in their little Frigidaires we took on the aspect of lightly steamed vegetables in our own private oven. Hot weather was a rare luxury to be cherished back home and we were not about to toss it aside lightly. As the days wore on the human vegetables that were us altered from a pleasant *al dente* to an overcooked parallel of the gastronomic atrocities I can still recall with horror from the days of school dinners.

Dusty would arrive by limo each morning, her mascara truck following behind and taking up a whole of the block. She had style. La Springfield had turned the kind of eyes that Tyson used to inflict on his opponents as punishment into an art form. Topped by the kind of haircut that could have been a mansion to a colony of bees and draped in beaded gowns that reflected the light of the Supertrooper and caused permanent damage to the vision of her devoted fans she was the epitome of a true star in an age of working class heroes. She exuded glamour and fantasy. And it was all quite unnecessary, for the former Mary Isobel Catherine O'Brien, late of The Springfields, was the owner of a voice that would no doubt have achieved a stardom of its own had it been inside the body of a three legged wart hog.

She was invariably to be found bunking in with Martha Reeves and her Vandellas. Martha was a big, bluff gap-toothed native of the Motor City enjoying her first real flush of success with *Dancing In The Streets*, unaware that the lowlier Supremes were about to leave her behind with the Fords while Diana Ross and Co streaked off in a Cadillac of stardom never again to be equalled in Berry Gordy's roster of girl groups. Partly perhaps because Gordy was in love with Diana Ross and all his energies were directed towards making her a success. The only person to try harder than Gordy was Diana herself.

Dusty's sexuality had always been in question and there was a rumour that she and Martha had been an item. I doubt it. I simply believe they enjoyed the same music, the same sense of humour and occasionally the same dressing room. I have often found that rumour and reality are rarely bedfellows. Whoever her bedfellows were and whatever Dusty did or did not do either in or out of her own bedroom should have been of no concern to anyone. I just hope that whatever she did made her extremely happy and I hope she got more of what she wanted than I did. That, by the way, would not have taken much effort. I have known Catholic priests who had a more active sex life than mine.

I can however proudly boast that Dusty Springfield once fiddled with my willie. And that is all you are about to hear of that - for now. I shall leave you in suspense with that tantalising little carrot, a tale of my own tantalising little carrot, in the hope that it will encourage the purchases of any biography I may write in the future. But then again, why wait? I might as well spill the bans.

The year I think was 1972. I left the raunchy red E type Jaguar behind and set out from my modest but rather nice mock Tudor detached house in Hayes, Middlesex in my little red Mini for Dusty's luxurious town house in Holland Park. It had cost her around £25,000 or so Peppi told me and it was an outrageous amount for a medium-sized London property in those days. Peppi Borza was her American dancer friend who was a constant companion, on-tap-fun and all round good guy. After arriving to settle in England from his native Florida, he had made a brief bid for fame with the advent of the new dance craze that swept the land at the beginning of the swinging sixties under the impressive handle of Peppi and the New York Twisters.

I remember a dance hall in Catford where the bouncers physically restrained anyone who attempted to dance the Twist when it first arrived on the scene. The owner thought it was like copulation three feet apart. My, how times do change. I wonder what he'd have thought of Channel 4? Anyway, after a while Peppi soon learned to stick with what he knew best and carved out a good living as the dance captain of several West End musicals.

Dusty was sharing her Holland Park home at that time with a young American singer called Norma Tanega. A name not exactly on everyone's lips but famous for a while following her self-penned hit *Walking My Cat Named Dog*. It had reached the dizzy heights of number twenty-two in the April of '66. Her follow-up hit here was noticeable by its complete absence and she was now making an attempt to establish herself as an artist. Once I arrived we all decided we should hit the clubs. All except for Norma that is who would not be talked into it. She was up for nothing more than a quiet night so without even her cat named dog for company she stayed back at the house while Peppi, Dusty and I piled into the little red cube and gunned off to Kensington High Street.

Yours and Mine was the 'in' club of the moment. Basically a predominantly gay establishment that was situated underneath a restaurant called The Sombrero. The people were beautiful, the atmosphere was intoxicating and the music was good. Some of the boys looked like girls and many of the girls looked like boys. And there were others who were probably only there to ogle boys who looked like girls and girls who looked like boys. We soon settled into the spirit of the evening and the place was more than buzzing that night because the diva herself was there.

Pretty soon Dusty and I were engrossed in a conversation which covered a lot of things, among which was the surprising fact that she had a 'thing" about soccer players and that in particular she quite fancied Gary Sprake who was keeping goal for Leeds back then. Shock, horror Dusty fancied men, do I hear you say? Well she did. I wonder if Gary Sprake ever knew of her secret passion?

Dusty was quickly getting smashed. I think it was vodka and coke but I really can't remember. I was remaining absolutely sober. It was a good five years before I would resign my membership of the worshipful company of teetotallers. In those days I was terminally dull. Boring was a giddy height I could only hope to reach once I learned to chill out a bit. The hours flew and when we looked up Peppi was nowhere to be seen. We learned later he had felt ignored and went off in a bit of a huff. Finally we quit the club, me leading and La Springfield wobbling dangerously behind.

We made it to the mini and I started her up but before I could put it into gear Dusty had reached across and rested her hand on my thigh. What on earth was happening? She began to tell me of a yearning she was having. The desperate need to have a child. Her body clock was ticking away, she explained, and she really had to do something before it was too late. At that point, I don't think I could utter a word. I was caught totally off guard. She, however had a theory.

'If you and I were to have a child it would be a really great looking kid', she suggested. My mouth was probably gawping like a goldfish but nothing was coming out. Inside, however, words and thoughts were trampling each other to death while frantically trying to assemble themselves in some sort of cohesive order. I knew the analogy was not a true parallel but the tale of Marilyn Monroe and George Bernard Shaw came to mind.

Marilyn had suggested to Shaw that, with his brains and her beauty a child of theirs would be the most incredible being.

'Ah yes,' replied Shaw, 'but what if it had your brains and my beauty?'

I was no Shaw. No such glistening spears of wit were waiting to swallow dive off my tongue but I garbled some excuse about not being quite ready to face up to the responsibilities of being a father. By this time her hand had moved over onto a part of my anatomy where a hand should really not be placed without prior permission from the owner. Thee appendage, that was only separated form the superstar's skin by the thickness of a piece of cavalry twill, was certainly not rising to the occasion as one might expect would be the case. Instead it was starting to shrink to the point where it was beginning to resemble a particularly malnourished earthworm.

Dusty appeared to suss out my discomfort and tried to allay my fore-
bodings by explaining that she would take sole responsibility for the offspring and that it should be no burden on me, financially or otherwise. I
was not convinced. I could see this coming back to haunt me in years to
come. We were not talking simply a 'bit of naughties' here. We were talking a real live, breathing baby. I tried to qualify my earlier misgivings but
it was already too late. The moment was lost and magic had gone. The
hand was withdrawn and we set off back for the house.

In truth I knew in my heart of hearts that it was just the booze talking.
But my mind kept going back to that bizarre situation. I wondered for a long
time what the child would have been like had we actually managed to get it
together. He or she would now be hurtling towards its thirties at an alarming rate. Was I a fool? Should I have simply taped it to a lolly stick and done
the dirty deed? I really don't know. The thought was very intriguing though.

We got back to the house that night to a Norma who was highly
amused at the totally legless state of her chum. She couldn't resist picking
up my camera and capturing the moment for posterity. My final true
shame was not the inability to deal with the aforementioned incident in a
mature and sophisticated manner. It was looking at those photographs
many years later and knowing that we had both been wearing the most
appalling clothes in Christendom.

Dusty's suede harlequinned trousers and waistcoat were however a tad
more forgiveable than my ball crushingly tight bell-bottom trouser which
looked as though they'd shrunk at the cleaners or had an argument with
my patent leather shoes. My tweed jacket would have been worn with
pride by Norman Wisdom I'm sure. As if that wasn't enough, my Jason
King haircut made Dusty's beehive look like a short back and sides. How
the fashion police didn't get us that night I will never know.

The outcome was that, once the alcohol had worn off of course, she did-
n't remember a thing about it. When I finally brought it up years later I had
to describe the whole farcical episode in graphic detail. Oh the disgrace.
The embarrassment. Not of failing to be a man. Or of merely behaving like
a completely unsophisticated dickhead. Even those awful clothes paled into
insignificance up against the tragic truth that my idol had absolutely no rec-
ollection whatsoever of fiddling with my willy. Sometimes life is very cruel.

Dusty had her own unique way of letting off steam when it all became
too much. She would send a minion out to buy a box of cheap crockery and
spent as long as it took to either exhaust the supplies or purge her demons
by hurling them at the walls of the corridor outside her dressing room.

Anyone around would be invited to join in the orgy of destruction. I never did. Even the cheapest material item came too expensive for me to get involved in its wanton destruction. But it worked for dear old Dusty and she could afford it. Anyway, it was probably cheaper than the price of a therapist.

The Supremes were luminaries in waiting. *Where Did Our Love Go?* had charted and *Baby Love* was waiting in the wings. I never saw that much of them. They tended to stay tucked in their dressing room planning how they would conquer first The States and then the world. Maybe they drank Coca Cola or perhaps they were already celebrating with champagne. Pretty soon saucers of milk would have been more appropriate fare for the cat-fights that were about to start as Florence Ballard and Mary Wilson saw Miss Ross, as journalists were eventually instructed to address her, edge herself into an entirely different galaxy.

In her autobiography Mary Wilson wrote that Ross, who apparently was Christened with the rather more proletarian tag of Diane, suddenly announced in '65 that there had been a mistake on her birth certificate and that from henceforth she would be known by her true name of Diana. When I read this I checked with my signed programme and there was her signature, inscribed in the September of '64 and it clearly states Diana. Maybe she was just practising.

For seven days we were incarcerated in that art deco mausoleum, entering at ten each morning and obtaining day-release twelve hours later. There were six shows in rapid succession and each preceded by a film of unutterable awfulness and banality. It was an Arabian adventure featuring Sinbad or some such character flying about on a magic carpet and its sole purpose was to get the people out of the theatre. If that sounds a little bid odd I must explain. The kids would stand in line from dawn for tickets and once they were in they were entitled to stay for as long as they could stand to hear *Be My Baby* or *Bread and Butter* etcetera. Eventually even the most devoted or mentally challenged of juvenile delinquents would crack at the prospect of having to watch Ali pratting about on that bloody rug for another hour and a half.

As the day wore on the colour of the audience would subtly alter. The insipid pink of the Caucasian teenyboppers who would scream their lungs out over current idols like us gave way to the shade of midnight soul. The people then known as coloured but who, in these politically correct days have become either black or native American, would roar their approval of the tall, handsome and oh so wonderful Marvin Gaye. Marvin was a real ebony star. His voice was a pure instrument that could move lightly and effortlessly from one range to another, *Wherever I Lay My Hat* slipping into *The Days Of Wine And Roses* like cream into coffee. I watched in admiration from the side of the stage most nights. He would say 'Hi' as he passed but I was never brave enough to engage him in further conversation.

Smokey Robinson was altogether more approachable and was happy to talk about the blessed Motown organisation which had unleashed such a huge battery of talent from that small clapboard house in Detroit at 2648 West Grand Boulevard. He was on the rise in the Motown firmament, not only as an artiste and writer but as a company executive, eventually becoming a vice president of Gordy's baby and nurturing the careers of the new young dudes brought in to straddle the changes in popular music culture. These were the truly great days of Motown when it had an edge and a bite to it. When Stevie Wonder was still little and he worked his way through *Fingertips* like a road digger through tarmac. I saw him years later at the Wembley Arena at the beginning of the eighties and the sterile banality of his newer wares left me despairing. By this time he was purveying the insipid pap of *I Just Called To Say I Love You,* a song that would haunt us over and over again whenever any over-sentimental lover wishing to score brownie points would request it on the radio. It was the blind leading the bland.

Occasionally I would wander into the dressing room of The Ronettes. I loved the Ronettes. Veronica's voice, with its sharpness and its tremor, was as sexy as anything that ever came out of a pair of lungs. And they had a look to match. Exotic features due to their Spanish/Black/Indian genes enhanced by a makeup technique that gave even Dusty a run for her money. Their beehives were black, their darkened eyes took on an almost Chinese aspect, and instead of long beaded gowns they tantalised the audience with short, tight and split-sided oriental print dresses.

Ronnie and Estelle frightened me. They were worldly looking and made me feel like a virgin child in their presence, which I almost was. But Nedra, the third member and a cousin of the two sisters was smaller, more prone to smiling a friendly smile and seemed as bemused by it all as I was. We became friends and exchange side stage 'snogs', an activity that was much more a case of posturing than anything overtly sexual. I don't think either of us intended, or even wanted, to take it any further. We were just enjoying a bit of a holiday romance mixed up with the ego boost it gave to immature and impressionable kids like us in this environment.

The Ronettes' career was short lived, possibly due to their personal svengali Phil Spector's obsession with their lead singer whom he married a few years later. Nedra eventually married and became a born again Christian, possibly riddled with guilt and begging forgiveness from the Lord for having pressed her lips against mine back there in the darkness of the wings of the Brooklyn Fox.

With the late nights followed by the early mornings we saw little of New York. The fans around the block kept us prisoners for most of the time and for snacks and such we had to rely on a small black lad called Sam. He was our 'gofer'. Gofer this, gofer that. If we wanted a hamburger or a sandwich Sam would take the money and fetch whatever our hearts desired. As far as I know Murray didn't pay Sammy. He did it for the glamour and the tips. I hope he had better bosses than us. We were not big tippers.

We did manage to break out on a couple of occasions and on those forays into deepest Brooklyn I discovered that nobody ever has to starve in America. There is always a cafeteria willing to give you a meal bigger and cheaper than the next one. Sandwiches were a revelation. They bore no resemblance to the anorexic squares of nothingness we were used to in Britain. Here in the land of plenty two thick slices of bread, which first had to be chosen from rye, whole wheat, pumpernickel and a dozen others, would be kept an inch apart by layer upon layer of your preferred filling.

If it was chicken practically the whole bird would be trussed up in there somewhere and fighting for space with lettuce, tomato, mayonnaise and coleslaw. Coffee would be regular, medium or large. The regular was large, the medium enormous and the large contained more liquid than you would normally use in your bath. My gob was well and truly smacked at the sight of such magnificent excesses.

Words were never wasted in the gruff, abrupt atmosphere of the efficiency friendly, but customer unfriendly, New York business place. But on the other side of the coin, neither did you have to wait half a working week to be served by a waiter or waitress with the brain power of a knitting needle. I liked this place very much. I just wished I could see more of it.

At the end of the day we would be too tired to check out the night life, not that we were night life people anyway. But one night our singer Mike and I went along to Joey Dee's Starliter lounge in the company of a couple of record company people and two of the Ronettes. It was good to see Joey again. The Star Club seemed such a long time ago although it had only been a little over a year. He was minus his Starliters backing group now, having quit performing in favour of the hopefully more enduring and age-friendly business side of clubland and his place appeared to be thriving.

Our party was given a prime position at the front of the stage and we watched a group called The Rag Dolls, not to be confused with The Paper Dolls who charted back home with a song called *Something Here In My Heart* and who were far superior to the slightly amateurish act set before us that evening. I do not say that out of any bias to my lifelong friend and soulmate Susie Mathis who sang lead with The Paper Dolls. I would if I had to but fortunately I don't have to.

As we sat and conversed, the Rag Dolls having warbled and scarpered by now, a young black man approached and spoke to The Ronettes. He had a sad, worn down look about his still young face and there was a familiar look about him but I couldn't put a name to it. Eventually I was introduced. It was Frankie Lymon. I was mesmerised as I held out my hand and shook his. *Why Do Fools Fall In Love?* I remember everything about it. Columbia Records. Green label, gold writing. The voice that launched a thousand other voices. A hero to every aspiring young black singer in the fifties.

My mind raced back to Sunday Night At The London Palladium, a show the whole nation watched religiously every week. Frankie Lymon was only thirteen at the time, too young to appear live on television after a certain time and so their segment had to be pre-recorded and the film shown instead. They were brilliant, the dance routines cleverly lifted from Jackie Wilson's stage act and executed perfectly. And Lymon himself looking cuter than cute with the others towering over him and a big broad smile spread right across his face.

We passed a minute or two in polite but inconsequential conversation before he moved on. I was not a good talker then. So often the phrase 'youth is wasted on the young' comes to haunt me. The youth that was once me wasted so many opportunities, but then haven't we all. And why do we feel we are the only one? A couple of years later Frankie Lymon was dead. He overdosed on the drugs that he must have already been addicted to when we shook hands that night. It's all too sad.

Our seven days in Brooklyn was an enormous success. The show raced like a tornado with a pace and slickness from beginning to end. Their likeness back in England could only possibly be found in the old Larry Parnes extravaganzas, and they were a thing of the past. We were getting a riotous reception at every show despite the fact that our puny white voices whining over a dozen or so scratchy chords was up against the finest examples of black American soul. Hardly justice, but I found it very gratifying.

The kids who came got real value for money, but even with modest entrance fees I expect Murray The K managed a goodly profit, as I doubt that the acts were overpaid. It was one of those 'prestige shows' that was looked on as an investment in exposure, although how a week in deepest Brooklyn can affect your standing in a nation that can have you at number one in the charts of one state and afford you total obscurity in the next I have no idea. But it was an unforgettable experience. It was now time to move on

The second leg of this great journey was to be a coast to coast tour with ourselves and Dusty being joined by Eden Kane *(Well I Ask You)* who had just flown over from the U.K. The first show was to be Tulsa, Oklahoma which, twenty-four hours before, would have been a song title. But Madam had enjoyed her fun. After a week in the company of her Motown idols who were by now both friends and fans, she viewed the prospect of boomy basketball courts in gloomy provincial towns with dismay. Upon arrival in Tulsa Dusty retired to her bed with a cold. I viewed this with the same suspicion that I reviewed court circulars announcing that 'Her Majesty has been confined to bed with a slight chill'.

I could sympathise. The Fox was a hard act to follow and a trek through a string of anonymous towns and cities would not appeal to some. But in truth I was looking forward to the road. New York was not America and there was a lot more I wanted to see. Over the next couple of weeks I saw a little more. Over the decades I was to see a whole lot more still. Some parts I liked and some I hated but I was still working on the premise that travel is a privilege and not to be dismissed lightly.

6

Go East Young Man

I could tell at the press conference that this was not going to be an easy ride. When asked what his remaining ambitions were Chris Curtis replied that he wanted to play Jesus Christ in a film version of The Bible. While there was no actual audible gasp there was definitely a noticeable pregnant pause before the interviewer glossed over it quickly and brought the proceedings to an uneasy close.

Our supporting act, Julie Rogers who had scored a huge chart success with a song called *The Wedding*, looked decidedly uncomfortable and disapproving and not without good reason. This was a violent place. She might soon have good reason to consider a follow up tribute entitled *The Funeral.* Ours. Had I known then what I came to know later about the Manila of the sixties I would no doubt have seen my life flashing before me. We were still in the days of innocence and guests in a country whose religious fervour was embodied in a Catholicism which made the Spanish Inquisition look like a meeting of The Ovalteenies.

The Marcos regime kept a totalitarian control over a mainly peasant population and a hint of dissent or rebellion could result in you meeting your doom with less limbs and more orifices than you started out with. In fact we were quite unaware of the delicacy of the situation in a country where there were more guns than shoes, that is if you first subtracted the number owned by the President's wife. Imelda Marcos, it transpired in the years following the revolution yet to come, could have run a small third world nation on her budget for footwear.

The Philippine oligarchy was not to be trifled with as The Beatles were to discover to their immense discomfort only a few months later. A snub to the sainted Imelda in the form of a refused party invitation, whether intentional or otherwise, led to a swift exit from the country, and a fab four lucky to emerge with their lives intact. With the exact science of hindsight we would all have behaved a tad better or perhaps not gone there at all. It was all brought vividly home to us a many years later when Marcos' political rival Benigno Aquino was assassinated on the tarmac upon returning from exile in 1983 to oppose the dictator in the country's elections.

But we were mere innocents abroad and more concerned with the odd behaviour of our always 'off the wall', though good hearted and normally amusing, drummer. It had all started out well enough. John McNally had managed to miss his flight to Hong Kong a few days earlier but that was par for the course and when he eventually made it the concert at The City Hall had been a riotous success with hysterical Chinese kids storming the stage in frenzied adulation trying to wrench us from the podium like some human version of a Chinese takeaway. I think I was a number three with a portion of fried rice. Spend a night with me and an hour later you'd need another one.

Mike Love and Bruce Johnston from The Beach Boys had been at the show that night and the newspaper the next day reported their comments, that we were okay: no better than an average American group apparently. Who cared what they thought? I wasn't that mad about them either. I hated those awful, cheap blue and white striped shirts they used to wear and as the surfing was not all that good in Hayes, Middlesex I didn't give a toss about what The Beach Boys said or did. Even then I thought they looked very old, more like The Beach Men. Sod 'em. We were still on a high having scored a huge hit with the kids.

Bruce Johnston was my equivalent in The Beach Boys becoming the new boy when the eccentric and unstable Brian Wilson had withdrawn from touring. I had no dealings with him and apart from the dodgy comments in the press never experienced any side of him be it good or bad. But many years later one of the group Sailor told me that he had been hired to produce one of their albums and he had come on very obnoxiously, informing them that he was going to give their music tits. I ventured that the reply should have been that he might as well since it appeared to have already acquired a prick.

One show and we were out of there, arriving at Manila airport the next day in a flurry of excitement. Hong Kong had been different. This was wild. It was February 1966 and the weather was more than a few degrees warmer than the chill we had left behind in England. The chaotic polluted roads were constantly snarled up by a mish-mash of vehicles as we made our way out of the capital to Quezon city where we were to perform.

Our strange convoy of cars made up of flamboyant fifties American relics, a Buick Electra and a Chevrolet Impala amongst them, were provided with an unofficial escort comprising of mopeds, scooters and jeepneys, the standard and unique form of local public transport hereabouts. These utility items, salvaged, swapped or stolen from the U.S. army contingent which was still very much in evidence on the islands, had been customised in the colours and fashions of gypsy caravans and trimmed with gleaming chrome, buzzing noisily alongside our raggle-taggle convoy as it snaked its way out of the planner's nightmare that was downtown Manila.

We tried to put all thoughts of the nearly disastrous press conference behind us as we were taken to our accommodation, a section of the stadium that would house our week of concerts. The Araneta Collisseum, named after its sponsor and benefactor who lived just a few minutes away in palatial and secure splendour behind the high walls of his estate and protected by armed guards, dwarfed us as we approached the enormous circular construction. Our living quarters fitted neatly into one curved area of the building and opened out onto a carefully tended garden enclosed by trimmed hedges and set round a large swimming pool. Off to one side was a restaurant which solicited no other customers but us. And the prices were right too. Our every culinary whim was to be taken care of day and night and at absolutely no charge whatsoever. Things were looking good.

We were presented with our very own servant, a young Filipino called Cruz. Whether that was his first name or his family name seemed immaterial. Cruz they said and Cruz it was. We could not go out alone into the town. Cruz had to transport us in one of the 'batmobiles' and protect us from harm. It seemed entirely probable we were more vulnerable to harm in the company of our employers.

Our liaison in the promotions company that had brought us there was a guy called Bobby Grimald. He was stern faced and intense, a character right out of a spaghetti western in which he would most certainly not have played one of the 'white hats'. His body bulged not so much with muscles as with flab but sheer physical strength was hardly necessary when we discovered that one particular bulge of flab contained all the power he needed. He was fully 'tooled up', as they say in the best gangster movies. If anyone threatened us Bobby would probably shoot them. If we threatened Bobby he would probably shoot us. We were learning fast.

We spent the first day acclimatising ourselves to the best sun spots in the garden and the most succulent items on offer in the kitchen. I developed a taste for pineapple pie and ice cream. That was about the most exotic any of us got as we invariably eschewed the local delicacies for steak and chips. We may have been idols on tour in far flung places but we had not yet outgrown our footballer mentality. Any foreign sauces were scraped off as if it were rat poison.

That night we got ourselves suited and booted for a party at Mister Araneta's house. His children and grandchildren were excited at the arrival of these English teenage idols and demanded to meet them. A request from Araneta was nothing less than a command. If we had not had accepted he would have lost face and Bobby Grimald would probably have had to dispose of us and deposit our remains in the foundation of a new coliseum or maybe another mansion. We were lucky that, unlike the Beatles, we had not yet suffered an overdose of glamorous indulgence and were always ready to take up an invitation.

It took only a few minutes to drive across the way to his sprawling acres. It took slightly longer to get from the front door to the reception rooms. Mister Araneta was certainly not living in reduced circumstances. The male guests wore their Barong Togalogs, the traditional shirts made from pineapple fibre with a delicate lace pattern effect down the front and worn open necked and outside the trousers for all formal and semi-formal occasions. The oppressive heat and humidity of The Philippines was not a black tie environment and these garments were cool in high temperatures.

The ladies and girls were all dressed up in wide petticoated party frocks like players in an Audrey Hepburn film. When you landed in The Philippines it was necessary to put your watches back five years. There was enough food there to eliminate the need for Live Aid, had we been in the eighties. And if we had not been teetotal we could easily have consumed enough alcohol to enable us to be sick all over the thick shag pile carpet within minutes before no doubt being shot for such a heinous crime.

During the evening Araneta took us out to see his garden and menagerie. There was an impressive display of birds and animals in various huts and cages as we weaved our way through the lawns and shrubbery. I knew this was no ordinary menagerie when we stopped at a small iron grilled construction and were faced with a gorilla that had obviously been removed from the rest of the family Kong at some time in its infancy. He was now living in grand style and probably sending money to the folks back home. Staring into his dark eyes I hoped at that moment that dad was not out looking for his long lost son and the bad guys who had taken him. Or their house guests. I stepped a healthy pace or two backwards. It made Blackie, our dog at home in England, seem like mere bagatelle in the pet department.

Over to one side stood a beautifully carved Polynesian style hut of a size and quality that made me want to move all my worldly possessions into it immediately. Araneta explained that Nat King Cole, who had played some concerts at the Coliseum the previous year, had been particularly taken with this and without a further word he had a replica shipped out to the black entertainer's home in The States as a gift. I believe I mentioned soon after that I was extremely taken with Rolls Royce cars but he must have mislaid my address at some time because nothing ever arrived.

At one point during the evening I indelicately asked him how he managed to become so rich. It was a crass, vulgar question born of the naïveté of youth, but he answered graciously that his secret was that he knew how to delegate. I nodded wisely as if we both now shared the secret of life. What Araneta did not realise was that I didn't understand any of it. I had no idea what the word delegate meant.

The inside of Araneta's world was like nothing I had experienced. From the numerous servants anticipating one's every whim and rushing to take care of it before you even knew what you actually wanted, to the elevator ready to silently whisk you to one of the luxurious upstairs apartments I was mesmerised by the sheer opulence around me. I had never before encountered a private house with an elevator. Office buildings had elevators, houses had stairs. Back in the sixties it would have still been considered quite outrageously extravagant to install an invalid stair lift for your incapacitated grandma.

The entertainment planned for the second evening was something else altogether. Mike, John and myself, along with our road manager Barry Delaney, were driven into Quezon City in one of the rock and roll cars. Chris had begun to separate himself from the rest of the group by this time and we left him back at the coliseum to do whatever eccentric people do in their private moments. We were ushered into what we assumed was a perfectly ordinary night-club.

Inside the long, low room was crowded and smoky and we were shown to a prime position in front of a small stage where the entertainment, which had already commenced, appeared to be a female dancer, petite and pretty and undulating in smooth seductive movements as she made eye contact with the largely male audience. There was a sprinkling of women in the place but the degree of prettiness and the manner in which they were groomed and painted seemed curiously at odds with the casual attire of the men which was casual to the point of being scruffy.

Before we had the chance to offer either our acceptance or refusal we were joined by five young women who, without so much as a 'May I?' distributed themselves evenly amongst out party. The penny, which to that point had been waiting patiently for my miserably ill-equipped brain to kick into gear, finally dropped with all the weight of a girder. I turned to the stage to discover that the all too few items that had been covering the vitals of the girl dancer had magically disappeared. I was staring wide-eyed at two fried eggs and a toasted sandwich. My God, I thought. I'll never go to heaven now. I've seen a woman's thingy.

The girls by our side put their years of learning the art of social interaction into practise and made vain attempts at conversation to probably the most reluctant customers they had ever encountered. We were simply not customer material. They could not even hope to obtain our compliance through the effects of alcohol either. The fizzy soft drinks we sipped nervously assured our absolute sobriety. They might as well have tried to seduce the Pope.

Trying to make conversation was hell both for them and us. Being hopelessly English we would go to any lengths not to appear rude but sentences stuck in our gullets as the girls struggled through one of the most intense and difficult training exercises they would ever experience. We stuck it out for the shortest time that politeness would allow and then, in the best tradition of the man from The News Of The World, we made our excuses and left.

Whether the girls were miffed or not we neither knew nor cared. I assume we were expected to whisk them off to places unknown where we would be expected to do unspeakable things. Unfortunately for them unspeakable things were not our style. We would not have been good at it anyway. We saved ourselves the embarrassment of premature ejaculation by prematurely ejaculating ourselves from that particular den of iniquity. We were probably stealing food from their babies' mouths as they saw their fees, no doubt taken care of by our promoters, vanishing towards the door but we just wanted to get our crimson faces out of that place and into our beds - alone.

68

As we passed the reception counter the owner, a large black woman whose appearance was a cross between the lady who sang *Happy Talk* in South Pacific and an overstuffed leather sofa, smiled at the exiting bunch of pale and pathetic British eunuchs and handed each of us a bag of M&Ms. She had us sussed alright. We were babes but this was not toyland. Any toys here can probably be found nowadays in a branch of Ann Summers.

Maybe Chris was having an easier time than us. There was no way of knowing as we hardly ever saw him. Our 'man of mystery' kept himself tucked away, only appearing for the shows, to do something odd or to cause a howling gaffe. He had inadvertently managed it during the very first show. The crowd, which must have numbered ten thousand or thereabouts, was going wild and Filipino kids rushed to the front to demonstrate their affection. So far so good. A young girl threw a garland to Chris who caught it and put it round his neck. That was fine. His next move was not.

In a flamboyant and generous gesture he removed the circle of flowers a few minutes later and tossed it into the audience fully expecting a roar of excitement as the fans would no doubt tussle for the souvenir. Wrong. This unfortunate motion was reward with an all too audible chorus of voices booing. Too late we understood that discarding someone's proffered gift was an insult quite high up on a Richter scale of insults in these parts. Poor old Chris could hardly be blamed. Not one of us knew any better but unfortunately, being the front man, it was his head that was in the firing line. Luckily our grovelling apologies and contrite expressions made it fairly clear to anyone with the brain of a teapot that it was a simple misunderstanding and that no insult was intended.

The moment of discomfort passed and we were quickly forgiven but, sure enough, in the newspapers the next day our *faux pas* was broadcast to the nation. The hitherto squeaky clean Searchers were acquiring a reputation for controversy. Of course, had we been a bit more knowledgeable in the ways of the pop world we would have played on this new image and built ourselves a whole new future in a field of entertainment where rebels thrived and wimps got trampled underfoot. But old habits die hard. We were beginning to feel very vulnerable.

Julie Rogers and her husband, a bandleader of the old style called Teddy Foster, viewed our antics from a distance. She from beneath a carefully coifed aurora borealis of hair and he from the sticky side of a hairpiece that looked like a road kill. We were not really of their world, as clean cut and sweet as we were reputed to be. We were still a pop group and pop groups were trouble. They couldn't help it. It is the nature of the beast.

The press conference had unnerved them a little I think and even in the confined space of the accommodation block our paths rarely crossed.

The closest we really got to Julie was when Barry Delaney found a pair of her knickers in the pool area and decided that the chance to feel what they were like on his person was too good to miss. He donned this surprisingly large and unflattering item of lingerie and pranced at the water's edge for our own photo opportunity. The next day they had been reclaimed and she never knew that a foreign body had been inside her 'smalls', or rather 'larges' as we had renamed them. I trust that they were suitably laundered before being used again.

Incarceration fatigue began to set in after about four days and we paced around the confines of our five star prison. On checking the local newspaper we decided a visit to the cinema was in order. There was a James Bond film showing, You Only Live Twice I seem to recall, and we searched for Cruz to provide the transport but Cruz was nowhere to be found. One of the other members of the staff set out to find him and returned with someone else in tow. 'I am sorry sirs, Cruz is absent,' he announced. 'This will take its place'. Feeling a bit like plantation owners we instructed 'this' to fetch one of the boogie-mobiles and set off to spend an evening in the fantasy of espionage, which was a few steps closer to reality than the fantasy of our own world at that point in time.

On our return from the city we were in a mischievous mood and needed something to relieve the tedium. After all we had been cooped up here for almost a week and the novelty of swimming in the pool or woofing down great wedges of pineapple pie was beginning to pall. There was an old sofa in the corridor out side our allocated rooms. I can't remember who thought of the wheeze but I imagine it was Barry (it usually was).

We decide it would be fun to prop the heavy item up against the door of the room that Julie and Teddy were using thus, we reasoned, preventing them from being able to open it in the morning. It is here that old chestnut of an homily 'the best laid plans of mice and men' comes into play. What we had failed to spot in our over hasty attempt at trouble-making was that the door opened inwards. The next day a very old man found himself pinned to the floor by a slightly younger and very weighty piece of furniture. And Julie Rogers narrowly missed becoming a widow. Bobby Grimald scolded us and as he sternly reminded us of the possible consequences. I kept my eye on his gun hand and prepared to bite the dust.

Still, the shows were going well and the house was pretty much packed for the whole of our stay. Chris kept any garlands firmly hoopla-ed round his neck and we smiled inanely throughout our time on stage, radiating nothing but goodwill to the people of the Philippines. One evening just prior to show time we were dressed in our smart stage outfits, which consisted of high cut three button black suits with neat black ties complementing our pristine white button down shirts, when we noticed that one of our members was missing. Chris was a trifle late. We were due on in a couple of minutes.

We sent Barry Delaney to his room but he came back both Chrisless and clueless. Bobby Grimald searched the restaurant complex. Nothing. It was getting desperate. We sent Bobby back to Chris's room and this time he returned with the tardy musician. Bobby was reluctant to tell us at that point where he had found him but later on all was revealed. He had discovered the missing drummer sitting on a chair inside the wardrobe of his room, guitar in position, door closed and attempting to write a song in that pitch black, claustrophobic space. Things were getting curiouser and curiouser. We began to get the idea that Curtis was a few taps short of a paradiddle.

Apart from his slightly odd behaviour Chris's antics caused no real snags in the routine. He was never in vision enough to cause any problems. Delaney, on the other hand, was putting us in mortal danger. The rest of us were beginning to get on Bobby Grimald's nerves, particularly because Barry, whose sharp-tongued skilful use of the English language was particularly lethal in the area of invectives and put-downs, was constantly winding him up by addressing him like a serf.

During a poolside larkabout one sunny afternoon (there were never any non-sunny afternoons) someone had thrown one of my shoes into the murky water which was opaque green in colour due to the formation of an algae thriving and untroubled by any recent chlorination. It says something about my lack of foresight or perhaps lack of funds that I had only packed one pair of shoes for a month long tour.

I stood on the side in my close fitting satin trunks, the kind that make you look as if you are smuggling a budgie down the front, and peered vainly into the unyielding depths. My swimwear was the fashion statement of the period long before surfer pants relegated them to a bygone era with everything else that had ever been deemed 'uncool'. Several dives failed to locate the missing item of footwear, which was invisible both from dry land and the floor of the pool and, in the absence of Jacques Cousteau, Bobby Grimald was summoned.

He shrugged as if to say that the shoe had gone and we had better keep diving or forget about it. Delaney was not about to accept that pathetic cop-out and suggested that the pool should be emptied. The suggestion sounded remarkably like an order to me. It sounded remarkably like an order to Bobby too who irritably pointed out that emptying and refilling a pool of that size was no small matter. It could not be done. Barry pointed out that we were international celebrities from a civilised country and it was outrageous that we should be expected to swim in such filth anyway. Like an insane tennis game after a Mad Hatter's tea party each continued to point out and counter-point out until they were completely out pointed. Delaney's sarcasm had reached a point that would have had Oscar Wilde on the ropes. At that point Bobby stormed off and the problem, along with any solution, was left in abeyance. There were no more points left. What was the point?

The next morning we entered the garden to find a swimming pool filled to the brim with crystal clear, fresh water and there on the side sat one black moccasin drying in the noonday sun. My experience of pool maintenance at that time was nil but in later years I was to realise that such an operation was not only long but extremely expensive.

Things were getting tense both in our camp and in the general environment around us. But the week was about to end. Financially the concerts had been a huge success and on reflection there had been much to experience and enjoy but I had a sneaky suspicion that Bobby Grimald would not shed too many tears on our departure. In a private moment in conversation with him during the time our luggage was being loaded into our transportation to the airport he confessed to me that he had had a great problem controlling his temper as far as Barry Delaney was concerned. 'I never before wanted to kill anyone but there were times when I wanted to kill him'. There was no indication in his eyes that he could have possibly been joking.

I got the feeling that we had escaped serious harm by the skin of our teeth and that it was time to vamoose. There were more important things to deal with now that the Philippine fiasco had been wrapped up. We were off to Australia and a date with The Rolling Stones.

1 Me and Cliff at Wembley,
   June 17th 1989

2 On stage and on screen at The Event

3 Falklands (John McNally, Jimmy Tamley and me)

Left:

4   Ambassadors Skiffle Group, c. 1957
From left: Tom Hanlon, Vic (front), Taffy Evans, John Botterill, and me

Below:

5   Coach trip to Ruislip (credit to Janet Mills) c. 1953 (Me, 3rd from left, front row)

Below left:

6   Family on aeroplane steps, 1952. Dad, Gran, Mum, Jackie and me

Below right:

7   Thames van with Cliff Bennett and me, c. 1961

8   Me and the Daimler
    ambulance c. 1962

9   Rebel Rousers & Stones
    touring, 1964. Dave
    Wendells, Bill Wyman,
    Sid Phillips, me, Moss
    Groves, Keith Richards
    (above), Brian Jones,
    Mick Jagger, Mick Burt

10 Me and Ford Anglia

11 Horst Fascher with me at Bad Segeberg in the 90s

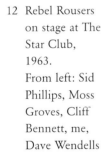

12 Rebel Rousers on stage at The Star Club, 1963.
From left: Sid Phillips, Moss Groves, Cliff Bennett, me, Dave Wendells

13 Kingsize Taylor & The Dominoes

14 Rebel Rousers, Joey Dee & Starliters, 1963. From left: Dave Brigatti, me, Dave Wendells, Joey Dee, Sid Phillips, Mick Burt, Willie Davis

15 With Bo Diddley and his 'curtain' stage outfit, 1963

16 On stage at The Star Club with Bo Diddley, 1963

TONY SHERIDAN

My Bonnie
(Mein Herz
ist bei dir nur)

The Saints
(When The
Saints
Go Marching
In)

Above:
17 Record sleeve of
Tony Sheridan's *My
Bonny*, backed by
The Beatles

18 Jamming with Tony
Sheridan in the 80s
(Tony Sheridan and
John McNally)

19 The Reeperbahn

Above:

20 Going by Cadillac to extend work visas, Hamburg, Jan 1963. From left: Dave Wendells, Moss Groves, Sid Phillips, Mick Burt and me

21 Me, Chubby (or is it Winnie?) and his manager Charlie

22 A singsong in the Basel Hotel lounge with Susie Quatro, Kate (backing singer), Henry Marsh from Sailor and Susie's keyboard player, Reg

23 Me and Dusty at her house the night of the mysterious 'willie fiddling' incident

24 Getting friendly. Same night, same appalling clothes

Right:
25 Me and Smokey Robinson backstage at The Fox, 1964

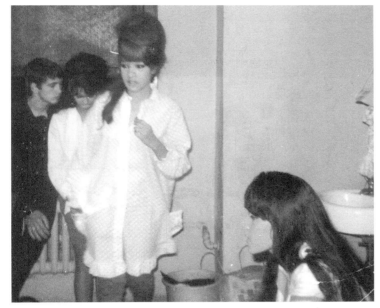

Left:
26 With the Ronettes in their dressing room at The Fox

Below left:
27 Eden Kane, John McNally and Mike Pender on Hollywood Boulevard, 1964

Below right:
28 Chris Curtis, Me and John McNally on Hollywood Boulevard, 1964

29 Tired little Hectors on the way home from Australia, 1964. Me and John McNally

30 The Araneta Colosseum, Philippines, 1966

31 A big welcome at Manila Airport. Bobby Grimald, John McNally, me, and Mike Pender

Above:

32 The fateful press conference. Julie Rogers, Me, John McNally and Chris Curtis

Left:

33 Mr Araneta, Mike Pender (seated), John McNally, me, and Barry Delaney (seated)

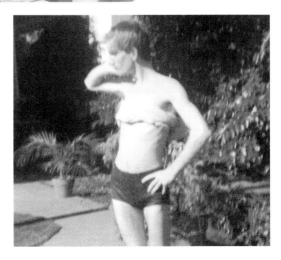

34 Barry Delaney in Julie Rogers' knickers

Above:
35 A week of capacity
crowds at the Araneta
Coliseum, Philippines

Left:
36 The Rolling Stones in
those mangy kangaroo
coats

37 Lunch by the Red Sea.
Me, Barry Delaney, John
McNally

38 Nazareth High Street. Me and Mike Pender

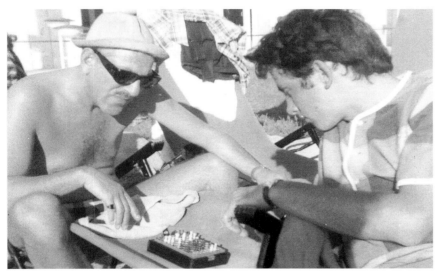

39 Trying not to get cheated by Tito Burns at chess

40 Ready Steady Go with John Blunt on drums

41 The 'chest from hell'

42 Our 'superior accommodation', Vitez

43 'spammed up' for action. Back - C.S.E. crew, Under Wraps, Christina, John and Lyn from Lynx. Front - Billy, Phil (Searchers' roadie), John, me, Spencer and 'fearless leader' Richard Asbury.

44 A café in Tomislavgrad - the town formerly known as 'shithole'

45 R&R in Tent City (Ploce)

46 Perks of the job. From left, Spencer James, John McNally, Lyn (Lynx), Billy Adamson and me

47 The forces' sweethearts. Eat your heart out Vera Lynn

48 Mummy's special soldier

49 Recording at Rockfield. Me, John McNally and Pat Moran

7

The Wizz Off To Oz

Keep going east and you will finally end up west. When you touch Australia your voyage has reached the point where it begins to turn back on itself and the sights and sounds start getting familiar once again. Continue and you will eventually disappear up your own amplifier. In one way that is quite reassuring but on the other hand seems a bit of a fruitless journey to travel so far and encounter people and places not too dissimilar to yourself. It's a bit like travelling from London to Paris only to have lunch with people from Balham. And only under exceptional circumstances would I even travel to Balham to have lunch with people from Balham.

We had been to Oz once before, in 1964 when we headlined a package which also included Del Shannon, Eden Kane and Peter and Gordon, not to mention New Zealand's own 'Queen of the Bluebeat' Dinah Lee. I can remember few things about Dinah Lee. At the top end she sported a Cilla Black haircut and at the other extremity she was firmly propped up by a rather large pair of feet. She sang her current hit record, a song that boasted the incomprehensible lyrics *doo way ackaway*. If I've misspelt those incomprehensible words I am sure that it is of infinitely less consequence to the world than if it had never been spelt at all. Another thing I remember was that she kept disappearing into Peter Asher's room late at night. Or he into hers. And Peter looked such a sweet 'butter wouldn't melt in his mouth' kind of a guy.

Del Shannon was still riding pretty high on the success of hits like

Runaway and *Hats Off To Larry* in those heady days before you could go out and buy a similar haircut to his for £6.50p a yard at Carpet World.

This time we were no longer headlining. Our career graph was on a downward course and our agent had glibly passed off the tour to us as being a 'double top' in a poor attempt to pander to our vanity and to salvage some of our self respect. But as our hits had sunk to a disappointing number twenty with *Take Me For What I'm Worth* and their last six releases had been one, one, one, one, one and two in that order it was pretty clear who were the mut's nuts in this little bunch of musical mongrels.

Their newest success was *Nineteenth Nervous Breakdown* but we had the feeling that Chris Curtis could well be heading for his first. He was not a happy bunny about our loss of status or the coupling with an outfit so much higher up the scale in our mutual workplace. Our last visit had been a *tour de force* and now we were forced to tour in a new position.

In truth Chris, who had always been more than happy to accept, or even demand, the credit for picking our hit records regardless of anybody else's input (sometimes true, sometimes not quite as clear cut) should have been equally happy to don the mantle of blame when they failed to deliver. The words cake and eat somehow spring to mind. But I have to say, right or wrong, pleasure or pain, Curtis was a malice-free zone and deep down there was a heart as generous as Santa Claus and as big as an ocean. He was becoming a bit of a pain but you couldn't help but like him.

The shows went well. How could they do otherwise? The Stones were huge and we were still very much a saleable commodity. Both groups got its fare share of screams. We were on little more than nodding terms with them although I found it quite easy to talk to Bill Wyman, and Charlie and Shirley Watts were a delight to socialise with.

Jagger and Richards I found a little more remote and in the main I steered clear, memories of John Lennon's sharp tongue still strong in my mind. But when we did exchange a sentence or two they were actually very pleasant, Mick in particular. Anyone with a twinkle that bright in his eye could never be all bad. Brian Jones was two years away from being eased out of the band he had given birth to but already he seemed to be on the perimeter of things, floating in and out of the action like an exotic but somehow sad butterfly. Colourful but at the same time fragile and easily damaged. Maybe it is only with the value of hindsight that I recall feeling that he almost appeared to be aware that things were slowly slipping away from him.

Australia was still fairly understated and open by London standards but it was a notch or two up from New Zealand. Aussies are a free spirited people willing to do anything and go any distance on a fun-fuelled impulse. If they weren't fuelled by fun they were most definitely fuelled by beer. Gallons of it. Most of the time it was both and I envied them their spontaneity and openness. At this early stage in my character development I was neither alcohol-fuelled nor spontaneous.

The weather there was warm and the air clear and clean. New buildings rose amongst the old Victorian terraced cottages with their cute verandas and wrought iron embellishments, some of which were maybe a touch overwrought. The controversial Sydney Opera House was still a building site with its enormous cowls inspired by the white sails of the passing ships and the even more enormous and never-ending cost that threatened to bankrupt the city.

We performed in the old Sydney Stadium, an edifice which to my eyes consisted of little more than sheets of corrugated iron and was fortunate not to collapse under the noise and vibration of the volume The Stones played at which, for those times, was pretty high on the decibel scale. I stood watching them, mesmerised by the energy if not overawed by the expertise. These were primitive times and there was much to be learnt by all of us. A fan by my side remarked that Keith Richards could make his guitar talk. I could see what he meant. And I could almost hear the guitar saying 'take your hands off me, you clumsy oaf'. But it was impressive, of that there was no doubt. This was not really so much a demonstration of music as a display of sex and power, and on that level it worked to perfection.

Over in our camp Chris appeared to be coasting through the days in a distant haze, his eyes dilated and staring even more than usual. Something was not right. We were all waiting for something to happen although we had no idea what. It was like Channel Five television. Everything was being observed through a haze of tiny dots and you had the feeling that if only you could join up those dots the greater picture would come into focus.

The next afternoon found us sitting in an exceptionally large bedroom in our hotel, The Sheraton, in the Kings Cross district of Sydney, an area that desperately wanted to be as sinful as Hamburg but had not yet found the courage of its convictions. It was about as naughty as your granny in a knees up. The sheer size of the room would have been impressive were it not that it had to accommodate four musicians, a tour manager and a road manager. Someone had messed up the bookings and like Jesus Christ we discovered there was no room at the inn until they found us this five star stable on the third floor.

We were sitting, all except Chris of course, chatting to Mike Rispoli, the representative from our mutual agency back in England delegated to look after the Rolling Stones and tend to their every whim and comfort. His 'oppo' in our group was Vic Sutcliffe who was delegated to make sure we completed the tour and got paid. Our comfort and whims, if this room was anything to go by, figured quite low down on the list of priorities. The Stones were staying just across the street in the Chevron Hilton. Back then the name Hilton still had a certain ring about it. Other hotels 'clunked' in comparison. The phone rang.

Vic carried on a cryptic and bemused conversation with whoever was on the other end. He put down the receiver and transmitted the news to us. The Australian Navy were holding one of our party at their local base and required confirmation of his identity before they decided what to do with him. He disappeared to rescue the errant drummer who had apparently strayed, for whatever reason, onto restricted territory. It said a lot about naval security there that he was able to enter the place with no sign of trouble. After all, with hair below his collar and slightly eccentric garb complete with large dark glasses he did not exactly look like your average matelot.

Later that evening we were ushered into cabs and transported to the local television show for a fleeting appearance during which we would mime to one of our hits. The dockyard incident was being avoided at all costs. No good would come of explanations or recriminations. We were just happy to have our front man back in the fold, a front man who at that point had retreated even further into his cavernous shell. Suited and booted we hovered in the dressing room waiting for the signal to get in position on the set. The young female assistant assigned to organising and looking after us mentioned to Barry Delaney that Curtis looked a little unsteady.

'Oh, don't take any notice of him. He's just being *affected*. He's always doing that', Delaney explained. The call came for us to get on the set. We all began to move, Chris included. The problem was that we were moving forwards while Chris was moving downwards. Before we knew it there was a unit of black clad cow-spanking humanity lying prostrate and motionless on the floor. Time was suspended momentarily as we all looked on open mouthed. There was no time to affect any form of recovery. We left the continuity girl to call the medics while the unexplained sight of a fab three lip-synched their way through a three minute classic.

We got through it somehow in a haze and came off to contemplate our uncertain future. It was as if we were slowly heading towards meltdown. We headed back to the hotel where we instituted a search of our hospitalised drummer's possessions. His large leather doctor's bag which he never travelled without was a virtual mobile chemists. A multitude of pills the colours and varieties of which would have made quite a cheery sight had we not been so depressed in the face of impending doom. We had no idea what they were or what they did. We decided on the only course of action. The whole lot went down the pan. The lid was lifted and a hypochondriac's dream was flushed away in an instant. A few seconds later a fairly substantial boom was heard somewhere in the bowels of the Sheraton hotel's plumbing system. Coincidence of course. Or was it?

One night in the infirmary saw our disintegrating member back to some semblance of health and an early visit to a local doctor saw his pill collection replenished. Things were no better and after a couple of incidents where Chris fell off the stage, plus another in which he managed to shut his finger in a door, we called in the heavies. This was ridiculous. We were the nice little goody goodies on tour with the big bad Rolling Stones. They were coasting through the whole thing completely untroubled by any hint of controversy while we were trying to deal with a medicinal nightmare.

Harry Miller, the promoter of the tour, was dragooned into giving him a severe dressing down and he undertook his task in a way that impressed me no end. Miller, a fairly passable Peter Sellers look-a-like, got straight to the point. No messing. One more incident, he informed the recalcitrant Curtis, and he would 'blow the whistle', as he so succinctly put it. We all assumed that meant the press, the police or both. At that point we were as frightened as the culprit. But it worked. Chris kept a fairly low profile for the rest of our time in Australia. Our two days in Sydney led on to one each in Brisbane and Adelaide followed by four days and eight shows in Melbourne.

While in Sydney, as a minor divertissement from our simmering internal problems I enjoyed a dalliance with a young lady by the name of Julie Adams. Well, I never actually said I was celibate, did I? She was forceful and outgoing in that Australian way that was years ahead of the women's lib that was still a barely believable speck on the horizon back home in the U.K. She was the owner of a small flat, large breasts and loose morals. Three attributes in the mind of most musicians.

She took the initiative in matters physical, which was fine by me. I would only have made a fool of myself. In those tender years me having sex was like a dog walking on its hind legs. It's not that it does it well. It's just remarkable that it can do it at all. Here in the 90s, I might add, not a lot has changed. Julie had a kiss like a cuckoo feeding its young. Every few seconds I would come up gasping for air. The entire situation was a magnificent exercise in role reversal, with Julie paying for drink and food without any argument from me. After all, I reasoned, I was the catch and she was the huntress. It seemed fair. And anyway, money in my camp was a bit tight so every little contribution helped. I have no idea where her money came from, but she seemed to have plenty of it I quite enjoyed this bit of mild whoring. It made me feel I had actual value.

When we flew on to Melbourne Julie caught a plane to join up for a couple of days. I was extremely impressed that someone would actually buy an aeroplane ticket to spend a very short time in my company. This kind of thing was not a common occurrence in my world. Luckily her money or her enthusiasm did not stretch to other parts of that vast continent, for which I was grateful. I was beginning to feel hemmed in and I was never any good at breaking things off. One of the great advantages of liaisons on the road are that the next night you are usually whizzed off to parts to where your temporary partner-in-sin finds it impractical to follow.

The affair, however, did not end happily. During an argument, that cause of which has long departed from my memory banks, she made a caustic comment about my lack of endowment in the genital regions, as women are sometimes wont to do when their backs are up against the wall. They know exactly how to wound. I was gutted, but I somehow managed to rally back and point out that when we met I never realised I was expected to throw it up a wizard's sleeve.

It was in Melbourne, I believe, that Delaney and I found our way blocked by a double parked car in a narrow street after we had dared to venture downtown. We waited for a few minutes but no one appeared. Barry went to check in an adjacent shop and returned with the news that a pompous and stroppy Melbourne matron who was not used to being rushed had promised to come straight out and remove it. She didn't and the by now irascible road manager tooted aggressively. Eventually she appeared and words of discontent were traded. An exasperated and angry Delaney punctuated his speech with expletives that those of a more temperate personality would have deleted.

'I've never heard such language before', she remonstrated, unfortunately for her, to the wrong person entirely.

'Oh come now, an old bag like you must hear it all the time', was the acid laced retort from a tongue with an A level in invectives.

78

By now the situation had calmed down to an uneasy truce and we could relax to a certain extent and enjoy the sun and surf of an Aussie summer. Chris's eccentricity quotient was still in the ascendant but it never caused us any more serious problems throughout the rest of the tour although things were a wee bit strained. Keeping things calm was a bit like walking on snow without leaving footprints.

The Stones observed all this at a distance and with much amusement. Jagger and Richards were, I recall, extremely intrigued when, while waiting for a flight in an airport lounge, Chris announced that he rather liked an aeroplane that stood on the tarmac outside and that on his return to England he would buy one. We just stared at the floor and pretended he wasn't with us.

In fact it would seem on reflection that such a purchase would apparently have been more in Curtis' power than Bill Wyman's at that point in time. In his book *Stone Alone*, Wyman puts The Stones' number one bank account that month as standing at £4,631 6s 9d. I had more than that in mine, and I was still a hired hand at that time. Maybe this is just an object lesson not to confuse with someone's wealth with their worth. Actual cash may have been scarce for them but their potential was priceless and they were well on their way to an immense fortune and even greater fame.

On the other hand I was highly amused at the Stones' purchase of kangaroo fur coats which some fast talking Antipodean shmutter salesman had managed to fob off on them as the latest indispensable fashion item. I was not at all convinced. I thought the decidedly dodgy garments made them look like a bunch of vagrant rabbits with a touch of the mange.

We were not the only musical celebrities touring upside-down land at that time. Somewhat incongruously the great classical guitarist Andre Segovia was a fellow passenger on one flight and as a tail end to their press coverage of the the rock and roll side of things they had seen fit to question the maestro on the merits of modern popular music. His opinion was not one you would like to have on your CV. Its parallel can be found in a quote by Sir Thomas Beecham who, when asked if he had conducted Stockhausen, replied 'No, but I've stepped in a lot.' Segovia on this momentous occasion insisted that the electric guitar was an abomination that should never have been foisted on the world. Beecham's bile was more to my taste but their sentiments were pretty much the same. It was not a view I entirely shared but, having listened to the sound in the Sydney Auditorium, I could see where he was coming from.

We landed in New Zealand to find it shut. Back in the mid sixties New

Zealand was not so much laid back as laid out. The weekdays were like an English Sunday and on Sundays it was like any day on the Moon. Virtually nothing moved apart from maybe some tumbleweed blowing down the deserted street. These are qualities that might have their own special appeal later in life as the body grows older and the mature mind begins to appreciate a slower pace. But the excess energies of youth demand sound, the louder the better, and movement, fast and furious.

We checked into the motel complex that the whole tour was using and checked out the pool and the grounds. While we were out a person or persons unknown decided to check out our rooms and remove any belongings they felt they needed more than we did. It was the one time I was glad The Stones were more popular than us. Our losses were trifling in comparison to theirs. In fact the only item removed from my room was an old pair of faded Levi jeans.

When I got back to England this little snippet was reported in the magazine Disc And Music Echo resulting in a reply from a gentleman called Paul, no surname supplied, who wrote that he was not at all surprised at what had been taken. He then informed me that if he had been the thief he would have removed items of my underwear and went on to describe in graphic detail what he would have done with them. I found it quite flattering. I am always of the opinion that it is much better to be fancied by anyone than by no one at all. I still have the letter. He never wrote again. That's the trouble with these fair weather fans.

While I was there I thought it might be interesting to look up my primary school pen-friend, a girl by the name of Heather Haines. Her family ran a butcher shop in a place called Te Kuiti. I must have been about ten when we began our correspondence and maybe six months older when it finally petered out. As with many a budding romance money proved a bit of sticking point. Letters in those times went either by sea or air. An airmail letter only took a few days but was horrendously expensive. One and sixpence. My pocket money for a whole week only amounted to two shillings. That was out of the question.

Sea mail was within my budget but in the time it took to get there and for the reply to make its leisurely way back over the seven seas I would have finished my education and been off out into the wide world earning an honest living. So Heather became nothing more than a distant memory and in the end I decided to let it stay that way. There was surely a greater destiny awaiting me than the dispensing of prime chump chops in a town where the highlight of the week was watching the traffic lights change, that is once the traffic lights had been installed. I often wondered if Heather ever realised that the small child who wrote those boring and barely legible letters was now travelling the world under the ludicrous and barely tenable guise of teen idol.

Our sold out concerts in Wellington and Auckland completed we flew back to Australia for the final shows in Perth's Capitol Theatre and as the exhausting, certainly mentally if not physically, tour drew to a close we had an uncertain future to contemplate. How the hell were we going to resolve this alarming situation? Did we have a drummer or not? As far as Chris was concerned he had played his last rim shot and was on his way to a new career as a record producer and songwriter. We were privileged to sample a little of the latter as he kept sending poems to us during the long flight via one of the stewardesses. These days of course they could only have been delivered by one of the cabin crew but we were still decades away from any sense of political correctness. We ignored the literary offerings and tried as best we could to rid our minds of the knowledge that the apocalypse was quite possibly close at hand and the world we knew was about to come crashing down upon us.

As it turned out our world did not end. It changed certainly but the high heavens did not fall around us. A lunch in the company of our smooth tongued agent failed to change Chris's resolve one iota, goodness knows we tried, and it was left for us simply to decide whether to give up on the spot or to fight on. There was no choice really. Our lack of talent in the musical arts was only exceeded by our lack of talent in every other sphere of employment. Skilled artisans we were not.

John's expertise as a seaman was not going to offer serious competition to any budding Lord Nelson while my previous aborted efforts as a dispatch clerk almost certainly assured any clients of the need to rescue their goods from the wrong address and any prospective employer of a collision course with the bankruptcy court. Mike, I believe, could lay a mean Marley Tile but that meant real work and who on earth wants to do that when the alternative is to prat about a stage for an hour of glory with a decent pay packet at the end of it?

We auditioned for a new drummer and spent hours at the Grafton Rooms in Liverpool listening to countless incompetent hopefuls making din after hideous din. As these frenzied sons of rhythm one by one clattered and banged themselves to a standstill it felt as though the pounding in my head would never stop. But it eventually ceased and if they were no further forward, neither were we. Meanwhile we had retained the temporary services of a young lad from Croydon called John Blunt who had been found for us by someone at our office.

Enthusiastic and nice as he was there could not have been anyone less suitable. When he played he sweated great globules of perspiration from the nose, the few years in age difference between him and us seemed like a millennium and his Keith Moon-influenced playing style and appearance meant that it was more appropriate to keep him in 'pop art' casual clothes at the back while we stood along the front, smartly suited like Eton schoolboys. But apathy, plus the fact that he worked very cheaply, kept him in our employ for almost three years. We might have conquered the apathy ingredient but cheapness was a harder element to argue with. We had though ridden the storm and the crisis was, for the moment, in abeyance.

Years on I would often reflect on the events and realise the truth in a sampler I had seen in a friend's house. 'Today Is The Tomorrow We Feared Yesterday, And All Is Well.' We headed into a new phase of our life as a 'popular beat combo' and set about to retrench and reorganise. It was not the first time and, as time proved, it was not to be the last.

8

Oh What A Lovely War

Courage is my middle name. But I so rarely use my middle name, so it was with a certain amount of trepidation that I flew into a war torn Israel in the June of 1967 following a break in hostilities between the fledgling state and the combined Arab nations. I was on a headlong course towards possible oblivion and immortality and more or less crapping myself. I did not even have the satisfaction of being able to live off immortal earnings. This gig was for free and free is a four letter word, particularly in the language of The Searchers.

Our Jewish agent, Tito Burns settled comfortably behind his large mahogany desk in the plush Vere Street offices, scratching at his moustache and picking at fingernails beautifully manicured and polished to a high gloss, and did what every patriotic Jew felt bound to do under the circumstances. He made the supreme sacrifice and sent four Christians into the front line. He might have had an attack of conscience but I was very likely to suffer an attack of the much deadlier kind.

But even I recognised the enormity of this perfectly selfless gesture. I am not totally devoid of feeling. If anything happened to The Searchers a large proportion of his earnings would go up in smoke, perhaps in flames too and possibly in many small pieces. Greater love hath no man. It is said that a gentleman is someone who possesses a set of bagpipes but refuses to play them. I would offer that another definition might be someone who possesses the ability to be a theatrical agent yet refuses to practise his art, or should that be artfulness?

But there was no going back now. I was on a jet bound for Tel Aviv and seated next to a performer and composer who appeared old enough to have discussed the finer points of diatonic scales with Bach or Beethoven. Larry Adler was a legend. There was no doubt about that. He was also a very nice person and if asked was happy to recount his amazing tales of his early life in America with a whole bunch of other legends, most of whom had long since expired. If not asked he would tell you anyway. George Gershwin. Cole Porter. Even Al Capone. He had met them all and I sat there, a fascinated if captive audience. Describing him as 'that shy Larry Adler' would be as much a mismatch as 'poor Andrew Lloyd Webber'.

His high forehead, which stopped abruptly in a straight line higher up than most foreheads generally are allowed to extend, was furrowed deeply like a washboard in profile. In a life as long as his I imagine you could accumulate a fair amount of worries. Or maybe it was just the accumulative effect of years of having to listen to your own harmonica. I am not a great fan of that particular instrument. I find that a harmonica is a bit like a packet of rice. A little goes a very long way. For me listening to a harmonica is like being attacked by a wasp with musical ambitions.

Our other travelling performers included Shirley Abicair and Leonora. Shirley Abicair had achieved some degree of fame in the fifties as a singer of lightweight, folk oriented songs to her own accompaniment of the zither, an instrument only slightly less popular than the harmonica. She was a pretty New Zealander whose prettiness and affable nature unfortunately could not halt her slide from fame. Her star was advanced in its path of descent in 1967. But she seemed either unperturbed or unaware, an eternal optimist.

Leonora had not yet reached any height from which she could noticeably descend. With a tuneful Joan Baez-influenced voice she made her living mainly providing ambient background music and atmosphere in the coffee-houses of London. Fun to be with and seemingly lacking in any pretensions, she was good company, easy going like her music and we hit it off.

At Tel Aviv airport we had begun the usual chaotic file along the gangway towards the exit when I noticed something on Larry's seat. His harmonica no less. I reunited it with its owner. He seemed pleased at its return in a matter of fact kind of way but was not offering the grovelling gratitude that I thought might be forthcoming, my having rescued him from a completely purposeless journey. Then it struck me that he probably had a couple of dozen more stowed away in his luggage. This one would no doubt be his Gracie Fields model. I took my harmonica to an airport but nobody asked me to play. Like a musical Paladin his motto was 'have mouth organ-will travel'.

As we stepped onto the tarmac it seemed as though the whole world was in uniform. If they were not garbed as airline employees then they were covered from top to toe in khaki camouflage. Combat kit can be quite a powerful fashion statement but here it seemed everyone had turned up to the ball in the same frock. Men and women alike were dressed ready for battle, which was hardly surprising under the circumstances.

Tension had been building up for sometime in an area that had always been in contention since the State of Israel was officially designated by the Allies in 1948. When the Arab Nations blocked the Gulf of Aqaba to Israeli ships, ostensibly cutting off their trade routes, the Jewish authorities considered it tantamount to opening hostilities. Not that hostilities were foreign to the two factions over the years. They were not exactly in the habit of nipping across the road to borrow cups of sugar from each other. They were much more likely to lob a few grenades over the garden wall.

Realising that the mother of all punch ups could be in the offing and that the most likely winner of any bit of aggro is usually the first one to deliver a kick in the matzahs, the Israelis crippled the Egyptian air force with a devastating blow on June 10th 1967 without so much as a bunch of flowers or a phone call to say 'Do you mind if we drop in?' How rude. In polite London society it is always *de rigeur* to give at least four days notice of any impending visit. And were those Arabs grateful? No, they were not. They immediately decided to pay a return visit to deliver their message that, as far as they were concerned, it was not a very nice thing to do and this year's barbecue and drinks party was off.

Our welcoming bigwig, a tall, thick set and balding man who would have looked like a building society manager in civvies and no doubt a pussycat but who, in his action man outfit, radiated power and control, brought us up to date on the state of play so far. They were ahead of the game at this point, something we were well aware of. If we hadn't already kept abreast of things through the British press his 'cat that got the cream' grin more or less told us that. In fact the tiny state, not yet twenty years old was now occupying four times the territory that had been handed out at its inception. We were now in a period of cease-fire and there was a rel-ative, if uneasy, calm.

He wanted to know how things were in London. Apparently he was a great friend of Topol, Israel's most famous thespian son who had become the toast of the globe after his stunning success in Fiddler On The Roof. On behalf of everyone he offered his thanks and said that it was a pleasure to have us there. Well, the price is right, I felt like saying but held my tongue. I was still unsure about the wisdom of being talked into this. One of the points of persuasion had been that we would almost be national heroes afterwards. I only hoped that any accolades would not be posthumous ones.

Our small convoy headed to the Sheraton Hotel sitting in stately splendour right at the edge of the Mediterranean Sea which looked inviting. It was a shame there would probably be no time for cavorting about in the waves. We were still at the age when our bodies would still look good cavorting and if the young, who invariably believe that age is something that only happens to other people, did but realise how soon the ravages of time attack the tissues they would do a great deal more of it. Each generation rather foolishly works on the precept that youth is something they have somehow achieved but in reality it is a fleeting and fickle thing that deserts us with indecent haste. A tissue, a tissue, alas in the end it all falls down.

When you are young you may pull faces in the mirror but as age descends the mirror eventually pulls faces back at you. Flaunt what you have while you can for when those ravages do finally attack they do so with a ferocity that makes this little spot of middle-Eastern bother seem like a few timid slaps on the cheek. But we were only there for three days. And it was all, laughable as the description of our trivial occupation is, work. Work? What we did was not work, it was a vacation.

We had stayed at this hotel before, on a visit in '65 when we played for civilians, and thankfully for real money. Most of the shows had been at a night-club in Jaffa but I recall an evening at a cinema in Haifa that was significant for the fans climbing to look through the windows of our dressing room after the show. If that seems tame I should point out that our dressing room was two floors up.

I had enjoyed the time here on that occasion. The scenery was without doubt spectacular. We would drive with soft dunes passing by, our travels leading to horizons of flat topped buildings in shades of cool, inviting white, their straight lines now and then interrupted by a dome or a stretch of castellated wall, finally to enter a city that appeared to be preserved in the mists of time. Here nothing seemed to have changed. Our European garments these days bear little resemblance to the ones we would have worn in the middle ages but here in the Holy Land where the preoccupation was with the practicalities of survival, fashion was an irrelevance, of little or no use, except perhaps to those whose lives took them to foreign climates and customs.

We visited the temple of the Bahai religion on that trip. The impressive cliché of a building I recall had looked strangely bare inside with little more than a few Persian rugs scattered over the polished floor. It could have been the last day of the Allied Carpets sale. Although I can't actually remember the Allied Carpets sale ever ending. Like the pyramids it seems always to have been there. We ate fish by the side of the Red Sea, sadly an unappetising meal due to the fact that they retained their heads and the eyes looked accusingly at us while we munched. It's no fun biting into something that is squinting up at you.

Nazareth High Street was smaller than its Hounslow equivalent but a touch more impressive to our English gaze. Maybe that was simply because of the very different look and feel of the place, or perhaps because its ancient history and mystical connections were embedded deep in our subconscious minds. But The Bethlehem Souvenir Discount Shop, complete with the tackiest neon star in Christendom, tended to drag one back from the romance of history into the harsh realities of twentieth century commerce. Nothing in the end I suppose is sacred. It reminded me of the anecdote about the Liverpudlian sales girl who, when asked for a crucifix, wanted to know if they required a plain cross or one with a little man on it.

The shows on that first visit had gone well I remember and, although the equipment was such that the status of 'basic' was a lofty tag it could only aspire to achieve, the audiences reacted wildly at the chance to encounter a real live rock group which, in that isolated land, must have been as rare as a perm on a daschund. Tito Burns had accompanied us that time. I would like to think it had something to do with our personal welfare and the advancement of our careers but, call me an old cynic if you like, I think it had a great deal more to do with taking advantage of a 'freebie' to visit the relatives. I think he turned up at one of our shows but it might have been a trick of the light.

Two years on it was basically the same land but this Israel, lounging lazily in the desert sun, was a sheep in wolf's clothing and dressed to kill this time. The atmosphere round the hotel was animated but casual and we were fussed over as we sat and discussed the itinerary for the next day. The hotel manager personally greeted the touring party, announcing that he was a great friend of Topol's. Hadn't I heard that before? Larry went into a banter mode that had me green with envy. It was years away from when I would be able to perfect the art of seamless drivel which was eventually to be my metier, my paltry offering to the world of entertainment in the absence of any genuine musical competence.

We had the remainder of the day to rest and relax as there were no actual shows until the next evening and it was easy to chill out in an environment that belied the realities of a war-torn state where buildings like the one we were in might well be flattened at any moment and at the merest whim of a hot and disgruntled potentate with a power complex from just over yonder. We may have been in the sophisticated swinging sixties back home but here in the desert we were in the land of camels and kings where a single man's word was the law as near as damn it. Just beyond the hotel wall the waves of the Mediterranean washed soothingly over the golden sands and as night descended the richness of the skies made a mockery of the guns and the bombs. It must have been a mistake. Surely they had no place here. This was the Promised Land.

The next afternoon we were herded into military vehicles and shipped out to our waiting audiences. It was here that we parted company with Larry and Shirley who had been paired up to service a different unit to us. No doubt if it came to hostilities Shirley could distract the enemy with a few intricate strokes of her zither while Larry talked them to death. The short journey took our group into the old section of Jerusalem that most Israelis had never set foot in but which was now in Jewish hands after their astonishingly successful David and Goliath act the previous week.

Our theatre of entertainment here in the theatre of war was to be the Hilton Hotel, once the last word in luxury which was now the last word you would use to describe the five-star bomb site in which we had set up our equipment. Smartly dressed waiters and Maitre d's had been usurped by scurrying groups of cuckoos in the guise of enlisted soldiers and order-barking majors. A snap of fingers and a demand for a pink gin in the current climes would receive short shrift. Our designated officer commandeered a suitable number of lowly cannon fodder to haul whatever equipment we had to whatever position we required it to be in. Our wish was their command, and why not indeed.

In between dispensing orders he managed to impart the surprising information that he was - yes - a good friend of Topol, a piece of news that did not exactly cause me to keel over with shock. I was beginning to envisage Topol's address book the size of Gibbon's *Decline And Fall*.

The very sound of his name was beginning to get my goat. What the hell was a Topol anyway? Was that a first name or a last name? It had a ring of Coco The Clown about it. Topol The Tumbler. Topol The Toucan? Maybe Topol The Twat. Was his wife Mrs Topol? I hope for her sake she was not. I could envisage her acute embarrassment at the butcher's greeting. 'A pound of lamb chops, Mrs Topol? Right-O.' To tell you the truth I was not even a fan of Topol, a truth it perhaps wise not to tell around here. He just seemed like a fairly run-of-the-mill Alfie Bass look-a-like to me. Maybe I was missing something. Okay, so the world was right and I was wrong. It's happened before. No big deal.

The assembled soldiers were hungry for entertainment and sat in eager anticipation as preparations went ahead and I observed them as I waited for the off. Now you can call me picky if you like, but I couldn't help but notice that many of these aggressively garbed paragons of stereotypical butchness were sitting there, hand clasped in neighbour's hand, with a lack of inhibition that would not surface in the glad-to-be-gay cafés of Old Compton Street for two or three decades yet.

It was sheer culture shock to a naïve young Hayes lad like me and my twenty three year old body in which was contained all the sophistication of a particularly dim boy scout. The customs and traditions here were a world away from our starch collar stiffness back in the U.K. where simply taking too long shaking someone's hand would have you marked down with accusations of rampant woofery. Try getting away with that one at Catterick.

The dilemma that raced round my head was this. If you really did have a bit of movement in the trouser region for your fellow squaddie how could you tell, in the light of the fact that you were already both digitally attached like a couple of pre-pubescent love birds, whether he had caught your drift and was responding to your overtures or not? I mean, in The Royal Engineers the very fact that you were holding another lad's hand meant you'd already gone too far and it doesn't do to push your luck with a broken nosed killer sporting a Kalashnikov by his side. One false move and the weapon in front of your face might not be the one you're after.

Showtime beckoned and we made our way towards the makeshift stage that had been erected in the large lobby. It was surrounded by a seething semicircle of khakis, greens and browns broken only by rows of milky white teeth that grinned appreciatively from the centre of swarthy suntanned young faces. You could almost hear the walls of that impressive pile of glass and concrete weeping nostalgically for the glory that had been so recently stolen from them and wishing upon wish for the return of the expensively dressed patrons who had treated them with all the respect and reverence that was due to the name Hilton. Personally I liked it better this way. The atmosphere was electric. It's just a shame the power wasn't.

Leonora had sung through her wistful and romantic acoustic set, no doubt reminding them of the loved ones from whom they were temporarily separated. They clapped and cheered and no doubt some had silently lusted. After all Leonora was a striking woman with dark mane of hair and high cheek bones that pulled your eyes to that strong and calmly enigmatic face. She could easily have been from this land herself. Maybe her parents were but somehow I never got round to asking.

When our turn came we clambered onto the platform in the only chaotic way we knew and, as speedily as we could, struck up our amplified jangle. *Farmer John I'm in love with your daughter*, we belted out with all the finesse and subtlety of a herd of rampant rhinos on heat heading for the best seats at the annual Miss Rhino competition. But not for long. As speedily as we had begun we ended. The power had cut out with an abruptness that would have been called very rude in polite society and we were standing there brandishing ineffective instruments that now began to look like just so much firewood.

The inevitable cheer of surprise rang out, followed by the equally inevitable babble of discontentment while we sheepishly milled about in the hope that someone would come to the rescue and restore our amplifiers' life blood. Whatever was happening was not happening quickly enough so Leonora returned in triumph to sing and to play her guitar which could deliver an audible sound without the benefit of two hundred and fifty volts of electricity thrusting up its rear end.

She was in the middle of *Plaisir D'amour* when Genesis was followed by revelation. Someone said 'Let there be light' and there was light, followed of course by the traditional cheer as the soldiers reacted like Pavlov's dog. Leonora ended the song and we retraced our steps. I think we got to the second verse, practically a concert by the way things were going, before the power failed once more. I was beginning to believe the electrician was a music lover. Or worse still. Maybe he was a Hollies fan.

We turned to step down again when we clanged into life once more as the watts raced through the wires and we strummed and yelled our way through a raucous set suitable for the situation, stampeding through the songs like men possessed in case we were cut short again. It was loud, it was frantic and the troops loved it. They stamped and cried out their approval and gratitude. The tension, mixed with the relief made us sleep soundly back in the comfort of our Sheraton beds that night.

The following afternoon we were shipped out to El Arish, one of the newly captured parts of the Sinai Desert, a longer drive but leading to a destination that was breathtaking in its difference to anything we had ever seen before. The makeshift base consisted mainly of tents silhouetted in the dusk as the sun went down and the moon began to cast its shimmering, magical glow over the scene. Tanks and trucks stood dotted around like grazing elephants waiting for the orders from their mahouts to move on.

We began to get hungry but no food had as yet appeared. It seemed that they had eaten some time before and we were in between canteen arrangements but they would hustle around to see what was available. A large cylindrical catering-sized can was produced and opened. The contents were dished out and handed to us. In our bowl the large chunks of meat, which having not been blessed by their introduction to any form of heat, looked like Kenomeat. Having put in our request however, we were reluctant to upset anyone by point blankly refusing their valiant efforts. I put a fibrous cube in my mouth. Quelle surprise. It tasted like Kenomeat. You'd have to be barking mad to eat that, I decided. I nibbled a bit and faked a lot and when they weren't looking, dumped it. My hunger dissipated, frightened no doubt that if it didn't keep its head down some other culinary atrocity might be forced upon it.

Our stage for this show was the deck of a flat bed truck out there in the romantic setting of the shifting, whispering desert sands with a generator supplying the power and, in the absence of anything vaguely resembling spots, strategically placed jeeps training their headlights towards us for illumination. Technically deficient it might be but atmospherically it was over-endowed. Once more the magical, silvery moonlight that appeared to shine with a more mystical diffusion there in the endless, open spaces of the Holy Land, framed the scene in a way that no theatrical designer ever could equal.

Beyond the confines of our encampment we could hear the occasional crack of rifle fire as the snipers eased the boredom of cease-fire that followed the adrenaline rush of war. It never felt frightening. Nothing about all this seemed real. We performed that night in a trance-like state, letting the sights and the sounds and the smells seep into our consciousness, and the primitive power source held up heroically throughout our set. If the snipers out there had their weapons trained in our direction we would have made a pretty good target with the headlights picking out our fragile bodies, sharply focused in their beams. If the soldiers had been pleased the previous evening, tonight they were ecstatic. Maybe it all had to do with the surrealism of the setting, or the sense of isolation they felt out there in the softly sweeping sand dunes, but at that point in time we were all one. Brothers in arms.

There had been much discussion as to how the convoy was going to get back to Tel Aviv. We were flying out the next day, back to Heathrow, London and streets and towns filled with ordinary people untroubled by the need to fight for their homeland. It was mooted that helicopters would be sequestered but there had been a problem with that idea. I don't know what, but choppers were out while travel by road at night was fraught with dangers. This was bandit country. But in the end, if we were to make our connection, then road it had to be.

We piled into minibuses and set off, trucks of armed guards at the front and rear to protect us. We were treating it like a game. Playing at soldiers, just like those old black and white films. A little way into the journey the line of vehicles came to a halt by a ramshackle compound and soldiers jumped down with their guns in the firing position. We had stopped for fuel, it was explained. This was the most dangerous part of the journey. It was fairly standard for enemy troops to be waiting to ambush foolhardy adventurers such as we.

Oops. I wanted to tell them that I wasn't a foolhardy adventurer. I was a shit-scared musician, and a not very good one at that, who had not quite understood just what we were taking on. Could we have a little rethink here, please? Perhaps we should hang about till morning. After all I didn't really need to be home for a couple of days, and my mummy would prefer me in one piece, if you don't mind. She's Presbyterian and wouldn't really appreciate my dying for Israel, no offence intended of course. She does have another son but I think she'd like to keep the set intact.

In the end all was well and we spurred on towards the twinkling lights on the far horizon, making the Sheraton in the small hours of the morning. The next day we breakfasted on the patio and said our farewells. I was ready to return home. I think we all were. Enough is as good as a feast. Our senses has been heightened and stimulated and to tarry would have put us in danger of overexposing to the point where our sense of wonder might have started a downward curve.

In later years I often thought back to our agent's musings that we would be treated like national heroes in Israel. We were never again asked to play there. We have however performed in the Emirates many times. Could we have been one of the Arabs' secret weapons?

Whatever our function there it was not to be our only foray into the field of battle by any means. A couple of decades down the line had us playing so many concerts in the rough and ready environment of military establishments we almost wondered if, perhaps in the midst of a drunken stupor we had mistakenly enlisted in the British Army.

9

Bugger Bosnia

I have changed the location and paraphrased the original wry comment. The comment was uttered by a very sick and grumpy King George V upon being told that he would be sent to recuperate in a Sussex resort more famous these days perhaps for its annual Festival of The Sixties. A place where thousands of nostalgia-constipated pop fans, some so far gone as to be suffering from a kind of anoraxia nervosa, gather with an almost unhealthy fervour to celebrate their dear departed salad days. For many the salad has begun to wilt and curl up at the edges. The principal difference between Bognor and Bosnia is that, although it has been well and truly buggered with the kind of viciousness that only a close neighbour can dredge up, and with all the fire power that such hate can muster, Bosnia remains for the most part the more beautiful.

Wednesday, August 30th, 1995. Its patience stretched to breaking point, the United Nations had commenced its bombing of the belligerent Serbian forces the previous night, unloading many tons of deadly screaming shells onto the town of Sarajevo. But was the talk in the base camp at Split of the unbelievable havoc that had been wreaked on what was once a picturesque Yugoslavian city? Was it hell! All the lads could talk about was a humungous pair of breasts that had been seen wandering about the area, followed at an impressively generous distance by their proud owner, a statuesque lady sometimes called Lyn but otherwise known as Lynx - Europe's Most Glamorous Illusionist. In fact Lynx were a three piece act, with another girl and one male completing the trio, but the three pieces that really mattered were Lyn herself and those two magnificent spheres that appeared to be welded to her chest.

I had first encountered these fearsome weapons the previous afternoon at Heathrow Airport as we assembled in front of the Croatia Airlines check-in desk. They flopped up and down like two plum puddings nestling in a sling shot and my taste buds began to make me salivate. As I wiped away my undignified dribble I remember thinking that if she bent down too quickly to tie her shoelaces she could have a small child's eye out! Had they been packed with Semtex the resulting bang could make Canary Wharf seem like a cheap birthday cracker.

We were gathered in our separate-but-together groups, jockeying through timid but friendly introductions at the outset of yet another Combined Services Entertainments tour like a bunch of kids on the first day back at school. Wars in the eighties and nineties were beginning to play a major part in our working lives. When the troops needed a mild diversion from whatever current hell they were in the midst of, we were sent for. Some of the company we had met before. Ruth, slim, sweet and Scottish, was in charge of Under Wraps, the trio of girl dancers, a vital ingredient in any CSE touring party. That ever so slightly sexual element guaranteed to make the spirits, and indeed a few other parts of these totty-starved squaddies, rise. Ruth, as well as being the dance choreographer, this time constituted one third of the act herself. Megan was a little shorter and darker and the possessor of a cherubic baby face. Tamsin had that cheeky Scouse humour that comes as part and parcel of any lass from the Wirral. They seemed pleasant enough.

We stuck mainly to our own groups to begin with, the girls chatting animatedly, as girls tend to do. (Gratuitous sexist comment). Our sound engineer, Phil Hayes, discussed the logistics and complexities of the vast amount of equipment with the CSE crew while we introduced ourselves to Lynx.

Christina was pretty and fair with an open and friendly personality. John was short and stocky. No, strike that. Let's not be precious about this. He was fat, bearded and dressed entirely in black, his voluminous clothes draped over a body borrowed from a sperm whale. He cut a sinister, somewhat demonic figure resembling nothing so much as a lead player in a German porn flick. On first meeting John was a bit scary.

And then there was Lyn, which was another thing entirely. Well, another two things entirely, to be correct. It is difficult to keep eye contact with someone when there are a couple of voluptuous mounds of pink flesh just calling out to you. They are magnetic. They draw you to them. I can only imagine it would be similar to a conversation with Charlton Heston. Talking to Heston would, I imagine, be like being held face down on a carpet. No matter what you do you can't take your eyes off the rug. I was in exactly the same state, mesmerised by these treasures. I wanted to say 'If you're drowning those puppies can I have the one with the pink nose?' Their custodian was tall and Amazonian, with sharp facial features that sent out an impression - quite wrongly as it turned out - of a personality that was cutting and hard. We exchanged pleasantries and I got back to crowd watching. It was amusing to watch male heads turn in gob-smacking astonishment at these marvellous promontories displayed so brazenly in the concourse of Terminal Two.

Richard Asbury appeared on the scene, a thick-set gentleman of medium height and a fine distinguished head of silver grey hair and appearance that reminded me of a somewhat understated Michael Aspel. An ex-deejay-turned-Head Of Services Entertainments, he had an engaging personality and laughed easily. We left the crew to take care of the mundane process of checking in our truckload of equipment and cases. In a typically extravagant fashion that only occurs during the spending of public money, it was destined to travel as excess baggage. Seven thousand pounds worth of excess baggage to be exact. We adjourned to the bar where, over several spritzers and beers, we firmed our friendships and bonded to perfection.

I have always looked on airlines as the last bastion of 'the customer is always right' mentality. The days of grovelling obsequiousness are, alas, virtually gone. I remember the days when shop assistants and bus conductors, waiters and counter staff would smile and try to attend to your every whim. Long past, I'm afraid. But travel on an aeroplane and the cabin crew are imbued with a resilience that has to be strained to its absolute limits before it cracks. Always a smile and a 'What can I do for you?'

Except, that is, on Croatia (pronounced Cratcha, it seems) Airlines. The faces on 04491 to Zagreb could have chilled our complimentary wine or turned the coffee cream sour with a single withering glance. I immediately renamed it Crotchety Airlines. It seemed more fitting. But I suppose that as their country was being bombed out of existence, they may not have had much to smile about. We were served with a hot meal, free drinks were dispensed and the aircraft did not crash, so maybe I had less reason than they to complain.

The arrivals hall at Zagreb was an ocean of blue berets. This was obviously the indispensable fashion item of the day, along with cute little combat outfits in a rather fetching camouflage pattern. The Dutch had the edge, having been issued with boots in a very attractive desert sand finish, unlike the other forces who had to make do with boring black. Dedicated followers of fashion they may have been but whatever semblance of cool they had was quickly blown when faced with the chest from hell. It was a most memorable and edifying sight. Dozens of blue-topped heads turning in goggle-eyed astonishment to mouth that most immortal and most expressive of phrases- My goodness, or similar.

One of the advantages of performing for the military is that there is no shortage of manpower to load our equipment onto the trucks. Meanwhile the artistes clambered aboard Land rovers and minibuses for the short trip to the hotel. This was our first chance to check out the countryside, and it was impressive. The feeling was somewhere between Greece and Spain. I suppose you could call it stock Mediterranean, picturesque and inviting and unsettled only by the scores of white painted U.N. vehicles to-ing and fro-ing like so many ants who had inadvertently traipsed through a decorator's spillings.

We checked into the Hotel Split and made arrangements to meet for dinner in an hour. The place was well appointed; the rooms spacious and clean and from the window the sea looked inviting. Down below the pool was clean and sparkling in its setting alongside the marbled terrace. It was full of water but empty of swimmers. The missing ingredient here were the tourists, but it seemed a reasonable supposition that, in the current climate, there would not exactly be a rush for deck chairs on this trip.

I showered, shaved and picked out a short-sleeved, leopard-skinned print shirt to wear. It was refreshing to get out of my comfortable but too casual travelling clothes. John McNally followed me into the elevator. Spencer and Billy were already downstairs in the lobby bar where the tour party had gathered. And, of course, so too were they. Nestling comfortably in a gold lurex hammock, for want of a better description, they rested peacefully under the watchful gaze of Lyn. It felt like they were becoming good friends by now and I was beginning to become very fond of the little rascals. They needed names, I felt. Bill and Ben seemed somehow appropriate. Only their mother can tell them apart, as the film blurb said. They looked like they were snoozing and I didn't want to wake them. 'Hello Bill. Hello Ben.' I could have sworn one of them said 'Flobalob.'

Dinner was pleasant despite being served by a woman with the looks of a russian shot-put champion and the temperament of a condemned Rottweiler. At some time in her life she had obviously been rode hard and put away wet. The wine and the conversation flowed in equal proportions but I called it a night early.

The following day the whole bunch of us grabbed breakfast and lugged our kit down to the lobby for the journey to Zepce (pronounced Zepchay) by Sea king Helicopters. But first we had to head for the main base at Split in order to get fully spammed up in flak jackets and steel helmets, all in that mandatory shade of U.N. blue. The identity cards that we were presented with at the same time proved that we were now official members of the United Nations Peace Keeping Force. I borrowed a couple of machine guns to pose for a photograph like mummy's special soldier. I'm not sure if Bill and Ben were issued with cards, but there was no doubt that within minutes every man on the camp knew of their existence. Empty corridors within seconds looked like the London Underground in rush hour.

We were taken to a room for a briefing on safety by one of the officers and given a convoluted run-down on the history of the region and its conflicts. It appears that Yugoslavia had been created after World War Two out of a number of countries. Under the iron fist of its dictator, Marshall Tito, (hmm.. a dictator named after our old agent and manager. How interesting) a guy they would have happily queued up to hate if they had not been in danger of being wiped off the face of the earth at the merest hint of dissent, the people lived a lasting, if phoney, peace. When Tito died there was no one of sufficient strength or authority to maintain that status quo. It is the nature of dictators not to groom successors. He who is worthy of being one also possesses, by nature, the strength and the naked ambition to overthrow his benefactor. The original idea was to have each of the countries share a term of rule but no country wanted to be ruled by another and muscles started to flex.

The first country to defect was Slovenia, an action that was accomplished with relative ease. The rest were soon to follow. Bosnians, Serbs and Croats who had been neighbours for decades suddenly upped and killed people with whom they had been drinking coffee and croissants the week before. In the view of the soldiers to whom we spoke, there were no good guys and no bad guys. The Serbs were the villains of the moment media-wise but the lads suggested that the Muslims were just as bad but much more sneaky about covering up their atrocities. Feeling no loyalty to either side, the soldiers would have preferred to leave them to shoot it out on their own, and may the worst man win. It is a volatile area to say the least, and born of an inglorious past. Let us not forget that it was here in Sarajevo that Archduke Ferdinand was assassinated, bringing about World War One - The Great War. The War-To-End-All-Wars-That-Didn't. We were due to set off at one-thirty in choppers but one of them had apparently developed a vibration in the rotor blades and the support acts formed an advance party in the fully working model. I was tense and my stomach was home to a family of manic butterflies. There is something mildly disconcerting about waiting to get on a helicopter that is still being put together.

At three-thirty we left the Officers Mess to fly as planned. Sorry, came the retraction, not ready. Back up to the mess for more tea and biccies till four-thirty. This time, it seemed, all systems were go and before we knew it we were zooming over the beautiful formerly-Yugoslavian countryside. We should have been doing a show that evening but the delay in the flight, plus the fact that the road convoy transporting the gear had been turned back in the night due to incorrect paperwork, meant that the timing was now out. But, as it happened, things worked out rather neatly.

We had landed in this hotbed of war on the very day that the United Nations started to bomb the shit out of Sarajevo. The venue of our first performance, Kissiljak, was deemed to be too close to the extremely violent conflict that had erupted the previous evening and which showed little sign of being halted. Thus our debut was simply put back by one day and we had another night of socialising to put up with. How sad.

Our billet for the night was one room in a requisitioned air conditioning factory along with the male member of Lynx and our fearless leader Richard Asbury. There were four bunks, making room for eight people. The two spare were not to remain that way for long. This was war and empty beds were fair game. That night they were occupied by two Ghurka officers. A wonderful regiment, the Ghurkas, which apparently consists of white officers with black privates. Very contemporary, and an amazing sight in the showers, no doubt. We got our own back for the intrusion later that night when at bedtime they were kept awake by the noise of pop stars giggling like schoolboys in the dark.

That evening was spent in the Sergeants Mess, having first feasted on the staple army diet of curries, chops, fish and pasta, not to mention the crumbles and custard, the pies and the tarts or the five different flavours of ice cream. This was nursery food with a vengeance. an army might march on its stomach, but I couldn't have marched anywhere after that little lot.

Most of that night was spent getting pissed with a six foot twelve Vinnie Jones lookalike called Steve Cunningham, who had apparently heard from someone who had seen us on another show that we were, as he so delicately put it, the dog's bollocks. I modestly explained that, yes we did always seem to go down extremely well on these events. Okay, promised

Steve. If we really did turn out to be the dangly parts of the said animal, he would present me with his Queen's Royal Lancers tee shirt which he had worn into almost mortal combat.

The following night, after a daytime trip into town with our hosts, we ran on stage to a packed house of four hundred soldiers, most of whom had been spoon-fed and burped after their earlier meal. We came, we played and we conquered. By halfway through they were all on top of their chairs doing the Wayne's World bow and chanting, 'We are not worthy'. It was a pretty awesome sight and in truth it was us who were not feeling worthy.

Earlier in the show the dancers had pleased the lads with their gyrations, skimpy outfits and set of three raunchy routines. Big John entered to the cry of, 'You fat bastard' and Bill and Ben had received an ear-shattering roar when they bounced on stage with Mummy for Lynx's display of fire-eating and illusion. But remarkably, none of this glamour detracted from the astonishing reception we got from this bunch of female-denied squaddies. We were indeed the pooch's gonads. Steve Cunningham presented me with his prized garment and I wore it with pride. One down, five to go.

The road journey to Vitez (pronounced Veetez) was beautiful but it was sad to think that such a magnificent country was being ripped to shreds in the cause of race and religion, the lamest of all excuses in the view of a heathen such as I. From the vantage points of the hilltop roads we were treated to an endless vista of mind-numbing beauty. Lakes and forests glorifying a deceptively peaceful landscape, the rich foliage occasionally marred by the intrusion of a bombed-out dwelling sitting in shamefaced ugliness like a festering sore.

Every now and then the rolling hills would rise and dip to frame an expanse of tranquil waters from which the rich red splinters of sunlight would rebound into our eyes. Was this Croatia or Serbia? I couldn't quite get it sorted out in my head yet. Whichever it was it was glorious. Thoughts of war were put aside till another shell of a house hove into view. After a couple of hours we reached Vitez and, leaving our bags to the hired help, headed to the cookhouse for more comfort eating.

Comfort was something we needed at this point because we had seen our accommodation. To call it a house would be the equivalent of elevating it to the peerage. We were in former Yugoslavia and what we were being billeted in was a former dwelling. Into the shattered shell of what only shortly before had been someone's bijou residence, electricity cables had been stretched and basic beds had been thrown. After the beds, the next thing they threw in was us, clutching clean sheets and dirty blankets. We were four to a room, except for our roadie Phil, who had lucked-in with a room of his own. This superior single in former Yugoslavia was a former cupboard with about six inches to spare on either side of the bed, but luckily Phil was a slim lad.

What had things come to? I had spent thirty-five years on the road with some degree of success and here I was, practically in my dotage, squatting. As the days wore on we almost got used to the layer of brown dust that covered everything. It was omnipresent. No one cared much about the muck and the grime or the fact that if you went to the bathroom you had to wade through two inches of muddy water and came out dirtier than when you went in. Or that the enticingly hot water from the shower turned to liquid ice two minutes later. There was little point in caring. It was not about to disappear with a wish. And anyway, this was Boys Own stuff. An adventure you couldn't pay for.

The show that night was, if anything, better received than the first. Four squaddies joined us on stage towards the end of the act, cutting loose like they had just been told they had won the lottery. Thrilling stuff. But nothing was more exciting than the sight of a khaki-clad soldier doing the Chuck Berry duck walk across the stage to the strains of *Johnny B. Goode*, a machine gun replacing the traditional guitar. It was also a night for celebration. The youngest of the dancers, Megan, was twenty-one that very evening and touchingly tearful when a candle-lit cake was brought on o the stage while a few hundred soldiers sang *Happy Birthday*.

The following day saw us on another mountain journey through scenery even more spectacular. It is a verdant and sunny land without the dryness of Spain. The serenity of the occasional quiet waters complimented the surrounding greenery, the moisture lending a rich vibrancy to the colours of this deceptively calm country. Yet again the splendour was marred by the ruins of ethnically cleansed houses along the way; homes reduced to rubble by the warring nations who all apparently have God on their side. Well, that makes it alright then, doesn't it? And if I am being irreverent to whatever deity is, or is not, up there then I know God will forgive me. That's his job.

From time to time we were stopped by mountain patrols of local militia. It was the only time we experienced any real sense of danger. Bombs and guns, if fired from a distance, are relatively easy to deal with. They are too removed from you, too abstract and distant, to constitute a part of real life unless of course they score a hit in your immediate vicinity, in which case you probably won't know anything about it anyway. But on these narrow mountain passes we were confronted by unfriendly faces whose eyes told us they bore a grudge against the world. Everyone was a potential enemy and we were intruders in the land of someone who was pointing an automatic weapon loosely in our direction and ready to fire on a whim. The rules here had been more or less tossed aside and one more dead stranger was of little consequence to one with even less to lose and whose family may have been wiped out the day before. Yugoslavia was raping itself in a vile and cruel display of national incest.

To make the long journey pass more speedily we played I Spy, much to the amusement of Simon, our fresh-faced street-wise driver from Stockport, who sat there smiling sardonically at this bunch of musical fossils that had been placed in his care. They were living out their idea of a rock and roll lifestyle perhaps, but not his. We told jokes. Some were even funny and if they were not, the company of the others made them so. The pleasure of a tour often depends very much on your travelling companions and three days into the tour we had bonded nicely. There was no arrogance. No petulance. And no stand-offishness from anyone. *Fearless Leader* was a joy and ready to laugh at anything. If Lynx's John had the look of a demon, he possessed the temperament of Father Christmas. Lyn and Christina asked for no special treatment as women and became part of the gang without fuss or favour. We persuaded Lyn to tell a joke.

Q. What's the fastest cake in the world?
A. Scone (Get it? - s'gone).

It was very much a John McNally joke, that doyen of schoolboy humour. He chuckled away, as did we all, including Bill and Ben who were having a whale of a time. The miles passed quickly and we eventually reached our destination, a small town called Gorni Vakuf (pronounced Gorny Va Koof).

The camp this time was larger and constructed of dozens of steel portakabin rooms. This truly was heavy metal city. At least now our bunk-style accommodation was clean, even if it was on the second floor of a two tier quadrangle and the rooms had no facilities. If you wanted to wash or shower or even go to the loo it was a five hundred yards hike up camp through the dust to the ablutions block. At least when you reached them the showers spewed hot water in abundance. The problem was that you got covered with dust again on the way back.

I opted for a rest in my pit while the others took the opportunity for a recce downtown to witness the devastation. The whole place had been

101

decimated only weeks before to uninhabitable cubes of brick and concrete. Maybe I should have gone with them but seeing all that destruction would not have made me feel any better. It's a small world, they say, and indeed in the canteen I ran into an old acquaintance, a bouncer from Legends, one of the trendiest London clubs back in the late seventies. In those days the club was owned by a friend of mine and Ollie the doorman had been augmenting his meagre army pay by moonlighting from Chelsea barracks where he was stationed. Now he was a captain or higher. There was a lot of gold on his uniform anyway. No longer any need to moonlight.

The show that night was held in a hangar and thousands of soldiers went hog wild, but we were beginning to get quite used to that by now, although not complacent. The food and drinks were once again in the Officers Mess. Some of the young lads from the ranks told me that the entertainers were always whisked away to another mess and they never got to speak to them. I suggested to the girls that they should visit a while and, to their credit, they were happy to do so, if I went with them. In the end their thoughtfulness was betrayed somewhat by just a few of the less mannered of the engineers hurling insults at them. Only a few, but enough to make things a little unpleasant, so we made our excuses and retreated. To some it's like giving strawberries to pigs. We returned to the mess and the television set on which Frank Bruno was winning his fight with Oliver McCall to become heavyweight champion of the world. Spirits that night were high indeed.

From Gorni Vakuf we headed for Tomislavgrad where, once again, we were given container rooms to rest and change in while we were there. After the show we would be travelling back to the hotel at Split. We decided to take a trip into town with Under Wraps and the drivers. Tomislavgrad consisted of one not very attractive main street and little else. Again, the people looked morose. Indeed, the features of the whole nation veered wildly away from good looking, but maintaining a facial expression that makes you look as though you've spent your whole life swigging vinegar does not help matters.

Richard Asbury offered the information to our drummer Billy Adamson that the town had not always been called Tomislavgrad. Years ago it was called something else. 'Yes. Shithole', was the dour Scot's reply.

We found a bar with seating outside where we could get coffees and beers. As a bonus the owner was actually quite pleasant, as well he should be with the amount of passing trade that had suddenly invaded his premises. The tourist industry was not exactly thriving in those parts. It was a nice, sunny day and we were in the best of moods. The tour was going extremely well to say the least and turning out to be one of the more memorable trips of our career. Far from being a danger-ridden sacrifice, it had turned out to be a pleasure and a privilege that few would ever be able to experience.

That evening we had yet another large hangar-type building for the show and a crowd that was off and running from the start, although the start was nearly delayed by John still being in the loo a hundred yards away when our non-adjustable intro tape started. Talk about being caught short. But, with a supreme effort and a quick wipe of the arse he made it in the nick of time.

Communicating with an audience of barely post-pubescent squaddies was becoming easier by the day. I now had the hang of just what buttons to press and the onset of mania had moved forward from mid-show to halfway through the first song, with the officers, always seated in comfy front row armchairs, going as apeshit as their charges. Soldiers are just big kids. And officers, in the end, are just big kids with power.

The end of the show wasn't enough for them. They had done the 'We are not worthy' bit again and now they were chanting for more and wouldn't stop. We had changed out of our stage suits and still they shouted. There was nothing to do but get back out there and give them *Nutbush City Limits,* a deafening rocker that was rarely in our set unless we really needed it. That night seemed a perfect way to end a rock and roll show.

We were still on a high for our two hour trip back to Split. The conversation was animated. We were looking forward to sleeping in real beds again, in single rooms and some semblance of hygiene and normality. Ruth, the choreographer, had an endearing habit of making *faux pas* by getting her words wrong and this night she managed to come out with a classic. The conversation was over a fighter pilot who had crashed his jet the day before. Was he killed, she wanted to know?

'Well, there's not a lot left when those things come down,' I replied a trifle sarcastically. I have an A level in sarcasm.

'You never know,' she reasoned, 'he might have ejaculated.'

Priceless.

Lunch the next day was a sad occasion due to the fact that the *fearless leader* had to leave the tour due to other CSE commitments and was flying to England via Italy that afternoon. He tried hard to make a sincere, moving speech but those things do not sit well with musicians or footballers.

We were musicians with the mentality of footballers. But we all knew Richard meant it and we were going to miss him.

His departure meant that he missed the wildest night of all. Ploce (pronounced Plochay) truly was tent city. Four and a half thousand serviceman, the third largest deployment of troops anywhere in the world at that time, all under canvas. It was a mind-blowing sight in the moonlight with soft lights shining from the acres of khaki tenting on a harbour sight setting, a re-enactment of a scene from a modern dress production of Lawrence of Arabia. In their off-duty daytime moments the tanned troops played volleyball or did their washing in makeshift outdoor ablutions to alleviate the boredom and discomfort. Romantic as tents may appear they are, in reality, no fun at all. When it rains you get flooded out. Tents do not have floors. These guys were existing in as near a state of hell as you could get.

Neither did this temporary city, reminiscent of a scene from Mad Max, have hot water. Try four months of cold showers and see how quickly romance fades. But the sight of the jolly entertainers from the modern day equivalent of ENSA brought a roar of approval from the lads. At least, that's what I thought. By now I had got so used to them that I had almost forgotten the effect that Bill and Ben could have on these boys. Ploce was tent-town but the sight of Lyn's boobs had caused a few extra temporary erections. At least the showers were cold.

I spoke to some of the guys and they seemed to accept their lot with a stoic good humour, even if they did not like it. Most appreciated the intrinsic beauty of the country that was their temporary home. I was glad. One particularly surly natured squaddie, ungracious of spirit and unbending in his desire to denigrate the place, remarked that it was the arsehole of the world. I suggested that he would just be passing through then. The irony was lost on him.

Ploce was the scene of one of the most memorable shows we have ever given. Or, to be more correct, one of the most memorable reactions we have ever received. Two and a half thousand battle-hardened soldiers took us to their hearts and sang and yelled themselves hoarse through what was for us an awesome experience. The officers mounted the stage to do a *Tiller Girls* routine. At one time it seemed the whole audience was up there with us. The stage began to buckle but somehow it held. We had been given *the bow* every night so far but arms raising up and down in such vast numbers and voices chanting at such an ear-splitting volume is hard to take without the heart beating a little bit faster and the eyes beginning to fill with moisture.

This was something else again. We got some good shots of the crowd but without movement it could never begin to convey what was actually happening. Maybe someone, somewhere has a video of the evening. I hope so.

The next day, along with Ruth, Tamsin, Megan and the drivers, we went into Split and were impressed by the architecture and sense of history. Once again it is hard to dispel the feeling of upset that stupid prejudices were ruining this uniquely beautiful spot on the globe. We all sat in a courtyard surrounded by intricately carved stonework of majestically weathered buildings, the like of which will never be erected again, and drank our coffee in the warm and pleasant afternoon air.

The town was not crowded which did not, of course, surprise us, although the Germans apparently still arrived in droves, having the good sense to realise that what you are seeing on the television news does not necessarily convey the truth of what is happening. This place must have been heaven to them now that they no longer had to spread out their towels on the sun loungers before retiring for the night. Split remained a peacefully picturesque idyll just there for the taking. It was such a shame there were so few takers.

Our final performance was at the main base just outside Split itself. In effect it was a repeat of the night before scaled down to about a thousand in the audience. Still wild. Still yelling. Still dancing and singing and demonstrating their unworthiness with a humbling energy and enthusiasm. There was however one thing that stood out during this show. Let me correct that. There were two things that stood out. Halfway through Lynx's act and due apparently to a technical problem during a costume change the little sods made their debut. I kid you not. Bill and Ben popped out to see what all the commotion was about. Pink noses pointing proud and perky in the stage lights, they were welcomed in deafening style by a goggle-eyed horde of gobsmacked troops. And in the way that little 'uns do, they seemed to have grown in the ten days they had been there. Well, you know how kids seem to shoot up every minute.

After the final celebrations in the mess we drove back up the coast for a nightcap at the hotel bar. For some of our party their nightcap was a piece of headgear that would have made Gertrude Schilling proud. I do believe there were two who just about made the room in time to pack for departure. For once I was practising moderation, finally hitting the sack around three in the morning.

By the time Crotchety Airlines had whisked us back to dear old chilly

Heathrow we were all shattered but happy. The promises to exchange photographs were made and, for the most part, kept. I wondered if I would ever return in times of peace to whatever the former Yugoslavia will be called then, but somehow the reasons and the drama and the conditions which governed this occasion were all part and parcel of what made the trip into a true adventure. Had they asked me to go back the following week, Mummy's special soldier was ready to sign up.

10

Breaking Up Is Hard To Do

For a brief, frightening time in 1985 it seemed that my privileged life of travel and adventure was about to come to an untimely end. We were on a short tour of Scotland, on the mundane round of social and cabaret clubs that had become the staple income of a working band which had found it necessary to exchange the galloping high horse of success for a steady trot on the knackered nag of life. In fact the eighties had seen a slight improvement of both our image and the work available and the trot was slowly building to a pleasant canter.

I was staying at the small, pleasant and unpretentious home of our Scottish agent Robert Pratt, a big, bluff bearded Scot with a look of Rob Roy and the mischievous humour of an errant schoolboy. He was good company and his enthusiasm infectious. The rest of the group were billeted in a nearby hotel. It was a nice arrangement as far as I was concerned. I enjoyed a welcome rest away from the company of my workmates with an added bonus that I got spoiled rotten by Robert's wife Cath who dished up appetising Cairngorm-sized meals daily in the way that only a Scottish mother can. It proved to be a deceptive calm before an unprecedented storm.

At the outset of the decade we found ourselves installed in the Rockfield Studios just across the Welsh border in order to complete a couple of albums for the American 'new wave' label Sire. Its enterprising owner Seymour Stein, a virtual human pop almanac, had discovered that these revered icons of his musical youth were no longer cutting discs. It was an oversight on the part of pop music that bordered on mortal sin in his eyes.

Stein was the man who had signed up the unknown Madonna and nurtured her into a global superstar. His roster of acts included Talking Heads, The Ramones, The Flaming Groovies and The Undertones, every one of them a success, and now The Searchers. There was no doubt that it was a coup for the bunch of fallen idols that we had become. The seventies had been a bit of a non-event for us. It wasn't a tragic time. Our career had not stopped by any means. It had not suffered a breakdown, but it was certainly in need of a good service. At that point we could not get arrested and if Stein wanted us to stick conical brassieres on our chests or spit great gobs of phlegm at our audience we would not have dismissed it out of hand. We were not exactly up for grabs at any price but our integrity might perhaps be susceptible to a little mild whoring.

For six weeks at a time the four of us, John, Mike, Billy and myself lived, slept, ate and worked at a converted farm that had become a serious environment for serious projects in a world of recording. A world that had changed beyond recognition since the 'twenty four hour, one-take' albums that had marked the simplicities of our hey day. What we had once looked on as technical wizardry was now 'state of the ark'.

We were now on a thirty two track recording system, involving countless overdubs that had never before been available to us, in that ever elusive search for perfection. Perfection of course always remained just beyond the horizon. It is the nature of the beast. But we ended up with a couple of fine albums for our efforts, *The Searchers* and *Play For Today*.

Our guiding light was a terrific producer called Pat Moran whose patience and appetite for work rivalled that of John McNally, a man whose industrious nature made workaholics feel inadequate. As for myself, I was a bit of a lazy git and the greatest periods of enjoyment for me during arguably the most fruitful segment of our recording career was elsewhere. I enjoyed nothing so much as woofing down the mountains of home cooked food that was placed before us each evening. I would then settle my bloated body in front of the television while somebody else committed their greater talent to tape in the studio next door, popping in as and when required to provide the bass or harmony lines

Moran was a dichotomy in the brash world of rock music. He was shy and introverted in himself but possessed a love of rock music and a finely tuned ear for the good notes and sounds. His constantly sought after talent assured him of a long and healthy career, if his work rate didn't put him into an early grave first. The only fault I could attribute to the affable Pat was a handshake like moist and slightly overcooked spaghetti. Most disconcerting. But, what the heck. I have quite a firm handshake and an ear like a boot. I wouldn't know a hit record if it came up to me and said 'Excuse me, you stupid pillock, but I happen to be a hit record'.

Alas the resulting albums were critically acclaimed but commercial failures. They stood up well against modern new wave groups whose sounds were in fact based on the heritage of jangly guitars that we had pioneered. But the singles failed in the charts despite acres of articles devoted to us in the N.M.E and Melody Maker. Disc jockeys were, as usual, treading more carefully lest the stigma of association with anything less than ultra trendy would taint them. To them we were infected and untouchable. Disc jockeys live in fear of the ageing process in a culture that will always belong to the young. They cling desperately to a youth that they know will eventually desert them. Most of them were 'Smashey' and 'Nicey' personified.

For a while we discarded our uniforms in favour of a carefully orchestrated casual look and enjoyed the applause of London's young trendies who frequented Dingwalls, The Venue and The Nashville Rooms while we plugged the albums. Yet another prestigious gig came out of the blue in the form of our first-ever Royal Variety Show. Tim Rice had been given the task of assembling a 'history of British' pop music segment for that year's spectacular and this high profile Searchers fan wanted us to be a part of it. But not as much as we ourselves wanted to be a part of it.

Mike at first apologetically informed Tim it was impossible as it fell slap, bang in the middle of a Scandinavian tour. John McNally however, who loved nothing so much as a logistical challenge, was not about to miss out on one of the most important and prestigious nights in the showbiz calendar. If it can be done it will be done was his motto.

We opted out of two nights of the tour, paid our own return air fares from Sweden and flew home to perform in front of Her Majesty The Queen at The Theatre Royal, Drury Lane on Monday the 23rd of November 1981. We had played in front of many queens before, but this one would be wearing a tiara and ball gown. Come to think of it, so were some of the others.

The line-up was pretty impressive. Cliff Richard, The Shadows, Lonnie Donegan, Adam & The Ants, Marty Wilde, Alvin Stardust, Donovan and Lulu. And all that was just a fraction of a bill that also included, among others, Andrew Lloyd Webber, Mireille Mathieu and Itzhak Perlman. It was a memorable evening indeed. It got slated in the press, as Royal Variety Shows are wont to be, but the atmosphere in the theatre both out front and behind the scenes, was almost alcoholic.

Meanwhile our critical success album-wise had not translated into charts positions and hard cash, but as compensation our profile was lifting slowly and we were getting on with the day-to-day business of being respected 'has beens'. We were riding high on the hog and doing okay, but behind the scenes all was not as calm as it looked. I was contentedly coasting through life with a smile on my face, but I had been viewing through rose tinted blinkers.

A group is often a very good approximation of a marriage. In fact we had probably spent more hours in each other's company than with family or spouses. We did not always get on but then neither did things erupt into the blazing rows that seemed to be the norm for a lot of other outfits. In the main we realised that, while life was not always perfect, what we had was too good to throw away at the first signs of discontent. It had become a marriage of convenience. Divorce had never been discussed. So Robert Pratt's words came as a bombshell.

'Mike is leaving the band.' My jaw hitting the floor with an almighty thud was a sound that could only have been heard by me. We were in Robert's car heading back from a show in Glasgow to where he lived in the small suburb of Condorrat. Outwardly I think I managed to maintain my composure. 'He wants to see if he can make it on his own before it's too late.'

Before it's too late? He was forty five, for goodness sake. It bloody well was too late, at least in my eyes. This was not the first flush of youth we were talking about here. In fact we had all passed the last flush some time ago. It wasn't going to be long before we were all flushed away permanently. Forty five was practically geriatric in pop terminology.

Apparently Mike had asked Robert to help him with a solo career and to all intents and purposes it was a *fait accomplis*. And I was told all this in confidence which was a bit of a bummer. It was like being told your home town was going to be hit by an earthquake very soon but would you please not tell any of the inhabitants. A dilemma by any standards.

In fact my problem was soon solved by the fact that promoters began to ring up John to ask why the group was breaking up. Things had been moving fast behind the scenes. More had been happening than met the eye, the ears or perhaps more appropriately, the nose. Something was rotten in the State of Denmark indeed. Needless to say John was slightly surprised. He telephoned me and we discussed what our options were.

We could of course give up and try to make our way in other fields of employment. That was not a very acceptable option, partly because we did

110

not actually have any other skills with which to find gainful employment but more importantly because it would mean total surrender to our defecting partner. Neither of us were in the mood to do that. If this was a marriage that was breaking down then I was so enraged that I could have happily indulged in a little politically incorrect spouse battering at that point. If this was dog eat dog then I wanted to be the dog that got fed.

We decided to retrench and reorganise. We set about putting our plans into operation almost immediately, scouting round for a replacement singer/guitarist who could reasonably fit the requirements. Any new Searcher had to be of clean cut appearance, reasonably scandal-free, and of the right shape and height so as to fit into the empty suit, as we were not about to buy a new one without a fight. The height, or rather lack of it, was important in order not to dwarf the senior members.

Luckily John remembered a young lad who had fronted a support band at a pub venue in Brentford some time back and invited him to apply. Neither of us relished facing the horrifying prospect of endless, excruciating auditions and all the embarrassment that was part and parcel of them. For the moment we put on hold the dozens of hopefuls who had sent in tapes and pictures. Word had got around very quickly on the musical grapevine.

It was arranged that Spencer James, ten years younger than us but steeped in the music of the sixties and seventies and a former member of the group First Class who had once hit the charts with the summer anthem *Beach Baby*, should pop round to see me and talk it over. John had telephoned to ask if he had been just as I saw the car pull up at the end of the drive.

'What does he look like?' he asked.

I wasn't sure quite how to answer this and still retain any chance of ever passing my entrance exam to the Diplomatic Corps. I watched the rather odd looking figure striding purposefully towards the house. He was small, so size was no problem. I mentally lopped £120 off the budget, the price of a new suit. He was wearing a white cheesecloth shirt with chopped off three-quarter length sleeves the like of which I had only ever seen in a black and white movie about the life of Tolouse Lautrec. His footwear, which came halfway up the calf outside a pair of sprayed-on jeans, was something I can only describe as a remnant of the principal boy's costume from Anita Harris's last pantomime. Everything screamed 'seventies'. I replied as tactfully as I could.

'Well, he doesn't look like a Searcher right now but I'm trying to imagine him in a suit'.

As it turned out he was perfect for the job. Vocally excellent with a rich powerful voice that was somewhere between Mike Pender and Tony Jackson in tone, he was also a skilled guitarist both in the solo and rhythm departments. As an added bonus his cherubic baby face was a real babe magnet. Women were smitten by the newcomer. Suddenly we had acquired a sex symbol.

As for temperament, he was a permanently cheerful soul whose child-like enthusiasm for seemingly everything skipped seamlessly from one new fad or project to the next. He was a person who lived his life like a pop record; in three-minute cycles. We formed our strategy and set all the wheels in motion so that there would be the minimum gap between the ending of one era and the beginning of the next.

There were of course a few legal niceties to hammer out and rubber stamp. This was the dissolution of a union and, while there might not have been any kids to argue over, instead we found ourselves in a curious custody battle over the name of the group. This was a new one on me. If someone was leaving to 'try and make it on his own' I failed to see where this little item came into the equation. Call me picky if you will but as far as I could see one person was leaving a band. The band was not breaking up. It had been continuous, with changes but without cessation since its inception. But Pender wished to incorporate the name into whatever new outfit he was about to put together.

We had a dilemma. Come to a compromise or risk a horrendous battle in court which could cripple us financially. In my simple mind it seemed unethical, if not illegal, for a person to leave a group which was a going concern and then purport to be that group. But what did I know? The law concerning partnerships was an area greyer than the cloud of doubt and despair that loomed perilously overhead. And it was law that we were dealing with here, not ethics, which I barely had a chance to say goodbye to as I watched them disappear out the window. After meetings with our accountants we settled on an acceptable form that Mike could use in his new venture, while we would continue to be The Searchers, plain and simple. Plain and simple it seemed but plain and simple it was not turning out to be.

Our new line-up kicked into gear with a smoothness that made it all seem too easy. Crisis, what crisis? The audiences did not just warm to the new lad. They boiled over. He was hard not to like and the talent was there for all to see as he stood there singing and playing his heart out and grinning away like a hi-tech Cabbage Patch Doll. We thought that we had finally put all our problems to bed. But we soon found we were constantly being confronted with abuses of the agreements we had so carefully laid out and signed back there at our financial offices in London. It was a minefield trying to pin down who was to blame. There was no doubt we were being sinned against but who was doing the sinning?

John and I finally had to agree that the only way to settle this was in a court of law. Never apologise and never sue, someone once said. I have nothing against owning up when I know I am in the wrong or indeed fighting for what are my rights, but it is wise to take the second part a little more seriously. Dealing with lawyers is akin to solving a particularly difficult problem of nuclear physics by mail with a granny who is deep in the throes of senile dementia. After weeks of correspondence you still don't understand what the hell is going on and you are no nearer to a solution. The normal rules of logic seem to have been heaved out the window with a careless abandon. The difference is, of course, that your granny is not charging you hundreds of pounds for the benefit of this fruitless communication.

Things began to take on an aspect of surrealism. It was as though a giant force had beamed me up and zapped me down in the middle of Las Vegas where I was forced to stand and pump money relentlessly into a giant slot machine. Unfortunately this slot machine was not at all interested in loose change. It was only prepared to accept very large cheques.

The first time we got a hint of what we were in for was when we were asked if we owned our own houses and what they were worth. That question, put to you when your feet have barely crossed the threshold, does tend to ram the danger home a tiny fraction. It was then that I realised how wealthy I actually was and how poor I was very soon likely to be. But there was no going back now. We pressed ahead with an action against our former partner, signing cheque after cheque to support our case which was only halted outside the courtroom on the morning the case was due to be heard. Our adversary decided that the better part of valour was to formalise the original terms through our lawyers rather than risk the big bucks that were about to mount up in costs once barristers and judges became involved.

And that was the end of it - not. Some time later we came across an infringement that caused us to take the matter back to court for a contempt action and finally we found ourselves sitting on a wooden bench flanked by high priced legal experts who struck terror into our hearts. Partly because the environment of the high court and all the pomp and circumstance that accompanies it was completely alien to our understanding and partly because we knew that every word uttered was totting up a bill with greater speed and ferocity than a till at Tescos. We felt as though we were about to be royally screwed. And not even with the pleasures or advantages that accompany being screwed by a prostitute. At least when you're screwed by a prostitute she has the decency to tell you what it is going to cost.

The courtroom, with its elegant carved oak furniture populated by impressively robed academics, was awe-inspiring in its sheer majesty. Any resemblance to a scene from Rumpole of The Bailey or Perry Mason ended there. In those television representations of the glamorous world of the legal giants, bewigged paragons of confidence and verbal dexterity construct sentences of such beauty and unanswerable logic that mere mortals like us can only gape in admiration. So much for the theory. This was real life.

In one hand our barrister held a pen with which he emphasised the salient points of our case. He was, to my absolute horror, standing on one leg. The other leg, out of sight of M'lud but in plain view of two horrified plaintiffs, was being held up behind his back by the free hand while, in disconcertingly faltering sentences he put his arguments for our worthy cause.

Our financial and artistic futures were at stake and here we were being represented by a bloody flamingo. Halfway through the proceedings John turned to me and spoke.

'We've lost this.' He was speaking aloud what I was already thinking. I nodded, my face no doubt a graphic picture of dejection. I began to wonder if Penguin Books would like one of their old invoice clerks back. By now they would even have forgotten how useless I was at the job. And most of the firms whose goods I had misdirected would surely have been liquidated by now anyway, even if they had been angry enough to hold a grudge. Even the six pounds ten shillings they used to pay me was beginning to sound good in the face of my impending ruin.

The judge, who had the appearance of one who had reached the age where all further worries about age were a completely pointless exercise and who I swear had nodded off more than once during the interminable and unfathomable points of law, began to sum up. As he spoke my ears pricked, my blood began to race as I attempted to keep track of his words. I could swear the tide was turning. Finally he gave judgement in our favour, plus costs. Being an agnostic I silently thanked the Great Pixie In The Sky for looking after me.

Meanwhile we found ourselves also litigating in a number of actions against unscrupulous venues who were taking advantage of this extraordinary situation and quite blatantly misrepresenting our name. In fact it got so bad at one time that we wondered if it might not be sensible to sue in bulk. 'We are currently suing in the Sussex area and invite you to take

114

advantage of our special offer open for the next three months at generous discounts.' Stressful as it was, we were successful in every instance, although we had to play a strong game of legal poker when our bluff was being called. In fact our strength was that we were not bluffing at all. We could not afford to. If we gave an inch they would take a mile and pretty soon they would own the whole motorway.

Each time we had our costs taken care of and accepted an out of court settlement, the amount varying a token sum to quite substantial piles of currency that went some way to giving us back a little of the faith we had lost. Our solicitor was particularly impressed with the compensation bestowed on us by an errant venue in Hammersmith. 'Very nice,' he said 'but I don't think it would be wise to attempt to make a career out of this.' I have since discovered a very interesting fact. It is apparently illegal for a solicitor to sue a client for his fees. What a wonderful rule. I think that the next time I get involved in expensive litigation I shall simply refuse to set-tle my account. It works for me.

So far, so good. But in the little spare time we had in the gaps between what seemed like full time legal employment there was a career to be nur-tured and a future to be planned. I had no intention of seeing my living grind to a premature demise. In the end this little ripple was to prove a blessing in disguise but right now the blessing appeared to be very effec-tively disguised indeed. We had to dig our heels in if this singing lark was to be an ongoing concern. There were still so many places I wanted to see, so many things to do. We had managed to overcome this tiny blip on the computer screen of life. It was time for the journeying to begin again. For this travelling man there was still a lot of travel ahead yet.

11

On The Road Again

We settled ourselves in the Business Class section of the Pan Am 747, our faces affecting a suitably superior sneer in the direction of the 'chicken and geese' slumming it back there in steerage. We were, in fact, pretenders. This hallowed ground was a totally unexpected bonus. Even in our hey day our trips to the U.S.A had been completely devoid of the trappings of luxury. And we were too dumb or too insecure to demand it. Now, October the 8th 1986, it was twenty-two years on and we were being treated almost like stars as we set off for The British Invasion Tour of The United States.

The American promoters had paid fine attention to detail when setting up this coast-to-coast extravaganza and were meticulous enough to have the whole party use Pan Am 101, the same flight number that carried The Beatles on their triumphant entry at the outset of Beatlemania in 1964. I imagine the subtlety was lost on most but I had to admire their strategy. In fact it was only the principals that were afforded the wide seats and the free champagne. The Searchers, Gerry Marsden, Freddie Garrity, Chad Stuart and Jeremy Clyde. The Mindbenders were a featured act but considered to be too much of a later mutation to merit the same degree of comfort and expense as the front runners. They, along with backing groups such as The Pacemakers, The Dreamers along with the road crew, were consigned to the cheap seats. As was the unfortunate Mrs Garrity.

Fred had decided to treat his spouse by having her accompany him on the tour but either his generosity or his budget had not managed to stretch to Club Class. But, thoughtful to the 'n'th degree, every now and again Fred would trot down the aisle to the rear end with a glass of champagne somewhat in the manner of an Eastern potentate trying to keep one of his favourite wives sweet. I think if I had been Mrs Garrity there would not have been a stick big enough to hit him with. Off hand I cannot think of too many rock and roll partners who would have countenanced such cavalier treatment. In the end the marriage did not last. Maybe the waters were not quite as calm in economy as they seemed on the surface.

It was a good start to the new phase in our career. Six weeks lording it up from New York to Los Angeles and all points in between while we contemplated our future at profitable leisure. The combined hits notched up by the bill on offer were considerable and we had quite a good pedigree. *Needles And Pins*, *Goodbye My Love*, *Bumble Bee* and a number of others had achieved high positions our there, the pinnacle being *Love Potion Number Nine* which had peaked at number two in the spring of '64.

Gerry And The Pacemakers had charted strongly with *Ferry 'Cross The Mersey*, *Don't Let The Sun Catch You Crying* and a bunch of others although oddly enough his signature anthem, the Rodgers and Hammerstein classic *You'll Never Walk Alone*, had been a stiff States-wise and was better known that side of the pond for being the accompanying song to the annual Jerry Lewis Charity Telethon. A bit of a bummer when you launch into the biggie and the audience stares back quizzically, wondering why on earth you're singing about cripples. He had enough others, however, to be able to throw away that particular crutch. No pun intended.

The original bunch of Mindbenders had been in the best sellers there, both as an act in their own right as well as with their one time lead singer Wayne Fontana. The group that paraded under the title on this occasion however was simply a workaday outfit put together to back Wayne in the seventies, but the name looked good on the bill and they played the hits.

Freddie, without any doubt at all, had captured the imagination of the Yanks in a way that eclipsed even his considerable success on home shores. *I'm Telling You Now* and *If You've Got To Make A Fool Of Somebody* made it for him but he was maybe best known for *Do The Freddie*. This was a maniacal dance-based song written especially for him to capitalise on the rather peculiar stage actions that punctuated his rock-comedy act. In my mind what he did was not rock. And in my mind it was not comedy either. But comedy is always a subjective thing. One man's Tony Hancock is another man's Chubby Brown. Leaping about in the air as though a Pekinese was snapping at your dangly bits while screaming out 'Just a minute' in a squeaky voice does not signify a high plateau in the realms of humour to my mind. But a star in America he certainly was, and he had a fair number of hits under his glasses.

Chad Stuart and Jeremy Clyde's sum total of chart success in the U.K. was a highest position of thirty-seven with a frothy ditty called *Yesterday's Gone,* a song not on everyone's lips in Britain. But for whatever reason, they had captured the imagination of the sixties American record buying public and their discs sold by the bucketloads out there. In fact for a number of years they had made the country their home. The promoters had flown the duo over there to rehearse with an American band. To maintain the 'invasion effect' that to them seemed so vitally important in marketing terms they went to all the trouble and expense of flying them back home again simply so that they would be seen to arrive with the rest of us. Had they seen the profits they were not going to make on the tour they would no doubt have dispensed with this bit of pretentious piffle. On top of which they would probably have seen fit to find the rest off us more suitable accommodation further down the aircraft, somewhere near to Freddie's wife.

As we set of on this great adventure we were experiencing déjà vu. This whole thing was more or less a mirror image of the nation-wide treks we had undertaken over two decades before. Way back then we would bus it from one side of that great continent to the other meeting up with other British acts who were also looting and pillaging in the current rage for all things long-haired and Anglo. In '65 our partners in crime had been The Zombies, another British group whose modest star had risen higher in the west. There, songs like *Time Of The Season* and *Tell Her No* achieved the acclaim that they deserved but which was denied them at home. Together we would arrive in a new town each day. And each day, at the first sight of our long-ish hair, we would be asked if we were The Beatles. Some times we were and some times we weren't.

In Jacksonville, I remember, we joined up with The Beach Boys who were riding on the crest of the surf, Sam The Sham & The Pharaohs, The Shangrilas and Lesley Gore. I was quite friendly with The Beach Boys, Dennis Wilson in particular. It was still a couple of years before their unkind comments in Hong Kong. The words 'pots' and 'kettles' dangle precariously above my head here. Given the fact that I often find great enjoyment in the delivery of a nifty line in vitriol with little or no encouragement, I am the last one who should complain. But nobody ever likes to be on the receiving end. The phrase 'just desserts' is always hanging about accusingly at the back of one's mind, or should be.

Along the way, in Richmond, Virginia, we were recruited into the mightily impressive Dick Clark Caravan Of Stars to strengthen a bill that included Peter and Gordon, Brian Hyland, Tom Jones and a bunch of others. Tom was high on the hog with *What's New Pussycat?* and ready to threaten the moral safety of American women, an act of which I am very sure he was eminently capable. American women had every reason to feel threatened by the boyo. The U.S. at that time, did not possess stars as macho as Tom. They either pretended to be or pretended not to be. Tom was always up front and in your face. It was start of the knicker-throwing season in Virginia.

Chicago, Nashville, Louisville and Terre Haute. Montgomery, Pensacola, Columbus and Oklahoma. Unprepossessing towns for the most part but having names that radiated style and glamour. Rock and roll names. Not like Cleethorpes and Dewsbury. Twenty four hours from Cleethorpes just does not cut it. The Dewsbury Lineman will never conjure up quite the same picture. The dream towns of my youth flashed past the windows of the coach as it raced along the miles and miles of relentless freeway. Vast, sprawling fields of grain gave way to parched desert lands which in their turn melted in to fairytale communities where folks like The Waltons no doubt still lived their unbelievably wholesome apple pie existence.

The down home charm of meticulously maintained white painted clapboard houses of Cape Cod, cute enough to be surreal with their perfectly trimmed lawns and picket fences and flags of the Union waving proudly, contrasted starkly with the urban downtown decay of metropolises such as Baltimore and Detroit. For Detroit the time of the 'Renaissance City' was still far off. Most of the old art deco buildings had yet to be restored to some semblance of their original glory. At night the downtown area was more or less deserted. It was safer to listen to Motown on your radio than to head downtown and look for it.

The crumbling brownstones of Baltimore seemed to be held together only by a network of rusting fire escapes, clinging to the brickwork like stopping off points on a giant game of snakes and ladders. In the streets and alleyways that separated the buildings the druggies and the winos staggered from bar to poolroom to garbage can in a search for some semblance of pleasure in what they loosely called a life. In the song, the lady came from Baltimore. In real life she took the first bus out of town.

If the towns were sometimes less than impressive, the names we only knew from the radio and the record labels were still held in awe by impostors such as we. Even the also-rans we encountered supporting us on the bills along the way were heroes in my eyes. They were American and I had bought their discs. It was enough. Billy Joe Royal whose *Down In The Boondocks* fell flat here because no one had the faintest idea what a boondock was, existed as a name barely on the tip of a few tongues. Arthur Alexander whose songs, *You Better Move On* and *Anna* were better known for their Stones and Beatles covers, tried to salvage a career out of audiences who were not even aware that the songs had been covers in the first place. What the hell was this old black man doing singing a Beatles song, they wondered?

Those days of my youth I remembered with extra sweetness perhaps because of the distance in time. The years erase the bad things first. And now here I was in 1986, the trauma of the split still fresh and our minds full of doubt and insecurity. It was the ideal opportunity to take stock and think about the rest of our career. At this point in time we were not even sure we had a career to think about. I ordered a glass of champagne and settled down on my flight to a temporary helping of glamour.

Our benefactors had set out to give the tour a high profile sure enough. Our hotel, The St Moritz, was elegant, expensive and in a prime position on Central Park South. John McNally and I decided to risk life and limb, although only in the bright light of day it's true, by crossing that oasis among the skyscrapers to visit the Dakota Building. By night we would never have made the other side alive. On the way we passed by the tiny bridge that shared a scene with Robert Redford and Jane Fonda in the film *Barefoot In The Park*.

As we strolled, weirdos rollerskated deftly along the pathways, defying gravity by clutching sideboard-sized boogie boxes on their shoulders while they slalomed in and out of the walkers. Bums and bag ladies shuffled aimlessly, no doubt justifying in their own minds the point of a journey from here to there in a life that seemed to have no point at all. And those who were just about managing to hang on to the next level up simply begged brazenly. We eventually arrived at the exclusive apartment complex where, on the 8th of December 1980, Mark Chapman shot John Lennon. Everyone remembers where they were on the day Kennedy was assassinated, when Armstrong stepped onto the surface of the moon and when John Lennon was shot. John had been in the process of giving him an autograph. I wonder how Mister Chapman would have reacted if Lennon had criticised his harmonies.

The impressive and solid chateau-style edifice was an eerie and fascinating sight, a curiously elegant spot for someone's life to be blown away. The ever-present clusters of fans stood for the most part in silence as they reflected on that dark, depressing moment. They were without doubt cursed by the current occupants who must have wished that Mark Chapman had picked any other spot in the world but this one for the culmination of his insane obsession. I assume they now cursed John and myself too.

We moved on down the road to visit the Café La Fortuna where John Lennon and Yoko Ono breakfasted daily. Here the occupants did not curse. Their trade had been boosted by the legions of devoted Beatles fans who simply wanted to sit and sup in the same spot their idols once had. The walls inside were decorated with signed photographs and album covers. It was light and airy in the small courtyard outside the main building where we sat and drank our cappuccinos at plain green metal pedestal tables which were surrounded by a bright red painted fence. It was a paradoxically cheery day to dwell on such a morbid subject but we were glad we went. And as a bonus the coffee was good.

The tour kicked off well the next day at Madison Square Garden, a prestige venue to entice the media for the benefit of boosting the shows to follow. The audience reaction was encouragingly enthusiastic as they wallowed in the anthems of yesteryear, almost word perfect to the simple unthreatening lyrics that held sway before rap and grunge kicked their butts. The reviews next day ranged from tepid to good. That was pretty much par for the course. Young writers out to make a name for themselves are not known for their addiction to the sounds of an older generation or for the generosity of their thoughts. Cruel wit has more impact and bite than polite approval. But somewhere along the way they also managed to give some praise without being effusive.

The next morning we left the lobby of the St Moritz to be confronted by our tour buses. Garth Brooks eat your heart out. What we faced were two cowboy wagons straight from the heart of Nashville, every panel and rivet ringing with the sounds of Merle Haggard and Willie Nelson. You only had to step on board to know in your heart exactly how it feels when your gal has left with your best friend, your dog has died and some theivin' crittur has driven off in your favourite Chevrolet pick-up truck.

Gone were the basic models on which we had ridden the freeways in '65, with their rigid front facing benches promising discomfort in every mile of your journey and guaranteed to deter even the most ardent traveller from a life on the road. These latter day custom-constructed leviathans were spray painted outside with garish western paraphernalia while the interiors were divided into sleeping and travelling compartments in a décor known as 'early dreadful'. They were lined in a combination of 'faux wood' and white buttoned plastic. The upholstery was of a design I had last seen being ripped out of a holiday caravan in Skegness on the grounds that it was dragging the place into bad repute. On top of all that the fumes from the huge diesel engines seeped into the passenger area and so we were in constant danger of either dying by asphyxiation or being taken into custody for offences against good taste.

The sleeping area consisted of twelve shelves stacked in threes and with red plastic curtains for privacy. They were like toasters turned on their sides. At times of tiredness we would slot ourselves in where the bread would normally go. When we were done we would pop out again. Anyone arising too quickly would concuss himself. In the lounge areas, one at the front and one at the back, there were tables to play cards on or to talk across and televisions and hi-fi built into the walls. It was all so hideously tacky. I loved it. We were off to see America in these fun wagons and for the next six weeks they would be home second only to the hotels and motels along the way.

America is an extraordinary place. A melting pot of creeds and cultures in which the sights and senses are stretched to breaking point in every direction. Overloaded cities where towers of steel and glass scrape towards what little is left of the skies while ant-like people scurry back and forth to sacrifice their sanity in praise of the great god Mammon. Sparse farmland communities where meagre livings are eked out from the flimsy covering of shotgun shacks are a world away from grumbling ghettos where a once slave population is kept as near to its former state as is inhumanly possible.

In the midst of an arid, unforgiving desert they created Las Vegas where vulgarity has become an art form. Here time is banned and you can take a break from gambling with your wealth and gamble with your future instead by having an Elvis Presley look-a-like marry you. And in both cases, if it doesn't work out you can always come back and try again. Further west in the la la land of Los Angeles a blond haired Baywatch babe walks the same street as a gargantuan woman whose body size, divided into more manageable portions, would provide us with a perfectly acceptable audience any night of the week.

Here acolytes worship in the temple of the body as they pursue what is for most the impossible dream of celluloid immortality. Nobody is a waiter or a waitress. They are all actors and actresses simply biding their time until fame steps forward and begs them for a date. It is a place where someone once described a starlet as any attractive young woman under thirty not at present actively employed in a brothel. The people are either too fat or too skinny. The newspapers are too thick and the toilet paper too thin. They don't speak the same brand of English and the humour is different. The average American thinks that irony is an optional extra in a Chinese laundry. It is a society of extremes. It is the place where size really does count. Something we knew all along but tried to ignore. It is weird and it is wonderful. Somewhere in there are the sane, ordinary folk but you get the feeling that they are a dying breed.

It's true that we were never going to see the real heart of the country beyond the edges of the freeways or outside the boundaries of cities where one derelict downtown is pretty much like another. There were too many towns in too short a time for their individual assets or otherwise to insinuate themselves into our memories. American cities on the whole are not like their British counterparts. Most are constructed in what one might call '20th century shoddy', with a handful of classic exceptions that almost, but not quite, throw you off the scent. In the main, erosion is all around. Permanent is not a word that readily springs to mind.

New York will never really rival London for the supreme quality of its architecture. Sheer scale is no substitute for pure aesthetic splendour. With the possible exception of that beautifully imaginative nineteen twenties spaceship the Chrysler building and a handful of others, the Big Apple has nothing to compete with The Tower Of London, The Palace Of Westminster or the recently rediscovered magnificence of The Natural History Museum. The Statue Of Liberty is impressive in an amusing way but in essence it is merely an overblown piece of kitsch. A monolithic fairground saleswoman in an illuminated headband trying desperately to sell her last ice cream cone.

We have demolished more buildings of true worth than were ever erected there. With a criminal disregard and a misguided belief that our apparent surfeit of architectural riches makes it excusable, we British callously raised the Mappin and Webb building to the ground a few years back. It could be argued perhaps that a land like ours that feels it can perpetrate such an act with impunity does not deserve to have so many riches to begin with.

The charm of Greenwich village, however, does manage to give London's Soho a run for its money. Here the eminently practical but mind-numbingly sterile grid system gives way to streets that lie refreshingly at odd angles and the human-sized buildings sit in quaint states of decay like squatters in a doorway, broken but unbowed in the shadows of Manhattan's towers. But New

York is without doubt one of the world's most exciting cities. A simmering melting pot of colour and culture that constantly threatens to boil over and cleanse itself in preparation for a fresh start. One simply has to stand in one spot for an hour to watch the whole of human life pass by. It is essential to visit New York just as it is essential to leave it again to adjust the horizontal hold on the television of your mind. We left the very next day, not for home but to traverse the rest of that great continent, or at least some of it.

Day by day we burned rubber on those great highways and tumbled out each afternoon to offer our musical wares to the devotees of popular song who gathered in venues of varying size, age and design. Long Island's Westbury Music Park and the Oakdale Music Theatre in Connecticut were technically efficient in their modern purpose-built construction but lacked the charm and history of dying relics such as Proctor's theatre in Schenectady. This lovely anachronism was clinging desperately to a gilt and velvet elegance that had been created in 1929.

We strutted our stuff on every kind of stage. Theatres in the round where you could be facing our grins one minute and our arses the next. Theatres in the park where the twilight of evening on the foliage surrounding an open sided auditorium provided an atmosphere that combined both calm and romance. Theatres in decay as they contemplated their approaching doom. Where our visiting troupe sometimes provided a reprieve and sometimes, when the crowds did not turn up, a death sentence.

Enjoyable as our times on stage were, the fun moments were in the bars and on the buses. The constant parrying back and forwards of stories and banter made the long hours of travel pass quickly. Sometimes all too quickly. There is nothing so fine in life as to spend time in fascinating conversation with friends old and new. The great teller of tales was Alan Mosca, the bass player with The Dreamers, with an accent as broad as the city of Birmingham from whence he came and the pepper and salt bearded appearance of a Yasser Arafat wannabee. The story of his amazing life one long night took us through one state and out the other end with twists and turns to rival the wildest novel. It is worthy of its own volume and I would not even dare to begin to tell it. His command of language in those outrageous Black Country vowel sounds was a feast to the ear.

We had entered Milwaukee but finding the hotel was proving difficult. After driving blindly for what seemed an age we instructed our driver, a stocky black man who we knew only by the name Red, to pull over while we asked a passer by for directions. The young woman opened her mouth to reveal a set of both upper and lower teeth braces that contained enough metal to rival the railings around Hyde Park. Kissing her would be like chewing an anvil. Mosca listened carefully and tried to absorb her words. He thanked her and we moved off. Fifteen minutes on, having driven by places we had passed a few minutes earlier, we were no nearer our destination and the bus stopped again. We shouted up to the front asking Alan what the problem was. In those stentorian Brumagem tones the great man spoke.

'We've just been stuffed up like kippers by a tart with a mouthful of brass'. What poetry. We were mesmerised by the sheer brilliance and spontaneity of that pure and unbroken sentence.

If Madison Square Gardens had been a high point on the tour there was no doubt that Tuffy's K.C Opry house was a low. A last minute substitute for a cancelled show in Denver, Colorado, this decrepit Kansas City theatre, like an actress of indeterminate years and well past her sell-by date, lay in dishevelled desperation and ill-prepared for our visit. Nothing appeared to work too well. There was a sound system that was unsound. It delivered an amplification of sorts but not one that we considered fit to accommodate the noise that we intended to pump through it. While Gerry's audio engineer, Andy Cairns, gallantly stayed behind in an attempt to install some hi-fi into the pathetic low-fi set before us, Tuffy, the owner of the establishment, took us out for something to eat. His head boasted a beard below and a hat above and the rest of him was dressed in sympathy. He was all boots and buckskins. We were in cowboy country. The chaos that surrounded the preparations for the evening's shows did not appear to phase him one bit. Neither did he seem to be especially upset that our potential audience so far amounted to a sprinkling of patrons.

Having stuffed ourselves with southern fried chicken and French fries we returned to the kind of 'opry house' that was never graced by Callas or Gobbi. By this time we had sound. Well, that was a start. What we did not have were dressing rooms. There were a couple of cupboard-sized vestibules at the top but any excess were forced to disrobe on the stairs and landings. In an attempt to add gravitas to the production of this splendid review the producers had devised a video segment of archive footage to lead up to the start of each act. It was a nice touch - in theory.

The curtains drew back and the opening clips were screened in readiness for the Mindbenders. Unfortunately nobody had thought to check if The Mindbenders were going to be ready. The clips ended. The stage remained empty and silent. All that could be heard were the mumbled words of surprise from offstage and the rustle of garments as frenzied group members tried to tuck their surplus poundage into their optimistically tight fitting clothes in a fraction of the time normally allowed. The curtains closed once more as the pathetic smattering of patrons looked on with incredulity. Tuffy's K.C. Opry House tonight appeared to be presenting a Faydeau farce.

Eventually the entertainment commenced, stumbled and hobbled through two performances, with varying degrees of fluidity, to a welcome close. I had no doubt that both audience and cast uttered a sigh of relief when the whole ghastly affair was over. And to cap it all, as welcome as a jester at a funeral, Sod's Law came into play. That very evening, by a coincidence of sheer misfortune, the music critic of The Observer just happened to be passing through town. He must have thought Christmas had come early that year. I read the report when I got back home. I prefer not to remember the text. My mind has obliterated his words.

As we were closing the show that night it was going to be cutting it fine to get back to the motel in time for a drink with the rest of the party. When the money was slow to arrive in our tour manager's open hands the delay caused a mild depression to set in. There was no chance. It was almost 1 a.m. Luckily our tour manager was astute enough to carry a gun with him as insurance against defaulters and he eventually arrived back at the bus fully paid up.

When we got back to the motel we decided, with little hope, to check out the possibilities of perhaps just one nightcap. Lo and behold Alan Mosca had sweet-talked the manager, a die hard sixties fan, into organising a mass 'stoppy-back'. We were able to quaff to our hearts content. But the bonus of all bonuses was the discovery that, due to strict state licensing laws, they were not allowed to charge for alcohol consumed after time. The whole shebang was absolutely free. The gods were indeed smiling down on us that night.

Tuffy's was tough but the Universal Amphitheatre in Los Angeles was a different kettle de poisson entirely. Perched on a rise just a few hundreds yards away from the old Psycho house and the Bates Motel, the impressive and acoustically brilliant auditorium was packed. It was the last stop on the tour. We had been to Syracuse, South Bend and St Louis. Fort Wayne, Fairfax and Philadelphia. San Diego and San Francisco. Oshkosh and Omaha. Now here we were in the golden west and ready for our final triumph before the journey home. Pockets of ex-patriot voices yelled their encouragement as they revelled in a non-stop orgy of tunes that were well loved and tested by time. Songs they knew by heart and which they sang along with, word perfect from beginning to end.

Jeremy Clyde, once a simple songster and now a veteran thespian, began to ramble into one of his monologues recalling a tale that was based around one of his recent television roles. His swashbuckling character had apparently required him to be clad from head to toe in leather, complete with a feathered hat and a sword. From the midst of the crowd a bellowing voice with a Scouse accent as thick as a docker's biceps roared out.

'Did yer 'ave a whip?'

My Clyde was unfazed and unabashed. In carefully modulated tones borrowed from Donald Sinden, he offered his reply.

'Yes, I had a whip. And a mace'. He never got any further.

'Yer big tart', came the unbeatable put-down.

It was a sensational night and a fitting end to six weeks of good times that we all felt we deserved. At the post-show bash Alan Mosca and John McNally sat talking to a young British couple who were currently residing in Tinseltown. Mosca asked if it was hard to get work there. The man replied in the affirmative. Mosca then asked what kind of car he had. It was, it seems, a somewhat beat up old jeep.

'Well, that's where you're going wrong, mate', he advised with the wisdom of one who knows. 'You drive up in that and they look out the window and see you coming and think 'aye aye, needs the work, can't be any good'. You've got to hire yourself a flash car and they suddenly think you must be doing okay and that's because you're obviously good at what you do'.

'See, I've been telling you that all along', interrupted his wife. 'I told him that', she repeated directly to Alan. Mosca's chest swelled with the pride of a man who has imparted great knowledge to the woefully ignorant. Before moving on he thought to ask their names. She was Angharad Rees and he was Christopher Cazenove. At that point in time he was one of the stars of Dynasty.

12

Solid Silver Memories

The seed planted itself into our minds on the journey home to England. What we had just been through was the best time we'd had with our clothes on for years. Great shows, great audiences and great company. We had relived a period that was tucked away in the memory banks of our distant youth. The long lost theatre package tour. Somewhere along the way it seemed to have died out with the dinosaur and the dodo. At one time they were the lifeblood of our industry, the annual showcase and opportunity for the record buyers to yell and scream at the currents stars in the finest comfort and conditions available. If the promoters had not exactly made a killing on the back of this one, that was simply because they had not done their sums right. The scale of the production was a little bit out of kilter to the actual range of its appeal. They had misjudged. Not a lot, but enough to pay the price. Artistically, and in the eyes of the public who had paid their entrance money, it had been a success.

The budget for around thirty actual stage performers plus personal crew, sound technicians, production managers, buses and drivers, not to mention the nightly cost of hotel accommodation, was a hefty wage bill to meet. The margin for profit had been eroded. But there was an audience out there waiting to get along to such shows, of that we were sure. We just had to figure how many, what kind of ticket price would be acceptable for this kind of entertainment, and who would they drag themselves out from behind their television sets to see.

It was John McNally who first decided that a scaled down version of just such a package was perfect for our home market. It was a concept that had been out of vogue for so long that the wheel would surely have turned full circle as wheels are prone to do. As brown had become the new black for a while so 'out of date' could become the new 'in vogue'. We agreed in principle with Gerry Marsden and his management and when we got back to England talked over the possibilities with our own agent, Alan Field. Alan, the 'Silver Fox' of the world of agents, being a smart cookie not only in appearance but also in his thinking, fully supported the notion. He in turn spoke with the Flying Music Company, an organisation run by two enterprising young entrepreneurs called Derek Nicol and Paul Walden.

A while before, they had spotted a gap in the entertainment market and set about filling it. They had realised that a whole range of talent had been virtually ignored for some time and along with it an audience that was growing older in years but not growing into the new music that now permeated the pop charts. They were middle age, middle class and middle income, without an outlet for the spare cash that just yearned to be spent on something they could both understand and enjoy. To them rap was just a word with a letter 'c' missing.

Walden and Nicol had rejuvenated the careers of a few stars of yesteryear by putting them out in successful promotions, sometimes in theatres and sometimes on the lively round of ballrooms. It was a circuit that had become badly clogged up with new wave and punk. They were constantly on the lookout for new ideas to extend and improve their enterprise. The idea of a sixties package came like gold to a panhandler. They were up for it in a big way.

They envisaged a major tour, maybe thirty or forty dates, with The Searchers and Gerry & The Pacemakers sharing the headline. Such a tour, they agreed, did not warrant an overloaded bill such as we had just toured with in the States. Neither the time available on stage nor the income one could generate in a two thousand seat theatre would justify it. Gone were the days of the quick on/off sets of the previous generation of packages. Performances were getting longer and longer and they would eventually culminate in the four hour marathons of Bruce Springsteen and the like. Nothing of that length was needed here but fifty minutes to an hour each on stage was an acceptable performance time from a group in the eighties. One more act, a short one to open the proceedings, would round things off nicely. They found such an act in Peter Sarstedt.

Peter was one of three Sarstedt brothers, Anglo-Indians brought up for the main part in Croydon and all successful in the charts at one time or another. The first had been Rick who, as Eden Kane, had notched up a run of big hits in the early days before Merseymania and the general beat boom sent all but a handful of the solo singers packing. Eden was a regular touring partner of ours in the glory days. The youngest brother, Clive Sarstedt, changed his name to Robin for the release of a virtual copy of the original Hoagy Carmichael recording of *My Resistance Is Low*. He was a true 'one hit wonder'. Peter Sarstedt on the other hand was a 'two hit wonder'. But *Where Do You Go To My Lovely?* had been such a monster that it would have been hard to find anyone of any age who couldn't sing at least the chorus of this anthem to a life of jet-setting pretentiousness. In that one short piece of writing Peter Sarstedt had provided himself with a pension for life.

Kicking the whole thing off at the London Palladium was a masterstroke. At a time when a lot of seriously important rock acts were struggling to fill out their arenas and stadiums, our paltry little piece of nostalgia packed them in for two shows on Sunday. May 1st at London's premier theatre. For those who considered that a sixties show was a show for people in their sixties it must have been a revelation that the patrons that night spanned every generation. Some had come to relive their long gone youth while their children, and even grandchildren, came to see what all the fuss had been about. After all, it was the most talked about decade in pop culture bar none. The Beatles had become icons for not just one but every generation. They belonged not just to a time warp but to a musical eternity. And the songs of them and their contemporaries, namely us, achieved sufficient daily airplay to ensure that just about anyone could manage to mumble their way through a reasonable portion of *Sugar And Spice* or *Needles And Pins*.

I checked out the audience from behind the red velvet drapes, the same ones that had once parted so majestically to herald our appearance on the old Sunday Night At The London Palladium. It was the highlight of the television week in those old monochrome days when the big box in the corner was still a piece of technological wizardry and wonder. The whole nation would sit in to watch stars from all over the globe appear in their living room. There was always a buzz about this particular palace of variety. Despite its size there was an intimacy that was as permanent as if it had been sketched into the blueprints before the elegant edifice was built.

The house was packed. People were still seating themselves after the second bell, relaxed and smiling after a pre-show drink in the bar. The ones who had stayed away too long were no doubt curious as to how the idols of their formative years would stand up to the images imprinted on their minds. Maybe, like old flames meeting after too long an absence, they were as nervous as I was. Scared? Too true. My bum was twitching like a magpie's eyelid.

But I need not have been. The feeling that emanated from the throng was as warm as the weather on that fine, balmy May day. The deafening applause that greeted each of the performances was an act of sharing; of mutual comfort. An understanding that we had all been through the same things, suffered the same anxieties of growing up and growing out and realising that it really didn't matter at all. We understood at last that age was a state of mind. The body was another state entirely, one that you were either comfortable with or not. And if not, well, you had the chance to do something about it. And if you didn't, so what. Wasn't it the music that was supposed to count?

We had all changed and we all understood how everything must change. We were no longer the sylph-like rock gods of their teenage memories. And they were no longer the shapely young groupies and skinny-ribbed fashion dandies who had once hoped to die before they grew old. If that had once been their intention they had unfortunately left it a little too late. They forgave us our trespasses and we forgave those that trespassed along with us. Age is a world that nobody gets out of alive.

Suddenly we found ourselves back in the public eye and riding on the crest of a slump. Almost overnight the decade known as The Sixties had achieved a profile higher than it had been since the first stirrings we all felt with the raw naïveté and hypnotic simplicity of *Love Me Do*. The press coverage was extensive. They could not deny the resurgence in interest. But neither could they resist lunging viciously with their sharpened quills.

The Guardian reviewer unfairly called Sarstedt 'that incomparably bad lyricist'. Unfair, I cry. The words of *A Brand New Love Among The Ruins* must surely give the lie to that glib exaggeration. Had he ever listened to them? The same writer attacked Gerry Marsden for not remaining the slim-hipped teenage idol he had been twenty years before. But twenty four years on we were no longer selling sex. We were selling memories, slightly used and slightly flawed maybe, but it was a perfectly good commodity. Everybody with an ounce of sense knew that those memories would have to take account of constantly altering physical appearances. The write-up failed to point out that Gerry's voice was just as good and as strong as it had been more than twenty years before, still with that street-wise Dingle-raised throatiness that had once sent shivers down the spines of legions of barely pubescent girl fans. And if someone does not like what they see or hear, if it is just not their idea of 'cool' then it is such a simple act to just stay away. The years change our looks. There is no escape, that's for sure. But there's no reason to lay down and die.

No matter how many great reviews a performer receives it can never eradicate the pain of the lone poisoned quill whose vitriol-laced ink remains indelibly tattooed on the brain forever and a day. It will seem so unfair that you and your great talent are being vilified by some pimpled prat with a face like one of those newspaper games, where you join up the dots to reveal a barely distinguishable caricature of George Best. A no-account scribbler whose venom, I would like to believe, is probably fed by the shame that he has a penis the size of a button mushroom and the literary skills to match.

The trouble with the young is that they feel that youth is some great thing that they have achieved when in fact they achieve nothing. It is simply a fleeting passage of time before they, like everyone else, hurtle inevitably towards old age. Nobody gets away with it, not unless they have the misfortune to die young. No matter how trendy you imagine yourself to be at nineteen, eventually you are that 'old fart' you derided in your younger days. The rap and grunge of today is the 'old folks' music' of tomorrow. And don't you believe anything else. Abuse your elders simply for acquiring age and you subconsciously abuse yourself.

If there is an audience that believes it can enjoy an evening wallowing in nostalgia and is willing to pay an entrance fee then there is a reason for an artiste to haul his ageing body, whatever state of decay it might be in, onto a stage. Some bodies wear better than others. Some talents wear better than others. And it is only the people who make their way to the clubs and theatres who can judge whether the expanding waistlines and the receding hairlines have passed the litmus test. And if there are people who believe that this will not be an uplifting or entertaining experience then the solution is ludicrously simple. Do not go. But there is never any reason to suggest that others might not partake of something simply because you yourself do not wish to.

We suffered rather less in that particular review. The writer was complimentary about our music. 'Still sharp, still convincingly serious about what they do', he wrote. The only barb tossed at us was reference to our shirts and suits coming from Man at C & A. He was wrong. They came from Principles. Same thing really. High street chic. Or, more to the point, high street cheap. Anyway, we were happy to have got away so lightly. Of course along the way we took our turn to receive the brickbats. I will avoid repeating anything negative here. Why should I? It's my book.

For the next month our little caravan of memories criss-crossed the nation, playing to standing room only and finishing at the Kings Theatre, Southsea on the 28th of May. The venture had been a huge commercial success. Critical success was a subjective goal. And in the eyes of the paying customers they subjectively decided that yesteryear was definitely where it was at. Punk and new wave could wallow in its own mire for all they cared. Blessings were being showered from heaven.

Over the next decade we were to repeat this formula again and again with only the names being changed to protect the innocent, and the profits. The Swinging Bluejeans, The Marmalade, The Fortunes, Dave Berry, Bobby Vee, Chris Montez, Billy J. Kramer. It was mix and match all the way. If the audiences were wallowing like pigs in a trough of nostalgia, we were doing very much the same thing. And if the recent U.S. tour had rekindled recollections of our first trips Stateside, then this little jaunt was more or less a scaled down replica of the once hallowed Autumn and Spring tours of our championship season. Tours that had once been the life blood of every pop group worth its salt.

Heady days indeed. It was a ritual. A tradition. The tour coach would set out from Alsop Place, just around the corner from the Planetarium on the Marylebone Road, and dispense an entertainment of sorts to all parts of our good Queen Elizabeth's realm. Looking back I can't quite get it straight in my mind why we all travelled on the coach and why everything started out in London. Most of the best-loved groups of the era came from the north of the country. Maybe it was because there was a universal consciousness in those days that the world began and ended in the Capital. Like New York, New York, if you can make it there you can make it anywhere. London in the sixties was the swinging city. It was where the action was.

Maybe we coached it because we were still in a financial backwater where groups were still kept on a tight reign and ignorant of their true potential or their true worth. Limousines, or even cars, were certainly not the order of the day. Such things were extravagances not to be entered into lightly, except for Dusty Springfield who swanned around most elegantly in her silver grey Buick Riviera. Besides which you could have more fun in the mass company of your peers than in the claustrophobic confines of a Ford Zephyr or a Rover 3 litre.

These were the days when motorways were still a novelty and even though we had both the M1 and the M6 there was still an hour of hard travelling on the A and B roads between them. The greasy spoon cafes like Jacks Hill on the A5 and the Busy Bee just outside Watford were beginning to give way to modern motorway outlets like the Blue Boar just below Coventry on the M1. These new and relatively hygienic fast food cafeterias, supposedly built on the slick lines of American counterparts (so long as you never actually got the chance to compare them with the superior efficiency and fare of those transatlantic parallels), hiked both their standards and their prices. The Blue Boar on a Saturday night would often boast more stars than a London nightclub as The Tremeloes, The Searchers, The Kinks and others would stop on the way home to refresh themselves, recharge the batteries and swap exaggerated stories of the hysteria generated at the evening's performance.

In November '65 we headlined a tour that contained, among others, Dionne Warwick and The Isley Brothers. Way down on the bill and doubling as compéres was a comedy duo who were trying hard to break into the big time. Syd and Eddie had to wait a number of years yet before Hughie Green would rename the winners of his show Opportunity Knocks and the public would watch the 'overnight stars' Little And Large on their television sets each week.

Before the start of the tour Chris Curtis and I went along to say hello to Dionne and welcome her to England. With Curtis clutching a bulky portable record player underneath his arm, (these were the days before the conveniences of the Walkman and Discman), we trotted up to her room at the Mayfair Hotel. Or maybe I should have said 'suite'. Americans never seem to have rooms, I have found. It is always a suite. It doesn't matter if it's nothing more than a shoebox with the furry marks on the walls from where someone has tried unsuccessfully to swing a cat, in their parlance it will inevitably elevate itself to the status of a suite.

On stage they have a fondness for the affectation of using the royal 'We', as if by doing this it somehow gives their backing musicians a feeling of equality. Patronising or what? I have always longed for a horn player to stand up in the middle of a show and point out that 'Excuse me but 'we' noticed a little inequality in 'our' pay packet this week.' They have a tendency to mess about with our language too. The smooth pronunciation of aluminium becomes a slightly sloppy sounding al-oo-min-um. The hard sound of *skedule* for whatever reason softens itself to become *shedule*. Sometimes Americans are so full of *skit*.

But Dionne was friendly enough and the three of us had fun playing the latest vinyl discoveries of Chris whose energy and enthusiasm was as always boundless and infectious. I did however manage to make the slight *faux pas* of telling Miss Warwick that I thought Eartha Kitt was wonderful. 'Well, she can't sing. That's for sure,' was the dismissive reply. I suppose in strict musical terms she was not too far off the mark but when you go by that particular yardstick Van Morrison and Bob Dylan had better watch out. There are times when technical perfection is not the only thing to aspire to. There are little things called heart and feel to be taken into account.

I decided that it would be wise to offer praise to no one who was not actually present in the room from that point on. She seemed happy with that. By the time the management came to our door to apologetically forward the complaints of the other guests who were being disturbed by our private disco we had bonded nicely and were looking forward to the tour.

Our tour manager Vic Sutcliffe had seen The Isleys in The States. He put the fear of god into us by saying that they were the most dynamic act he had ever seen and that no one could follow them. That was why it was essential for them to close the first half while Dionne would open the second, appearing just before us. The fear turned out to be groundless. The Isley Brothers had certainly been grounded in that slick energy and professionalism with which the Americans seemed to be imbued. But you simply cannot tell kids what they will or will not appreciate. They went down well enough but the kind of soul-stirring acrobatics, both vocal and physical, that whip up a crowd in Harlem can leave a bunch of kids from Cannock stone cold and mystified by something that is a part of another culture entirely.

They were nice guys. Ronnie, Rudolph and O'Kelly Isley were making a living and enjoying a renaissance partly on the strength of The Beatles introducing their *Twist And Shout* to the mass consciousness but they were still years away from their real success. They could never have envisaged at that time that songs like *Harvest To The World* would eventually elevate them to the ranks of black royalty in the funk era yet to come. In fact they were living on a tighter budget at that time and, being used to the American system of hotels selling room rates rather than a per-person tariff, would try to get away with three people bunking into a twin much to the disapproval of the management.

I was fascinated by their method of shaving. Instead of a standard razor and blade they would spread a depilatory cream onto their faces which they would remove with a knife after a pre-designated interval. I thought it was wonderful. I hated shaving and this looked painless. It worked on them. I tried it. It did not work on me. At the end of the ritual my five o'clock shadow was still there and I looked like an anorexic version of Desperate Dan.

The Isleys had a tiny problem with timing. Not the timing associated with musical syncopation. It was the timing associated with being at a specific point at a specified hour. They had a hard time cutting it and Fred Perry, the camp-natured but iron-fisted tour manager was not to be trifled with. On one particular occasion his patience was overtaxed. He held back the coach for what he deigned to be a reasonable leeway and then ordered the driver to proceed on an 'Isley-less' journey to the Midlands.

When they finally arrived at a departure point that was significantly devoid of any tour transport they panicked. Instead of telephoning the office, which was situated a mere stone's throw away just off Oxford Street, they simply hailed a London black cab and instructed the driver to take them to Birmingham. He of course thought all his Christmases had come at once and zoomed off in a general northerly direction grinning like a man with a car full of daft singers. Three hours later, and with pound signs for eyeballs, he dispensed his load at the theatre and demanded recompense from Fred.

Fred was not amused at all. He divided the sum applied for by about half and sent the adventurer back down the motorway with a flea in his ear and a permanent dislike for black songsters and fey, white tour managers. I trust The Isleys were grateful at Fred's truculent attitude because I am sure as eggs are eggs there was only one source the cab fare would eventually be extracted from. A three piece vocal act. And I do not mean The Beverly Sisters.

Dionne Warwick was a strange one. Rather remote, I found. I do recall sitting up late one night in a hotel in Stockton On Tees discussing religion. She was a devout church-going Baptist. I was a shameless unbeliever. Neither of us convinced the other. But it was all very friendly and civilised. She did not however seem happy to be on the tour. I could sympathise with that. Although she had hit the charts in a big way with *Walk On By* and was over here plugging her new Bacharach and David-penned release *Reach Out For Me*, her world was not one of teen-idoldom and hysteria. She was meant for better things. Her musical habitat was a few cuts above the kind of pop pap that we purveyed.

The way out for her turned out to be a little drastic. I can only assume,

50 With Lonnie Donegan
  and Lulu at the Royal
  Variety Show, 1981

Left:
51 Hank Marvin, Bruce
   Welch & John McNally,
   Royal Variety Show

Below:
52 Fans in high places.
   Being presented to H.M.
   Queen Elizabeth II,
   Royal Variety Show

Touring chums in the
U.S.A. 1965

53 ...with Tom Jones,
Norfolk, Virginia

54 ...with Peter Asher and
Brian Hyland,
Norfolk, Virginia

55 The Beach Boys,
Jacksonville

56 The Shangrilas,
    Jacksonville

57 Arthur Alexander

58 Sam The Sham,
    Jacksonville

59 ...with Bobby Vee,
Oklahoma

60 Lesley Gore,
Jacksonville

61 Billy Joe Royal

62 With Jackie De Shannon, who originally recorded *Needles & Pins* and wrote *When You Walk In The Room*, Heathrow, 1965

63 '86 British Invasion Tour press conference, Kennedy Airport

64 The Café La Fortuna, New York

65 Card from La Fortuna

66 USA Tour Buses

67 Our sleeping shelves

68 Whiling away the
endless hours on the
road

69 A singalong round the
   pool with Gerry
   Marsden, Phoenix,
   Arizona, 1986

70 Relaxing in
   Tijuana, 1986. Me,
   Billy Adamson,
   John McNally

71 With Marie Osmond
   recording Solid Gold in
   L.A., 1986

72 On stage on a Solid Silver Sixties show

73 The finale. Pacemakers, Billy J. Kramer, Gerry and The Searchers

74 End of tour party at The Palladium, 1993. Back row: Paul Walden, (Flying Music), Billy Adamson, Spencer James, John McNally. Front row: Gerry Marsden, Billy J. Kramer, me, Derek Nicol (Flying Music)

75 Spencer James, John McNally, Helen Shapiro on the 1998 Solid Silver Sixties Tour

76 Backstage visitors at the Fairfield Halls, Croydon, Peter Sarstedt and Adam Faith, 1998

77 Touring, 1965 style. Searchers, Zombies, Heinz and others pull in for a 'cuppa'

78 Paul Atkinson (Zombies), Bobby Vee, me and one of Dusty Springfield's musicians, 1965

79 Programme cover for Searchers / Dionne Warwick / Isley Brothers / Zombies tour 1964

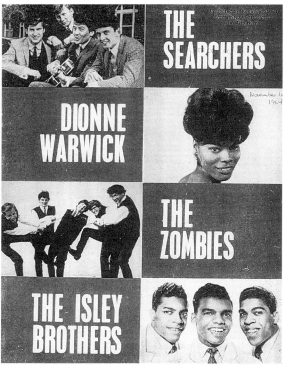

80 The famous Raffles Hotel, Singapore

81 The Hong Kong skyline

82 John McNally, my ladyfriend Lee Lowsley and me by the temples of Bangkok.

83 Me, Lee Lowsley, Mary and John McNally sampling the bars of Pattaya

84 A Bangkok riverboat, powered by Chevrolet

85 A grand old lady. Canberra in Gibraltar

86 Working hard on Canberra

87 A first class lady in
    a first class cabin.
    Edwina C. Trout,
    survivor of The
    Titanic

88 John and Mike posing
    by my red E-type
    Jaguar, 1967

89 Falklands, Chinook and 'tardis'

90 Alternative transport.
A Tornado

If Music Be The Food Of Love - Rock On...

91 Singing for their supper-clockwise from top
left, Bruce Welch (Shadows), Ed Bicknell
(Manager of Dire Straits), Susie Mathis (The
Paper Dolls), Mark Knopfler, Shirley Douglas
(The Chas McDevitt Skiffle Group), Chas
McDevitt. Centre - Me

92 Mike Berry, Peter Sarstedt

93 from left: David Wigg (The Express), Fiona Hendley, Paul Jones, Henry Marsh (Sailor), Bruce Welch, Shirley Douglas, me

94 from left: Dave Dee, me, Chip Hawkes (Tremeloes), Bruce Welch

95 Lionel Blair, Helen Worth, Bobby Crush

96 Me and Mike Read

97 Me and John, partners in musical crime

98 My first day with The Searchers, August 3rd 1964, The Coventry Theatre. Mike Pender, John McNally, Chris Curtis and me

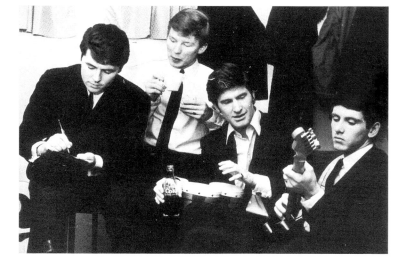

effective though it was, that it was unintentional. She got knocked down by a bus in Glasgow. It does tend to help, if you are a visitor from America in Great Britain, to remember that we drive on the other side of the road here. And that, for Miss Warwick, was the end of the tour. Complete with a plaster cast that resembled a badly made evening glove, she scuttled off home for greater fame and more sophisticated venues.

With regard to the number of acts packing the bill, audiences got great value for money on these shows. The length of each set though was shorter than a pixie's willy. My great friend Ed Bicknell was a still a young lad in those days and a fervent fan of all the current pop sounds. He went to just about every show that came to his native York, and his enthusiasm for the world of music eventually brought him a career and great wealth from managing Dire straits. On the programme Ed would religiously scribble down the running order of songs for each act. Our prestigious top of the bill spot for that particular tour consisted of an unknown opener, followed by *High Heeled Sneakers, What Have They Done To The Rain?, Someday We're Gonna Love Again, Needles And Pins* and *When You Walk In The Room*. Six songs in total. What a bargain.

Dionne was, in time, to prove her true worth and become a global superstar who could pack huge concert halls on her own without the aid of passing pop groups such as we. I saw her much later on at The Royal Albert Hall. By this time she was a major draw. She had also undergone a visual transformation that had changed the somewhat heavy looking and severe person with just a hint of moustache around the upper lip I had toured with into a beautifully groomed and gowned diva. Her makeup was now designed by experts and her hair coifed into flattering and perfect confections that accentuated a pair of chiselled cheekbones that I never recalled seeing before. She looked terrific.

Her voice had not really changed. She had always been good. In fact more than good. It was a wonderful voice. The quality was not so much its purity or sweetness. In fact it always had a cutting edge to it bordering on hard at times. But it was a unique sound and tugged at the heartstrings as it cracked between ranges. It felt like it had been lived in. Nobody else sounded like Dionne Warwick and uniqueness is the key to stardom. It was a voice that I continued to love throughout my life. I never tired of it. I suppose that, in a way, that is why I had so resented her dismissal of Eartha Kitt. It was their originality rather than their vocal purity that provided the greater part of their appeal. A short while afterwards, by the way, I had a run in with Miss Kitt that made Dionne seem like a perfect pussycat. But that's another story.

On stage I found Dionne herself a cold performer. It was as if there was a curtain between the audience and her. Or maybe it was just between me and her. To me the eyes had a dead look about them, as if she never really wanted to be there in the first place. And I could not understand it. In fact the most animated she became was when she was lambasting poor old Cilla Black for stealing her songs.

The end of her set left me totally baffled. The audience rose to its feet and gave her a standing ovation. She collected the obligatory flowers, enough to fill several greenhouses, and left the stage. The applause grew in volume as the audience rose as one to pay her a fitting tribute. She returned to take a bow and left once more. The crowd continued to stand and clap ready for the encore. The encore, sadly, never came. After much coaxing she was talked into taking one last bow, by which time she had changed into a very unprepossessing frock of the sort you might wear on a visit to your auntie in Croydon. The audience then shuffled out, mystified and disheartened.

It seems that Miss Warwick did not perform encores. During the performances she apparently always 'gave her all' and that was that. They came, she sang, they left. Well excuse me Miss Warwick, but what a load of tosh. We are not talking about real life here. We are talking about showbusiness, complete with all its idiosyncrasies and traditions, its tinsel and its tackiness. Here, very little is real. We are dispensing dreams and illusions and why on earth, or anywhere else come to that, should we not?

Traditions are very important in showbusiness, both to the artistes and to the audience. One of those traditions dictates that, as a mark of courtesy and appreciation for a good performance, the crowd will clap with extra verve and volume at the end of the concert. In return, as a mark of respect and appreciation for such a reception, not to mention paying a considerable ticket price which will hopefully keep the said performer in a fair degree of luxury not enjoyed by the majority of patrons, the artiste will round off the evening with one final song. It has nothing to do with pure logic. It is an accepted politeness. It sits happily in our comfort zones like a brandy sits on the throat after the coffee. Remove it and it is as if someone has just stolen the after dinner mint you were so looking forward to. If you play the logic game then you do so at your peril.

If the audience decided to apply the same kind of logic what would happen? Throughout the show they would applaud each song to its value. Some may be worthy of more applause than others. At the end of the final number the assembled throng would simply deliver the approbation due for the last three minutes or so of music and, without further ado, make a hasty exit to the car park. They could be out of the theatre before La Warwick reaches the wings, the silence broken only by the sound of her own stilettos as they tap dejectedly across the boards.

That, my friends, is logic. If Dionne cannot give more than her all then the sensible thing is to give one song less than her all, play the game, then return to the stage and give the audience the respect, and the final song, that is its due. It requires no more effort. It is simply an exercise in timing and stagecraft.

But despite that little niggle at my sensibilities, Dionne Warwick is the proud owner of a most majestic voice and one who has more talent in her little finger than my body could hope to amass in several lifetimes. When her accident forced her to withdraw she was replaced by *Up On The Roof* singer Julie Grant, I believe, and the tour continued to a contented conclusion. Apart from one of the Americans falling asleep in his room with a lighted cigarette and destroying a section of the County Hotel in Taunton, it had been a fairly uneventful few weeks, enjoyable and, thankfully, a financial success.

These yearly excursions were always fun. The constant gripe one hears about the rigours of touring life is to a great extent exaggerated. Sometimes it is not exactly a piece of cake but then it is rarely a cupful of castor oil either. The camaraderie was always something to be savoured. The life of a pop musician can become claustrophobic, surrounded by the same travelling companions, herded in and out of dressing rooms that deny the space or the personality of a home, and checking into yet another anonymous hotel that is so similar to the last that you almost felt it had somehow leapfrogged ahead of you and settled itself in the next town to await your arrival. Many's the time I've tried to open a door with the number of the previous night's room.

The package tours managed to afford me the rare privilege of seeing Britain, of being a tourist in my own part of the world and getting paid for it. Of course a round of one-night stands gives you very little guarantee of anything other than a bunch of city centres and any stretch of countryside still visible beyond the hard shoulder of a motorway. But there are people in Britain who have, excluding their home town, spent more time in drink sodden Spanish resorts than they have in any part of their native land.

Because of my travels as a musician I am aware of the difference between the oak framed Tudor buildings of Chester and the indomitable grey granite structures of Aberdeen. I know that Chesterfield has a curious spire that twists like a witch's hat and that the once downtrodden city of Birmingham has undergone a renaissance that has brought life and colour to its virtually neglected canals. There are times when the great highways are left behind as our clumsy charabanc is forced to manipulate winding roads that were meant for nothing larger or faster than a horse or a cow. And I revel like any gawping tourist at the chocolate box-cute villages of Devon and Cornwall, with their wigs of neat thatch and brooches of pink and yellow roses.

The world is full of beautiful places. What we must not forget is that Great Britain is one of them.

13

Faraway Places

To have travelled, to have truly journeyed in the real sense of the word, it is preferable to have experienced the senses of wonder, disorientation and fear in more or less equal quantities. A degree of poverty is probably desirable also for maximum effect but I was never good at that. My wayfaring has invariably has been conducted in tandem with patronage and privilege, and long may it remain that way. Maybe in my younger days I could have been an embryonic Jack Kerouac, making out with just a rucksack, a glib line in chat and a change of underwear, but my spoilt psyche now demands a degree of comfort and protection. I am, in other words, a spoilt brat.

My in-built sense of the romantic however still demands the kinds of unfamiliar sights and sounds that jar with all that is natural and commonplace in my day to day existence. Singapore does not quite cut it in terms of the 'difference factor', which is strange for a destination so far to the east of one's home port. It was a major disappointment in what has been a fairly extensive life of travel. Drained of character and colour, it has been homogenised to the point where the pale hue of milk would be like a rainbow in comparison. In the practical sense it works. It is efficient, clean and crime free, on the surface at least. In the aesthetic sense it falls down like a cripple at the hands of a less than successful faith healer.

It has to be said that when you touch down at Changi Airport during the hours of darkness the twinkling city lights lend an air of Christmas to the world below even in the height of summer. And the illuminated boats in the harbour bob up and down seductively enough in the black of night to endow even the roughest old hulk of a tanker with more than a touch of romance. The warm and humid night time breeze hits you like a gentle rebuke from a lady's velvet-gloved hand outside of what is essentially a gigantic shopping mall with planes. This terminal building is a monument to Mammon with its acres of air-conditioned, marble-lined space where this particular nation of traders makes its last pitch for a sale before you depart the shores. The quality goods of the finest emporiums are on display here in an atmosphere of sanitised tranquillity rare in such a busy travel terminus. It is clean to the point of sterility, a condition which continues to exist in the streets outside.

Singapore is a republic with an elected president, but so powerful was the leadership under Lee Kuan Yew, who held sway from 1959 until he resigned in 1990, that the authority over the population was about as totalitarian as you could get without actually being a dictatorship. There is very little crime. The penalties are extreme. Litter has almost been eradicated and even chewing gum is banned. If you've got any gum chum be prepared for a hefty fine. When you spot a stray piece of paper alongside the highway there is almost an irresistible urge to get out and photograph it. Or report it to the authorities as an undesirable alien.

There was a recent story in the newspapers that the tiny group of islands, 640 square kilometres which is 247 square miles, has a serious rat problem. Almost three hundred were found at the airport in the space of five days. It is hard to believe. The pavements outside looked clean enough to eat your noodles off. Maybe the crafty little rodents were hiding in an attempt to avoid a penalty ticket being slapped on their forehead the minute they stood still, the little scamps. In Singapore there is possibly nothing so unwelcome as a rat chewing gum.

It was 1996 and we were here to perform at two venues, a British club just around the corner from the main shopping thoroughfare of Orchard Road, and a new luxury marina at the other end of the island. Our accommodation was pretty spectacular. It was only a short cab ride from one side of my room to the other. Had I been there for any length of time I would have sub-let my bathroom to three or four needy families. The mirrors and marble glistened and reflected ostentatiously as I stood before the streamlined porcelain toilet bowl. It was all too splendid and made my dick look terribly shabby. I put it away quickly and went on a walk to take in the surrounding area.

Orchard Road was constructed as an appeasement to the shopping gods and each side of the wide carriageway was lined with suitable places of worship. Five and six storey malls crammed with shops and shops-within-shops selling anything from the lowliest tourist tat to the fashionable designs of Louis Vuitton, Donna Karan, Ungaro and Ferragamo. The smaller and cheaper stalls were manned for the most part by immigrants from the Indian sub-continent and I found it a trifle odd that so many should bear the rather 'un-Asian' surname of Armani. There was Vince Armani and Tony Armani. Frank Armani and Charles Armani. Those Armanis must surely have rogered like rabbits to have produced such a spectacular amount of offspring. There was even a Gianni Armani, which no doubt resulted from a spot of couture world in-breeding between Georgio's lot and the Versaces.

Here you can have a suit made to measure in two days. Less if you're desperate. And when you receive the finished product it looks exactly like a suit that has been made in two days. These garments have a definite 'bygone' touch to their cut. It is almost indefinable, but the curve of the waist, the width of the lapel and the length of the jacket, it's all slightly wrong. A nineties product with more than a hint of a '47 demob suit. Sort of 'Man at V&A'.

There is a culture difference between the Singaporean shopkeeper and his Indian counterpart when it comes to methods of selling. Stroll by an outlet owned by a local and you can complete your browsing virtually unmolested. Try that within a hundred yards of an Indian owned store and, like an unsuspected sperm whale, you will be 'harpooned' and reeled in to the kind of sales pitch that would make Don King seem like a monk under a vow of silence.

You don't want to buy? That's okay. You are his friend. He isn't selling anything. He is only giving advice. Anything at all you want in Singapore, he can get it for you or he knows a man who can. A shirt for yourself, sir? A pair of silk pyjamas for your wife or your girlfriend? The pyjamas are tacky. They looked okay on Susie Wong way back in the fifties and haven't looked good on anyone since. But it is hard not to cave in under this kind of pressure. He hasn't sold anything all morning. You have to buy something, please. He pleads. You refuse. He pleads some more. You dig your heels in. He pleads with even greater fervour. He is now becoming a very annoying little pleader, but your pride insists that you will not allow yourself to fall prey to this kind of moral blackmail.

Eventually you leave without a purchase and his face tells you that you are no longer his friend. It is difficult not to feel guilt. After all, the poor guy is only trying to make a living in a space ten feet square on the bargain basement level of a seven storey store where every few yards will take you past another shop selling the same thing that he is. No better and no worse. Life is a lottery and he is holding just one solitary ticket while fervently praying that today the numbers will come up right.

I wanted to visit the infamous Bugis Street but Lee Kuan Yew's monumental clean up had rid the once notorious red light district of its vice and its character. Once was when the crowded pavement restaurants were enlivened by the presence of the 'koi tois' (have I spelt that right? I think not), the transsexuals whose shapely beauty made a mockery of the rough old harridans who put on their drag to troll the clubs of Hamburg. The tables are still there, with a sparser amount of diners, but the 'girls' have gone and with them the atmosphere. These outrageous men dressed as women made our average groupie look like women dressed as men. It's a shame and so unnecessary. It is, I think, a mistake to attempt to rectify every little glitch and imperfection. Contain, maybe. But eradicate, no.

Early evening I wandered on down to Raffles, the stately hotel that had been the focal point of elegant Singaporean society in the thirties and forties when Somerset Maugham and Noel Coward would dispense their wondrous wit and timeless elegance in abundant measures in the Long Bar. I was clad in white knee length shorts and an open necked silk shirt. I felt badly underdressed as I approached this icon of gracious Colonial living. The building had grown over the years and the once lazy and tranquil surroundings of tropical gardens had been invaded by high rise hotels. It was inevitable. The virus that is, often quite inaccurately, called progress is a deadly one that attacks with no mercy. In mitigation the additions to Raffles itself had been constructed quite sympathetically and, like Elton John's hair, you knew that at one time there had been infinitely less of it but the join was very difficult to detect.

The Long Bar, decorated in the sober and reassuringly solid style of a gentlemen's club, was crowded with tourists all dressed as badly as I was. I would have much preferred the option of an emptier room with maybe just a sprinkling of guests preferably in black ties and shimmering gowns. A quietly restrained atmosphere where one could hear the tinkle of cocktail glasses as they sipped their cooling Singapore Slings beneath the ceiling fans. It had become a mission of mine to imbibe one of these legendary beverages while on the island. You cannot visit Raffles and leave without having had a Singapore Sling.

In reality this magical moment was as diluted and disappointing as the

144

drink itself. The bulk of this gin, cherry brandy and cointreau mixture was pre-prepared, ready and waiting in half filled glasses to be topped up with last minute essentials and shaken with the cracked ice on the receipt of each order. It wasn't quite McDonalds but in my mind it was heading that way. I was drinking a Slush Puppy with a slight kick. My innocence was gone along with those images from the black and white films of my younger days. What was that line from Peter Pan? Clap hands if you believe in fairies. I was not clapping.

And where was the gleaming grand piano from where a tuxedoed sophisticate would have at one time tinkled out a seamless string of ageless melodies? The sound of music came down the stairway from the room above. It was not a piano and there was nothing grand about it. And the music did not so much come down as stumble and crash to the ground in an obscene orgy of synthesised convulsions. I just knew there was a Filipino cover band hovering above us somewhere. This was the fare of a Majorcan beach bar or a holiday village in Sussex. What next, The Birdie Song? It was an ill-suited adornment to this dignified old dame of a hotel who deserved to live out her remaining days in a gin soaked haze of understated refinement.

The concerts went over incredibly well in the face of a national consciousness that does not exactly encourage overt displays of frivolity on formal occasions. When it came to making complete pillocks of themselves the British ex-patriots were up for it in a big way. No change there then. It was an enforced jollity born of a mixture of total boredom and the need to suppress the truth that, while they were leading a life of comfort and luxury, it was at a high price. They were birds in gilded cages. Away from the comfort zones of their homeland they were all too eager to present an image of a cultural group having a whale of a time which, I decided, they were not.

The average oriental audience on the other hand could make fishing look exciting. They were without a shadow of a doubt elegant to a high degree, the men shop-window immaculate and the ladies as delicate as fine painted porcelain, but oh so stiff. In this part of the globe it is considered unseemly to clap and sing and join in the general melée of a piece of entertainment. The general rule of thumb is that one sits with respectful attention dispensing an appreciative gift of polite applause at the appropriate moment. This I'm afraid is not good enough for us and a crowd that is still on its communal bottom at the point where we are taking our bows is an audience lost.

With all the subtlety of Jimmy Savile's jewellery, we pummelled them into submission, making them sing, clap and sway against their better judgement and natural inclinations. We launched an assault and were taking no prisoners. We ran back to our changing room to the sound of cheers that in England would have been quite passable but out here in sanitary Singapore was nothing less than a triumph.

From Singapore we flew on to Hong Kong, but not before I had succumbed to the lure of the boutiques. I could not resist the beautiful display of Mont Blanc pens. I have a thing about fountain pens. Goodness knows why. These particular ones cost a fortune and no amount of expense could ever rescue my handwriting, which resembles a spider drunk on a mixture of methylated spirits and lysergic acid. But I had to have one. Luckily these days I can usually have most things that I want. Helen Shapiro, in her new persona as a 'Messianic Jew', quoted to me 'Thou shalt not covet.' I pointed out to her that I had bypassed the 'covet switch' and was now patched straight through to 'own'. A few years on, by the way, I decided that a Parker Duofold, in the mother of pearl finish of course, was much more elegant and exclusive and so once again 'covet' was tossed aside and I was in like Flynn. I somehow feel though, that the need for such trinkets, these little symbols of pointless extravagance, signify a deep-set insecurity in my nature. Well, if I recognise my own failings then perhaps I may be on the way to doing something about them. Or then again, maybe not.

Hong Kong had changed little in the three decades since my first visit. People have remarked to me how many more skyscrapers there are now but it had always seemed that way in my eyes. There might have been a little less blue between those towers of glass and the clouds but we are talking about a huge population living on a postage stamp. It is the difference between a moderate sized colony of ants and a larger one. There still seems to be millions of the blighters. If people were cholesterol then Hong Kong was overdue a massive heart attack.

But there is a life in this tiny colony that Singapore lacks. The Star Ferry is still only a few cents and carries you gently across the waters to the mainland while charging you no extra for three hundred and sixty degrees of views. Slotted into the skyline I spotted what used to be the Bond building, a radically asymmetrical off-the-wall design of tinted glass that had been erected on the instructions of Alan Bond when his corporation was riding high. I had met the Bonds in their home town of Perth in Western Australia at the beginning of the eighties and had become a firm friend of his then wife Eileen, or Red to anyone who knew her. Red had taught me what fun life really was. She had no inhibitions and no 'side' to her. People were people, rich or poor and judged on their merit. She was, and is, one of nature's great ladies.

Sadly The Bond Corporation went belly up to the spectacular sum of $800m and Alan, since divorced from Red, was incarcerated for his demeanours in a case that seemed to have a touch of vindictiveness about it. At one time he had been the national hero, winning the elusive Americas Cup for his nation. It was the 'tall poppy' syndrome. If they look like they are getting too big for their boots, cut 'em down. It was a sad reflection.

There is a hustle and a bustle here. Abject poverty and children of the affluent society rub shoulders in the narrow streets of Kowloon. It is a tradition in China for a new home to employ the services of an expert in feng shui. This is an ancient art in which the contents of a room are so arranged as to ensure the occupant of a life of total harmony. Good luck will abound while the bad will be dispelled. This practice seems to have caught on in the fashionable salons of the west where an expensive professional will remove the clutter from your home and your bank account at the same time. Observing the dire circumstances that most of the Hong Kong peasants exist in it doesn't bear thinking about how bad their luck would have been without this invaluable ceremony.

Tenements that can just about be seen through the lines of washing stand in juxtaposition to hi-tech towers. The frightening fact is that no matter how hi-tech the tower the building methods are still likely to follow the ancient paths of centuries gone by. The flimsy looking scaffolding is bamboo tied together with nylon cords. What might seem permissible for the erection of a garden hut somehow seems preposterous as it reaches the fortieth floor of a future multi-national headquarters.

Chinese scaffolders skim up these rickety edifices with a surely misplaced confidence and an absence of any safety harness. They probably do exist. They might even be compulsory for all I know. But I suppose the average macho Oriental rigger would rather risk plummeting to an early death than have his mates call him a big girl's kimono. I toyed with the thought as I sat in my room on the eleventh floor of our hotel. It is disconcerting being that far above the ground in a building that had constructed with the aid of implements that last week might well have been holding up someone's Brussel sprouts.

I had grown fond of the tiny, but crucial, Crown colony and wondered, like everybody, how it would fare following its impending hand-over back to the Chinese Communist Government in 1997. A few years before, at Christmas time when the whole place was illuminated in a display of fairy lights that rivalled Vegas, we had spent December 24th performing in a Chinese brothel. A very elegant and expensive brothel I must emphasise, its working girls, petite and pretty in their virginal white organza dresses, resembling the cast of Swan Lake.

When we went on that night we faced an empty room. The girls and their clients inhabited the booths that formed a semi-circle in front of us at the edge of the dance floor and doing whatever they had to do. In the face of our din I trust they were using the rhythm method. The songs of the sixties must have been very low on their list of priorities. But that most golden of all decades is a powerful force indeed. By the time our set banged its way to a close we were being cheered on by the happiest and best looking bunch of hookers, and their paying customers, I had ever seen. It was a case of 'coitus interruptus' and a great compliment indeed.

While in the colony we were asked to do a television show for a predominantly Chinese viewing public, which was an intriguing idea to say the least. We had no inkling that our profile was particularly high in the ethnic community and when we entered the studio for the taping of what was a high budget and extremely popular variety spectacular we discovered that we were the only Caucasians in the building. Very odd, but a welcome opportunity to get our faces over and to let everyone know we were still alive and kicking ass. As an added bonus it was an environment where for once we could feel tall. *Love Potion Number Nine* was the hit they had chosen, not in fact a single in the U.K. but a monster record for us in The States.

Our fellow performers were dolled up to the nines in the latest threads from the Orient's finest designers. The collections from Japan in particular were very much 'in' at the time. Kenzo and others had at last given men something to wear that was dramatic without being ridiculous. We weren't lagging too far behind though and I thought we stood up quite well in our black shortie jackets with gold emblems appliquéd to the sleeves. They certainly showed off our bums well. Thank goodness we had kept our little botties in good shape. There is little point in wearing a bum-freezer jacket if you've got an arse like the Mauretania. Not an inappropriate analogy actually because the outfits made us look like four stewards off The Love Boat. My friends back home suggested that black masks would have been more a suitable uniform as what we were getting away with was highway robbery.

We waited patiently on our podium and watched the comings and goings

148

around us. Eventually we were approached by the director, an extremely camp character who spoke in sing-song sentences that sounded like cascading cutlery. I had never encountered a camp oriental before. The innate smallness that characterised his race served to emphasise his femininity.

'Prease, you leddy now? We pray tape and you sing.'

We asserted that we were indeed leddy and that he could pray the tape whenever he wanted. The tape prayed but we did not sing. The voices that came out of the speakers were not those we were accustomed to hearing. The recording of *Love Potion Number Nine* in the machine was in fact the original version made by The Clovers a few years before we got hold of it. They were American, older than us and their voices were an octave or so deeper than ours. They also happened to be black, which we plainly were not.

We pointed out the error. The camp director looked perplexed. We suggested that in this veritable temple to the hi-fi industry and bootlegged tapes there surely must be a shop nearby that possessed a version by The Searchers. They sent a minion on a mission and we waited for the outcome. Half an hour later he returned in triumph. We were able to be ourselves again. Meanwhile we had been discussing the options open to us had they been out of luck. We decided that in the worst scenario we might as well just go ahead and lip-synch to The Clovers' version. After all this was Chinese television. And to reverse an ancient stereotype, we probably all sounded the same to them anyway.

Hong Kong has an atmosphere and a life about it. In parts it is dilapidated and crumbling. A city has to have some dirt and decay. Not too much but enough to make you feel there is some sort of freedom reigning somewhere. But Hong Kong is not a place in which to linger too long. It is claustrophobic, as if you were trapped with ten other people in an elevator designed to hold four. And there is the omnipresent aroma of Chinese cooking. It is a sweet cloying smell that pervades every nook and cranny. Unlike the puke of my youth it is not a smell that dissipates when the nose has got used to it. The nose never gets used to it. Certainly not a European nose.

Bangkok, on the other hand, is heavy with another kind of nostril-rending stench. That of pollution, pumped out by the two-stroke 'tut tuts', the three-wheeled taxi substitutes that provide cheap transport, the unique charm of the city and the destruction of one's lungs in one fell, or should that be 'foul', swoop. We went there to provide the New Year's Eve entertainment at the luxurious Dusit Thani Hotel where an earlier appearance had impressed the management to the point where no one else was considered suitable to please their guests on that most important night of the year.

We did not work over New Year and Christmas. It was our rule. To get us there they had to use persuasion and bribery, two methods very close to our hearts. We were finally talked into sacrificing the traditional festive pleasures, those of having to entertain the usual bunch of freeloading friends and relatives and their inane drunken chatter back home, by the offer of tickets for our partners to accompany us, a holiday in their sister hotel in Pattaya and wads of cash. Needless to say, being The Searchers, our considered priorities were not necessarily in the order stated.

If you want 'different', Bangkok has it in spades. It has changed beyond recognition from the time that Anna sailed to those shores to be the governess to the children of King Chulalongkorn, absolute ruler over what was in those days Siam. The advent of the motor vehicle and the invasion of the mighty tourist dollar has choked up the once sleepy city where its gentle and smiling people lived out an altogether much simpler existence. These days a Bangkok traffic jam can put the M25 to shame. But traces of the old world still remain. The compound that houses the religious temples of glittering gold and red squats in the midst of the high rise office blocks. A spectacular anachronism in both its symbolisation of purity alongside the bars and sex clubs and a display of priceless splendour which contrasts the poverty of the Thai peasants whose every tedious day is a struggle for survival.

The temples are gaudy and ornate, rising splendidly in elaborately curlicued peaks studded with tiny pieces of glass that glint unceasingly in the sun. There is nothing restrained about this architecture. It is overdone to the point of being vulgar but it is hard not to be impressed. The grandest building holds the Jade Buddah, the crown jewel of their sacred artefacts. It is placed high up on a pedestal like an overdone wedding cake and looks disappointingly small from that distance, but the hordes come daily to gaze with reverence at the pot-bellied green figure. I'm a little short on reverence in that area but I was pleased to have seen it.

On the river bank, just in front of the renowned Oriental Hotel, one of the world's leading hostelries where the ultra rich rest their weary heads at night, longboats powered by huge V8 engines from abandoned American cars speed visitors on death-defying trips through the twisting, turning waters. The weighty power units are attached to the rudder and seem to move effortlessly up and down and from side to side in the hands of a skilled operator whose diminutive size makes him appear ill-equipped to lift, let alone perform such intricate manoeuvres.

The narrow river, surely too narrow for boats of this size and travelling at such ridiculous speeds, winds through dense tropical foliage. Every once in a while it spurts past a flimsy bamboo hut. A river frontage here bears no resemblance to the manicured lawns and mock-Tudor dwellings of Henley On Thames. Families clad in rags watch in suspicious silence as you pass and perch on their rickety dwellings to wash their other rags in the slimy green water. Once on this river you have finally left the world as you knew it. You feel like an extra in The Deer Hunter. It may not be Viet Nam but it is little more than a hop, skip and a jump away both in distance and atmosphere.

But let's not be coy about it. Probably the main attraction for visitors to Bangkok is the sex industry, even if the intention may be simply to ogle in wonder rather than to buy. Just a couple of hundred yards down the way from our hotel was Pat Pong, the short street that houses the highest concentration of bodies for sale and display that one is ever likely to see, or would need to see. Young girls barely in their teens, and occasionally one suspects a tad younger, come from their homes in the country to the city which affords the only hint of a chance to accumulate enough money to keep them and their families alive. The families suffer their sense of humiliation in a self-deluding denial and silence. It is easier to pretend it is not happening while pocketing the cash of a life of shame. Needs must when the Devil drives. In this case the Devil owns a sex club and he needs a constant flow of young nubile bodies for his customers. The girls live with the dream of finding a client they can transform into a husband who will remove them from this abhorrent existence and take them away to a better life in America, Britain or Australia.

We visited an establishment where the surface of a bar provided a runway for a steady stream of girls who had been trained in a variety of skills of the most extraordinary and unlikely kinds. As the naked performers strolled along at eye level to the patrons, objects of all shapes and sizes were produced from the depths of an orifice in which such objects were never meant to be deposited. Razor blades, cigarettes and bananas were drawn, brandished or expelled to the astonishment and amusement of the onlookers as they sipped at their Barcardi and Cokes.

The sense of the ridiculous reaches overload when, as her *piece de resistance*, one of the young 'entertainers' produced nothing less than a live linnet. The small bird emerged apparently unscathed and very little the worse for wear considering its incarceration in probably the most unlikely, not to mention cramped, dwelling it was ever likely to occupy. I fancied it was coughing a little but my fancification meter might have been knocked a little out of kil-ter under the circumstances. Hughie Green eat your heart out. Opportunity Knocks never boasted an act like this one. Let's hear it for the linnet, folks. And I mean that most sincerely.

And if all that stretches the imagination, word has it I missed a gem the previous evening. The American fleet were in town and the guys were, well, behaving like sailors on shore leave tend to do. One of the bar girls, in a most impressive display of muscular control, was propelling bananas from that part of her which should not be privy public gaze into the crowd and a particularly lively sailor was adding to the spectacle by catching the fruit. Upon catching it, urged on by the cheers of the crowd, he then proceeded to eat it. Whether it was the aim, the speed or just his lack of concentration he missed a shot and the banana fell to the floor and, with a highly com-mendable observation of the rules of hygiene, he refused to eat it.

14

Tips For Terminal Travellers

'If God had wanted us to travel economy he would have made us narrower'. Not my words actually but those of a friend, a particularly well-heeled lady of more than ample proportions and an understandable taste for the finer things in life. But for those of us with champagne taste and beer bottle pockets the world has been opened up by the advent of the package holiday and the blessed charter airline.

All I really require of my air travel most of the time is that it be safe, inexpensive and with a modicum of comfort. Any surplus cash rescued from the temptations of fleeting and unnecessary luxury can soon be put to good use in the cafés and bars of sunny Spain or Portugal. When corporate hospitality is gracious enough to provide the wherewithal I shall willingly propel myself to the sharp end of the plane at the speed of Concorde. But when I have to shell out the necessary readies from my own shallow reserves then mach-1 will be reduced to a slow shuffle back to steerage with the rest of the hoi polloi, my tail fin between my legs.

If, like me, you are economically well and truly allied to the common rabble you had better learn to make the most of the tricks of the trade and the shortcuts available to cheapskates like us. The most important rule is your mode of dress. Get that wrong and you are lost forever. Before you slip into your best faded Levis and Planet Hollywood tee shirt or that oh so comfortable shell suit that makes you feel like Roger Black but actually makes you look like an overstuffed bag of crisps, stop and think again.

First of all it is an illusion that jeans are comfortable clothes in which to travel. They are heavy and restricting. They ride up your legs severely restricting the circulation to your vital reproductive parts and effectively cutting off most of the circulation. By the time you are at your destination you may never be able to father children again. Your white tee shirt is a magnet to the sauces and relishes that have been diligently developed and trained to leap off of their plastic trays onto your once pristine apparel. Within an hour you will look like Picasso's palette.

I should not of course have to point out that the shell suit is nothing less than an offence against mankind. It is an abomination that has been foisted upon us by a money hungry leisure industry which has cleverly managed to convince a pathetically pear-shaped population that, by donning the equivalent of a couple of giant size carrier bags, the flesh beneath will somehow adjust itself into the perfect hour glass shape. It does not. Inside the wrapping you are still the bag of dough you always were. On the outside you are the fashion equivalent of a motorway pile-up in a multicoloured monstrosity designed by Jose Feliciano.

The wearing of matching shell suits is a crime of such proportion that in many less liberal countries it is probably punishable by death, or if it's not, it should be. In the most extreme cases you can come across whole families clad alike, and probably all sharing one brain between them although never quite making full use of it. Mummy and Daddy shells waddling down the street flanked by mini-shells and baby shells like debris from the dustbins outside of the Walkers factory.

Furthermore they are an actual danger to every person in their proximity. One shell suit too many and there will be enough static generated via the rubbing of sets of cellulite-filled thighs to ignite the after dinner brandies and start a mid air conflagration. Let us be honest. Rig yourself in this manner and you will look like dross. And if you look like dross then dross is what you will be treated like. You have absolutely no chance of catching the brass ring, of finding the Holy Grail, of having bestowed on you the most desirable freebee that the world of travel can endow. I am of course talking about - the upgrade.

Just beyond the drawn curtain there is another world. One where food comes on plates fashioned from delicate china. Where the champagne glass is filled without delay or expense. And where your legs are free to roam in front of you to a degree so delicious and different to your economy restricted postage stamp of space in the rear compartment along with the rest of the plebeians. Back there it is only the firmness of the seat back that prevents you from involuntarily committing an interesting, though not to everyone's taste, sexual offence with the person immediately ahead of you.

To gain entry to this Valhalla there are several possibilities. By far the surest is to cultivate a suitable contact in the airline you are travelling with. It's not what you know, it's who you know. It may be an old maxim but it's a true one. I never actually 'bunged' anyone to move me up a notch although I had heard of regular scams being operated in this way. It is of course quite illegal. Well at least it is for them as the 'bribee'. As for the briber, I'm not quite so sure. Certainly their jobs would be on the line if they were caught but we'll let them worry about that, won't we. If it's offered, I say go for it.

But this has never actually been necessary. Whenever this courtesy has been afforded me it has possibly been because they were suitably impressed at our 'star status', pathetically low on the scale of star statuses though it may be. Some people are easily impressed. Or perhaps it was a chance meeting at a social function when the wine has loosened the tongue and made them make promises they would later live to regret. Or maybe it was just because I'm such a hell of a nice person and it's no more than I deserve. Whatever the reason, whenever it comes off the feeling of elation is better than sex. Well, it's better than sex for me, that's for sure.

I recall being upgraded once on a trip to Detroit and not just to the middle section. Oh no. This time it was all the way up the nose. Or should that be nose in the air. I had paid about three and sixpence for my ticket. My father had worked for British airways and I was taking advantage of his staff travel concession. The 747 had been severely overbooked and, strangely enough, at times like this the companies prefer to upgrade their employees rather than paying customers from a lower fair structure. Whoopee. I was all for that.

It was an interesting flight. I encountered an old lady who, at the time, was the oldest living survivor of the Titanic. Her name was Edwina C. Trout and she was returning to her home in Hermosa Beach, California after attending yet another Titanic convention. She was sprightly and animated, and nicely dried out, as she told her fascinating first hand account of the world's greatest, and most notorious, shipping disaster. I enjoyed her company immensely. Almost without exception I never manage to sit next to anyone of interest on long flights. And neither, I am sure my neighbours would say, have they.

By coincidence, travelling on the same flight and upgraded as an employee of British airways, was an old school chum. We reminisced and he was suitably impressed and intrigued by the path my life had taken. Spring Grove Grammar School in Isleworth did not make a conscious attempt to churn out pop musicians. In fact, if I remember rightly, they actively discouraged it in favour of 'proper jobs'. Ones with a future. I am absolutely sure that thirty six years on they would still not consider what I do a proper job, or one with a future. But somehow Ian McClaghan and myself managed to escape the sausage machine. Me via The Searchers and he with The Small Faces. And I do have a pension. Several of them in fact.

As we chatted a stewardess sat next to us and joined in. 'Do you still manage to make it pay?' she inquired with the incredulity one who could well have been indoctrinated by the philosophies of my old tutors.

'Well, look at him. He's travelling first class,' my old school chum interjected.

'But I thought...' she began and then stopped. She had been trained well. Discretion was deeply ingrained into her make up. It was on her list. She knew exactly where I belonged. About thirty rows back.

I have stressed the importance of dressing correctly. No airline is happy to seat you amongst the elite of its clientele if you are attired like a passing vagrant. The main cabin of a jumbo jet is not a desirable pitch for a Big Issue salesman. And it is a complete fallacy to assume that smart clothes are uncomfortable travel wear. Not by any means. Lightweight, loose fitting, crease resistant trousers beat a pair of thigh throttling jeans any day.

My standard outfit used to be a double breasted black suit in a material that was sharp and not prone to rumpling up. The line of the lapels resembled the edge of blade and the slight sheen of the material meant that any crumbs and spillage could be wiped off with no trouble, leaving a glacier smooth expanse that was as impressive and unruffled at the end of a long journey as it had been at the outset. Of course these days I veer towards the rather more chic single-breasted jacket. The double has become somewhat passé.

The shirt should be white or pale blue with a collar slightly looser than normal. And if you can get a tab or pin collar which holds the tie in place like a sartorial banner proudly displaying that the wearer is indeed a very sharp cookie who will grace any orifice of your aircraft in which you should choose to place him. And you can always slip something a little more casual, like a tennis shirt, into your carry on luggage. If you don't get your upgrade, sod 'em. Just nip into the loo at the first opportunity and put on your bog standard apex (advance purchase excursion economy) gear. It no longer matters. Your back has not been scratched and so you are now free to look like a pile of dog poop if you so desire.

156

Occasionally, just once every blue moon, the gods are on your side. I was in the line for my return from Toronto and glancing with envy at the short, and hassle free Club Class check-in counter. Standing in front of me was one of the oddest characters I have ever seen. Five foot nothing and topped by a sadly depleted amount of steel grey hair with the section that was still managing to cling to life scraped back into a male menopausal pony tail, he was clad in a small flower print outfit the like of which I had only seen in the pyjama department of Mothercare.

It boasted, if that is the right word, a ruffled neck and a pair of culotte-style bottoms that I think I remember Dany La Rue might have once worn in a panto at The Mayflower Theatre in Southampton. Danny would have suited them much more than this oddity. I had little doubt in my mind that beneath this ludicrous getup he was wearing Pampers. This was not an adult. This was a renegade from The Romper Room. I stared anywhere but in his direction, willing him not to talk to me. Of course he did.

He began uncontrovertialy enough by grumbling at the length of the check-in queue. I mumbled a grudging agreement. He surveyed me up and down and it was clear that he did not approve of my garb. His remarks about my suit, its bourgeois conventiality and its unsuitability for an air journey were cleverly disguised just enough to prevent me from decking him there and then.

He asked as to my profession and the conversation took its predictable course to the point where the name of the group was mentioned. 'God, are they still living? I thought they went out with the velita.' This was a person who felt that the cut and thrust of an Oscar Wilde wit was both a weapon and a protection, something only to be admired by a mere plebeian such as I, as if to be put down by an aesthete were a privilege. That might have been true had he possessed one tenth of Oscar's word power and the merest fraction of Wilde's charm. He did not. I was not best pleased. I had simply been waiting patiently in the line and I now found myself being insulted by Andy Pandy.

'And what do you do?' I asked.

'I'm a fashion designer,' he replied. He surely must have seen my eyes boggle with disbelief. I pointedly ran a malevolent eye up and down his p.j.'s.

'Currently unemployed, I assume?' I was not smiling as I said it. His face dropped and he sniffily turned away. I had peace at last. It was at that point that I was approached by a lady member of the British Airways ground staff.

'Are you travelling alone, sir?', she asked. I replied in the affirmative.

'Well, would you like to check in over here?' She led me to the Business Class counter where I was processed and handed a boarding card that was infinitely superior to the lowly one my prepaid ticket deserved. Holding it aloft, I triumphantly walked past Andy Pandy who glared briefly before turning back to face the rest of his lengthy wait. What goes around comes around, as they say.

It is a fact that airlines overbook in an attempt to fill every vacant seat and every now and then they can get themselves out of a hole by bumping up one of the smarter economy passengers. Just once in a very blue moon there is, for the man in the right attire, a larger, more comfortable seat waiting. It was, I decided, time for a light snack.

While we're on the subject of food, nothing, I'm afraid, in the real world is perfect. I just have to point my accusing finger at airport eateries. In most areas travellers have got it made these days. Shopaholics have their addictions catered to at every turn with Harrods and Dunhill dispensing their luxury items alongside the unending lines of life's little essentials from Marks and Spencer, Boots and W. H. Smith. But for my working lad's tastes in the snack department they have been divided and conquered.

Sure, you can get a chic little croissant and a cappucino, hardly the fare of the trucker on holiday, and yes, you can sit down and be daintily served at a cutely decorated bistro. But the real nitty gritty, the self service joint with the kind of hot grub with which transport cafés for decades have nourished our great nation, continue to disappear almost before our eyes. Oh, there are a few still surviving but sadly the powers that be seem to have given the sublimely important mission of their improvement to a university graduate with a mile of letters after his name but who has surely never used such a plebeian form of body refuelling.

Consider the needs and then face the realities. You have stood in line for what seems like an eternity and checked in your stowed luggage. This is always a time of rising tension and you now need a calming rest over a hearty breakfast. Today you have struck lucky. You have fortuitously entered the terminal with the self-service area. This is very comforting. After all, your mammy never took a baby boomer like you into the posh places where the staff, dressed much better than yourself, would eventually condescend to bring you the menu after having studiously avoided eye contact for a full fifteen minutes, where the meal would take another half hour to appear and where the bill would use up all of your eating-out budget for a fortnight.

Your character has been set a long time ago. You want to see it, have it handed to you and push your tray to the till where the formalities will be completed in an instant without the embarrassment of wondering whether or not and how much to tip. Tipping was another thing we baby boomers never did.

As you are in an airport you are invariably carrying a shoulder bag, a large one in order to avoid straying into the dreaded regions of excess baggage. You probably have a couple of newspapers and magazines. These are not put away because the idea of a relaxing glance through the latest events and gossip over a cuppa is an inviting prospect. As your job training did not include the intricate skills of juggling it is now essential that you have a clear run on the tray counter right through to the cash point. Not a chance.

Some smart arse has decided that an arrangement of separate sections is more aesthetic and pleasing to the eye and every few feet the surface of parallel rails stops and presents a chasm which one must metaphorically leap. Your bag weighs down one side. The tray of purchases is an uneven counter balance on the other and delicate judgements must be accurately made. One wrong calculation and whole caboodle will crash to the floor This is not eating. This is The Krypton Factor. And it's not over yet.

Now think about things for a moment. If you head for the café you may want a sandwich. You might want a hot meal. The majority of folk will opt at least for a hot drink, be it tea or coffee. So where do they put the tea counter? Right next to a corner, that's where. This is precision placement, worked out down to the last minute detail so that everyone can bunch up into a wonderfully unruly rabble like a crowd leaving a football match. And what is in the adjacent corner, complete with a football crowd of its very own? Got it in one. The food bar, where one optimistically joins the milling throng.

Multiply the number of minutes it will take someone with the organisation capacity of a headless chicken to make up your order by the number of impatient and hungry customers waiting and you quickly sense an impending riot. The array of dishes are filled with the kind of things that please the taste buds and attack the heart. You pray that the person in front of you does not order an egg. They do. Oh no, not that. Now the customers have completely forgotten time as they witness an entertainment display of the most dazzling dexterity. But back in your own world the person behind the counter has their back turned to you. A dozen trivial tasks have suddenly become terribly important.

Bread is removed from its wrapping and the *'great buttering'* takes place. Nobody here has actually ordered bread but this is simply a diversion to avoid the customer's eye. Rare animals have become extinct in less time than this. More oil is flicked over the longest cooking egg in the universe. Plates are moved from one area to another, and possibly back again. The buttered bread is repositioned.

This bread is never toasted. My goodness no. Toast is another story entirely. When you want toast it has either been there for a decade and is completely inedible or it has to be freshly made and the preparation is rivalled only by the dreaded egg for its frustration factor. But your predecessor eventually gets their food, you choose your meal (avoiding the egg of course as the plane leaves in an hour) and in time you move on to-OH NOOO-THE TEA BAR! A golden rule has been ignored. As the manager of a Spanish sports stadium remarked when attempting to evacuate the ground through a solitary turnstile, never put all your Basques in one exit.

I really do want to meet the man who has designed this place of torture. I badly want him (or maybe it's a her, we must be politically correct) to witness this insane folly and to suffer like I have. But I must not think like this. There are thousands of hard working and dedicated people in airports all over the world doing splendid deeds and there are, without a shadow of a doubt, a multitude of unreasonably awkward customers making their lives a living hell. (If any cafeteria staff are reading this I just want to assure you it's not yours I am referring to. It is somewhere else entirely). And anyway, beyond all this frustration there is still the thrilling prospect of yet another wonderful journey through the azure skies to a land which with luck, for a short time, will seem like heaven.

Once on board you settle yourself into your seat. If the upgrade is just a shattered dream you should at least have had the good sense to either pre-book your seat or arrive early enough to gain an advantageous position in the cabin. Go for a bulkhead placing. Your legs have all the room in the world and you won't have to compete in the Olympic championship hurdles to get out for a visit to the loo. If the bulkhead seats have all been taken then my suggestion is scrap any idea of a window seat. The view is short lived. If you've seen it once that's all you need and it's not worth the disadvantage of being hemmed in by a fourteen stone couple (in shell suits of course) who need to be crane-lifted out by Wimpey in order to facilitate your safe passage of escape to the disgracefully scruffy steerage bog.

The on-board meal is a wonder in itself. The strangest concoctions are often forced on you as if they were things you found on your table in

Basingstoke every day. I used to hate travelling to Scandinavia. It was always herrings in oil or some other slimy and virtually inedible sea creature that had never seen the inside of an oven. Things have however improved over the years and pretentious chefs no longer feel the need to educate your taste buds in order to fulfil their own sense of destiny.

The main dilemma these days is how to keep it on the plate. In-flight meals seem to acquire a life of their own once the plastic wrapping has been removed. That wrapping, by the way, always reminds me of the indoor fireworks I used to have as a small child. There was a substance in the box that approximated the effect of snow. You took a red-hot poker (well, at least, a responsible adult did) and held it to a white tablet the size and appearance of an aspirin. Suddenly the room, the furniture of which over the years had begun to show an inordinate amount of poker burns, was filled with tiny white flakes, a vast amount out of all proportion to its pigmy source and which obliterated the sight of your parents on the other side of the hearth.

In the same way, the clear film which so neatly held you modest repast in place on its plastic tray now billows out like a monster from Star Trek completely filling the once empty space between you and the seat back. And there is now no way of scrunging this into manageable sized portions in order to give yourself room to move and breathe. Once loose, like Topsy, it grows and grows and grows. And while you try to handle this alien creature knives, forks and napkins are spilling over onto the cabin floor. This is not a meal. This is Challenge Anneka.

If you have chosen your carrier well you will have a wealth of entertainment at your fingertips to occupy your mind through the long flying hours. Remember, you have a choice, the commercial said and indeed it does make a difference. At the time of writing Singapore Airlines and Virgin were among those who had already upgraded to the multi-choice video system with up to twenty four channels, not to mention video games and audio or the personal cellular phone. For that last item you had better have plenty of credit left on your card or you risk meltdown before you've finished enquiring about the weather.

Gulf Air was still stuck, along with some of the others, with the old fashioned bulk head 'one programme fits all' screen. A form of torture cleverly devised so that only a portion of it is visible at any one time due to small children restlessly bobbing up and down in front of it. These brats seem to have the uncanny ability of knowing when the crucial moments are about to be screened and in an instant totally invalidate all that has

161

gone before. As far as I'm concerned, Herod wasn't such a bad guy after all. No doubt stiff competition will ensure that everyone will sooner rather than later fit their cabins with the latest gadgetry available, but until that happens it's worth checking before you commit yourself.

That all important space between the seats varies to an alarming degree but none of the airlines maintain a consistency here so it is difficult to point you in the right direction. Charter firms come in for the most stick but I think that's grossly unfair. If you are travelling on a charter you are cutting your budget as fine as it can be sliced and for a few hundred pounds you are probably being flown, fed and sheltered. And it will be damn good value for money so put up or shut up, I say. Get the free wine down you and knock out the Zs for the rest of the journey. And next time, don't be such a skinflint.

One of the most important arts to learn, particularly in the realms of air travel, is that of complaining. Not only is it a catharsis that can help release all your pent-up aggression, but there is money to be made. I was taught the finer points by a lady friend, a particularly feisty theatrical agent who had overcome the disadvantages of existing in a sexist world by cultivating a persona slightly more frightening than Attila The Hun.

She had a penchant for flesh several years younger than her own and was known to pursue aspiring actors, firm of body and fair of face, to the bedroom door and beyond when they let her. They had scant respect for her, even less love. It was mutual misuse. Not many of them could actually act. She knew that and so probably did they. But at least they would be able to attend the occasional premiere or enjoy the interiors of London's finest restaurants. Someone unkindly dubbed her 'the face that lunched a thousand shits.'

But she made me realise that, for the short time it took to sit down at a computer and construct a scathing missal to an errant airline, much money or its equivalent would come whizzing through my letterbox. The problem is that the British are not by nature a nation of complainers. A family will sit around a cafeteria table moaning and groaning bitterly about the pile of inedible crud that lies festering on their plates. A smiling waitress will approach and ask in her sweetest voice if everything is okay. The herd of human dissatisfaction is suddenly transformed into a compliant and submissive example of moral cowardice as they nod in gratitude for the heaps of pulsating botulism that they now pronounce as lovely, thank you.

The trick is to maintain the indignance that you originally felt. This is the hardest part. All resolve to take matters further are normally forgotten one hour later. Big mistake. Make yourself remember just how annoyed you had been. Work yourself up and keep your discontentment nicely on the boil until you get home. Then get on that word processor and let the venom flow. But it must be controlled and well constructed venom. They must be made to understand that their sin has been of such magnitude that it has become a matter of principle to right the terrible wrongs done. They must also be aware that you are not going to go away and that the better part of valour for them is to retreat with honour. After all, there is an office worker at the other end of your letter who has the power to dispense someone else's money at no cost to theirself.

Let me give you a few examples of the loot I have managed to pillage over the years. Preordered special meal unavailable on a Maltese airline - £30. (That's always a good one. They rarely get special meals right). The same offence, repeated a number of times, on a German airline - a rather swish suit bag delivered to my house. Luggage not arriving at my destination, requiring me to spend the night only a couple of notches up from the status of a derelict - £375 from a British company. And musical instruments inadvertently left off two consecutive flights to Holland - a pair of tickets to any destination on the carrier's schedule. Not bad, eh? And it gave me the opportunity to practise my writing as well.

So much for flying. If you are travelling by road there are a few important things to consider, especially if your journey is within the British Isles. First and foremost make sure your vehicle is in good order. Sitting on the hard shoulder waiting for the breakdown service is dead boring. It always has been and it always will be, although once again competition has forced them to get their act together. Time was when veritable aeons had passed before a man in a very small van, (or in the days of my childhood, a motor bike), would arrive only to shake his head and tell you that he'd have to send for a tow truck, which would of course be another hour at least. These days you've hardly time to listen to The Archers before a very very nice man pulls up and teases your ten year old Montego into life again.

RDS radio is a handy device. It breaks into your programmes to tell you that there is a huge hold up at Godstone, south of London near Gatwick. The fact that you are actually on the northern section of the M25 and about to shoot up the A1 pisses you off a little, especially as this useless piece of information has come just at the moment Poirot is about to announce who killed the village postmistress. You do however get very adept at flicking it back onto the proper station at the speed of sound once you have realise that this particular snippet has no relevance to your personal comfort.

But the single most important thing that has transformed my life as far as road travel is concerned is automatic transmission. For years I thought it was still a fly-by-night invention only fit for shiftless, mollycoddled Americans. For aeons the impression stayed with me that they were always breaking down and that British mechanics did not know how to fix them. It stuck firmly in my mind that you could not bump start an automatic and I remembered hours and hours of bump starting cars and vans in my teenage years. It was a method of getting the vehicle on the move that was used more frequently, it seemed, than the designated starter motor in those days. Automobiles had come a long way since those pioneer days but my memory had remained in the dark days.

I finally succumbed in 1994 and you would have to drag me screaming back to a manual shift. Along with the superhighway came the super traffic jam and for decades I would clunk clumsily in and out of first gear to propel my tired old wreck a few measly feet, getting angrier with every resented effort. With an automatic you simply lift your foot off the brake and the tickover will effortlessly glide you the necessary distance. Sheer bliss. Get one. Forget all that macho posturing boy racer stuff and go auto. You won't be sorry.

If you are truly well prepared you will be fully spammed up on when not to attempt to get on the M25. It's virtually a total waste of time heading north from 1 p.m. on a Friday. And even if you manage to sail through that bit rest assured you are going to come to a grinding halt where the M6 meets the M5. A good working knowledge of the parallel A roads is an asset, along with a sure-sighted and quick-witted passenger to scan the map. If you hit trouble you can whiz off the motorway, zoom around the back doubles like a rally driver and join it again at the next junction. Sometimes it can be fun as long as your time is not crucial.

Motorway cafés, by the way, are pretty much the same as airport cafés with the same apalling logistics applying and prices hiked up higher than a stripper's skirt. But they have a unique quality in that you can enter in the peak of the rush hour or the wee small hours of the morning with exactly the same result. By the time you are served you will be infinitely nearer death.

The mentality of British caterers does not equip them to deal with crowds. In the busy period you remain in the queue for the time it takes to view The Godfather, parts One, Two and Three. (Don't forget to add extra for the fried egg). Arrive when there is not a soul in the place and the result is the same but for a different reason. The staff have scurried off like frightened rabbits into their warren doing goodness knows what. The counter is a service-free area. What uniformed persons there are will be dusting the far reaches of the cafeteria in beautifully graceful and totally fascinating slow motion strokes that would earn rapturous praise from Marcel Marceau. Once at the till you will of course have to spend time filling in the forms for the mortgage application in order to pay for the only product more costly than titanium.

While we're touring our great British Isles let's talk about hotels. Have you seen the prices of those things? A week in a three star hotel at the published rates will make your mortgage look like beer money. Who pays those rates? Not us that's for sure. Get in touch with an accommodation agent. Let them do the deal. Most people don't even know of their existence but from the comfort of their anonymous offices they will haggle over the phone on your behalf and, believe it or not, it costs you nothing. Their meagre fee comes from a commission paid to them by the hotel.

That single with bath that they wanted seventy five pounds for is yours for forty or less. Hoteliers are pragmatic people. They know that an empty room brings in no revenue and in the end your forty pounds is better than a slap on the buttocks with a wet kipper, although there are places in London that would charge you much more than forty pounds for that particular service. (At least, they did the last time I was there).

If you can't find an agent and if you don't embarrass easily and have the nerve then you can still do it yourself. Just telephone and ask for the accommodations manager, state your case and your budget and you are more than likely in with a chance. Of course it is an advantage if you do it on the actual day and you're not in the middle of the peak season. By the way, bargains are always available at weekends.

Getting back to foreign travel, there is one particular system I have which most, I know, will look on as bordering on fanaticism. I have a check list installed on my computer and for each journey, whether it be a day, a week or a month I religiously make my marks in the appropriate adjacent tick boxes. I have listed every item I might ever want on a trip away from these shores beginning with passport credit cards and ending with cufflinks and film for the camera. I have spent far too much time pulling everything out of cases at the last minute because I'm not sure if have packed a particular shirt or pair of shorts. I spent far too many weary hours lugging around twice as much clothing than I was ever bound to need.

Okay, so I will almost never need everything that is on the list but it is a simple procedure. A tick means the item is in the case. A number next to a category tells me how many I will need for the time away and it gets a tick once they are all in. A dash means that this particular item is not required. And if there is something that I will not be able to pack until just prior to departure, a circle tells me to check before I leave.

And if all this detail makes me sound as though I am suffering from acute paranoia, let me tell you it works. I've got better things to do with my life than to spend it with my head in a suitcase. Once that tick is there I never have to rummage around because I can't remember what I have or have not packed. I need never check again. If there is a tick next to pass-port I know my passport is in my carry-on bag. With the amount of trav-el we do the least time these tedious chores take the happier I am.

By the way, this system does not work when applied to women. Like a budgie when someone has left the cage door open, logic flies straight out the window. It is virtually impossible for a woman to say, when going away for three days, I will need these three evening dresses. Their minds do not work like that. They require multiple choices that can only be made prior to the function at hand. As the writer said, men are from Mars and women are from Venus. Don't argue. Don't try to change it. And don't, if you care for your sanity, try to figure them out. Just enjoy them.

There's no doubt about it. Travel is an art. And, like all arts, the better you are at it the greater the rewards. But no one is infallible. I once went to Australia and could not get rid of a nagging doubt in my mind. There was something I had forgotten, I was sure of it. One month later we touched down at Heathrow and my local cab company picked us up. Roger, our regular driver, with a Humpty Dumpty body and an egg head to match, collected us. After the marathon journey I was not looking my best but, checking Roger out I decided that a bad hair day was infinitely better than a no hair day. We got out at my place and as I walked up the drive and peeked in my lounge window I knew what had been bugging me for the last month. My three-bar Belling Tudor-style electric fire was blaz-ing away with all guns. I was extremely fortunate to have a house that was still standing. Sometimes no amount of preparation helps.

15

It's Very Nice To Go Travelling

If you ever feel the need to witness a visual definition of the word desolate then The Falkland Islands can provide a pretty good example. To say they are bleak is a bit like saying that Galtieri was a bit of a naughty boy. The treeless landscape suggests that The Almighty has at some time taken a swipe with a giant G2 disposable, slicing away everything save a few patches of designer stubble here and there.

To the Argentinians they are Los Malvinas. To a couple of thousand inhabitants they are home. And to an equivalent number of British soldiers installed to protect them from further invasion they are a pain in the arse. Due south of Argentina and well on the way to the South Pole, this forbidding territory is the squaddie's least favourite posting. From the moment he arrives his time is spent ticking the days off the calendar till he can go back to Great Britain.

We made the tedious eighteen hour journey twice across the South Atlantic as headliners on a CSE touring party. The old style ENSA had been nicknamed Every Night Something Atrocious. The nineties version was dubbed Crap Show Expected. Life was good and work was plentiful throughout the eighties and nineties and we could afford to take on gigs almost purely for the pleasure and the experience. I stress 'almost'. We were paid, though not handsomely. It was very much a labour of love.

On each four month tour of duty there is a test of endurance for a soldier, cut off from any real creature comforts or semblance of social life and with a virtual absence of female company. (Soldiers do not consider lady

167

service personnel as female). The main base of Mount Pleasant is the principal camp, containing all but a handful of the troops. A rabbit warren of metal huts are joined together in a fascinating maze of temporary housing. Long internal corridors that have not always been there, protect the men from the icy wind that cuts relentlessly across the flat terrain. Before that they simply had to freeze on the journey between huts. Somehow it always seems to be winter there. Even the temperate summer climes seem like winter.

The remainder of the forces are dispersed among the mountain sites of Alice, Vernon and Kent, miniature versions of Mount Pleasant, where approximately forty men in each camp live out an even harsher existence in an atmosphere of male bonding gone mad. Tiny communities and as close knit as any family, nowhere is more than thirty yards from anywhere else. Here you have to like your mates. And if you don't, then it's best to pretend you do.

In the mountain camps life exists within a self-imposed set of rules and rituals and you break the rules at your peril. There are fines for everything. Ring the bar bell and the next round is yours. Bump your head on the low doorway and your forfeit is determined by a spin of the 'wheel of fortune'. Feet on the furniture, twenty pence in the charity box. I managed, in my short stay, to merit every fine on offer including one which had me sitting on a toilet, the seat round my neck and my trousers round my ankles whilst wearing a special cap and sucking my thumb. Don't ask me why. I don't know. It's best not to argue with a bunch of guys who have just kicked the crap out of a foreign force in one of the bloodiest conflicts since the Second World War. If they say jump, I ask 'How high?'.

Once a month the lads have a pub crawl. It begins in the Officers' Mess. There are three bars on each camp. When the drinking is done they 'catch a bus' to the next one. This requires them to sit on the floor, legs locked around the person in front, and shuffle *en masse* to the next watering hole. Miss the buss and the culprit must pay a fiver for a taxi. In other words he puts the required sum of money behind the bar for a 'slab' (a case of beer) from which anyone can draw until it is exhausted.

There are songs sung nightly, each one complete with a choreographed set of actions. Sit down on a line when you should be either standing up or banging on the ceiling and a slab is awaiting payment. When one of these anthems is in full flight at the end of a particularly riotous evening it is one of the most emotive and moving sights I have ever seen. Any given night usually ends up with the predictable performance of a song in which there is a great dropping of trousers. Naturally I was roped in to help out on this one. Not because there was anything impressive to be revealed (far from it) but I was the only one in our merry band who happened to be as drunk as they were.

The song came to its rousing end with the horrific sight of five strapping young soldiers and one fast-ageing pop singer, whose body was shot more than the enemy, bobbing about with their combat equipment swinging in the air. I confess that in any sizeable conflict my equipment would have been sadly inadequate. I might manage a few stray shots but I doubt that anyone would be seriously wounded. Nude singing, I might add, is not a sensible thing on the whole. The main problem being that not everything stops when the music does.

The close environment of the mountain camps quickly became a spiritual home for me. The only thing that puzzled me after watching them getting slashed up night after night is how on earth they ever got even the simplest chores done let alone emerge victorious in battle.

When you first arrive in The Falklands the number one priority is to go and see the penguins which, at that time of the year, were nesting in ovals of scrubland down by the shore among the dunes. A couple of hundred birds had constructed twig nests which filled the hollows they had made in the sand. Penguins are, without a doubt, cute as they scuttle about in their immaculate evening dress as though they are off to an embassy ball. The first shock comes when you realise what smelly little sods they are. The strong stench of ammonia pervades the atmosphere and clings steadfastly to the membranes of your nostrils until your sense of smell grows accustomed.

The second impression is that these are not at all the sweet natured cherubs their reputation or outward appearance would have you believe. They spend the whole time squawking and snapping at each other while constantly stealing twigs from their neighbour's nest for no apparent reason. One twig more or less could surely never make a difference to either their personal comfort or the survival of their offspring.

The Falklands provided the first opportunity for me to conquer a long standing fear and head skywards in a helicopter. They do not inspire me with confidence. A flight high above the ground on a device that is little more than a giant egg whisk was an unnerving prospect. And my debut was to be in a Chinook, a chopper with not exactly the finest safety record. Maybe it's my imagination but it seems to me they have gone down more times than a White House worker. Chinooks are those great big dark green airborne whales with dual rotors, one at each end. And yes, they do interlock in their synchronised rotary operation, a fact that it is sensible for the nervous not to dwell on for too long.

On takeoff and in fine weather the Chinooks usually fly with the end loading bay door left down. We had just flown over the infamous Goose Green, an insignificant little cluster of houses over which a very significant battle had been fought, when the load master signalled me to come to the open bay where he was standing. I obeyed him, very slowly. You do not race towards the open door of a helicopter in flight, not unless you're a rotor blade short of a vertical take-off.

He strapped a harness round my waist and hooked a cord onto it. The other end was attached by a similar hook to the 'copter frame and for the next fifteen minutes or so I sat next to him on the ledge of the bay. Legs dangling over the edge as we soared over the countryside on a modern-day magic carpet ride. After a few tense minutes the nerves subsided. The vast brutal terrain of the Falklands passed by beneath mesmerising me and my apprehension turned to an exhilaration that is hard to describe.

The locals, most of whom live in the largest town of Stanley, had been christened 'Bennies', after the slow-witted character played by actor Paul Henry in the long running, and now long gone, soap opera Crossroads. There was a love/hate relationship between the troops and the Bennies, whose tiny closed-in community and, of necessity, a certain amount of in-breeding made them easy targets for their street-wise protectors. But if Bob's not only your uncle but also your cousin and your father in law, who am I to criticise? When the choice is between shagging a sheep or a near relative then who can blame them if they put the lamb chops to one side and get on with something more familiar and appealing to the appetite?

The Falklanders were torn between gratitude at having their homeland restored to them and resentment at having to settle for an invasion of another sort by people who were not even the enemy. When the squaddies were ordered to cease calling them Bennies they change their pet name to 'stills'. When asked why, the answer was because they were 'still Bennies'.

Soldiers are not known for their diplomacy, in particular towards women. Not unless they are using it to further their carnal intent. Diplomacy after all, as any politician knows, is not meant to convey a compliment but rather to secure a convenience. Women, in such a posting, are rare and both sought and fought after, but everything changes as the plane speeds homewards. One rather tactless flight officer dropped himself into a whole bunch of trouble when he announced over the aircraft's communication system, 'We are about to land at Brizenorton. Ladies, how does it feel to be ugly again?'

Occasionally the performers suffer at their hands too. We had flown to Belize to perform for the troops stationed there. This jungle outpost in Central America, a land that at one time was known as British Honduras, is a whole lot more bearable than The Falklands. And, with its tropical heat and lazy lagoons that swish gently over some of the finest coral reefs, is second only in desirability as a posting to The Ascension Islands.

The dancers had done their bit. They were not the most co-ordinated or best looking of girls but they were female and under twenty and anything constituting a member of the opposite gender is usually a sight for sore hands. But the boys were coming to the end of their tour of duty and interested in little else than getting back home to Britain. Another CSE show, that they were in fact ordered by the officers to attend, was to them simply another annoyance and a waste of beer drinking time. The compere, an adequate, if not side-splitting, comedian told his jokes and introduced the speciality act, a magician.

He was not the best magician in the world. Indeed, he was probably not even the best magician in his street, and the lads were getting restless and dangerous. Finally, two or three appalling tricks later, a young soldier rose to his feet, threw and empty can at the stage and yelled, 'You're fucking useless. Get off and put the dogs back on.'

The logistics of getting a bunch of musicians and their accompanying baggage from one part of the world to another on time and without mishap can get a bit hairy from time to time. We have had a few tighter than tight schedules to contend with and mostly it was down to ourselves making rods for our own backs. From Singapore to Nantwich, an unlikely coupling you have to agree, was probably the most off-the-wall example of a potential disaster waiting to happen.

John McNally cannot resist a challenge. If it can be done it will be done, is his philosophy. Furthermore it goes against his principles to allow a possible gig, and therefore its accompanying fee, to escape into another group's hands. The complicated arrangement of connecting aircraft on this particular jaunt allowed only a maximum of two hours grace for errors and delays. Anything more and four hundred people would find themselves gathered in a Midlands civic centre staring at an empty stage. I pointed this out to John. 'Who dares wins,' was the succinct reply. So we went for it.

171

We went on stage at a hotel in Singapore at 11.45 p.m. and churned out our roster of hits for an hour and twenty minutes. The packed conference room was throbbing with demented revellers, a large party of information technology people rounding up their working holiday which had, up to now, been spent aboard a cruise liner. The fact that the ship had caught fire a few days previously had possibly given them a greater reason to celebrate not only the end of their stay but merely being alive. Whatever. They were in great spirits and our fears were for the moment assuaged. We hit our pillows around 1.30 a.m. Just enough time for a very quick cat nap before the minibus was due to take us to the airport at 4.30.

Sod's law was in operation that day and there was, inevitably, a delay to our Gulf Air flight to Bahrain. We lost something in excess of forty minutes while the craft stood idly on the tarmac. Once in the sky I diverted my attention from the tedium of the flight and the growing feeling that this whole operation was going to end in disaster by complaining bitterly about the complete absence of white wine. My irritability was fuelled by my memory of the same situation existing on the same carrier almost exactly one year before. I was not flying on Frankie's favourite airline. If the staff were unhappy with me I could not have given a toss, as they say in the smartest circles. Let them look on it as a training exercise. Life should never be too easy.

Time-wise, things were not looking good, but we made up most of the lost minutes and landed on time. It required a change of planes here but there were no snags and we touched down at Heathrow on schedule with surely enough time to make the internal connection. We breathed a communal sigh of relief. Strangely, it was here that we hit the biggest snag. We had to collect our baggage and clear customs before transferring everything to Terminal 1 for our domestic flight to Manchester, due to depart in an hour and a half.

We piled our luggage and instrument cases on to a couple of trolleys and set off at speed through the corridors and ramps that link the departure halls. It would have been wise, on reflection, to have taken our proficiency tests in the handling of these incredibly contrary contraptions before attempting a Formula-One trolley dash on such a crowded racetrack. But hindsight is an exact science. Trolley design, on the other hand, is not.

The inventor has seen fit to equip this unique type of carriage with the same steering mechanism that guides a water diviner. It has a mind of its own and mine possessed an especially vindictive mind that had apparently been trained in the deadly arts by someone whose usual pupils are Rottweilers.

172

Without warning the front wheel was wrenched at a ninety-degree angle by an unseen hand in a piece of sorcery that would have done justice to The Omen. I was on a severe gradient at the time and the silver metal beast hurtled at full power into a bunch of unsuspecting holidaymakers. Before I knew it I had impaled myself on a pair of skis which had recently returned from a pleasant vacation in Klosters.

Revenge though, was sweet. One of the heavy flight cases, the one containing the unfriendly weight addition of the twelve string guitar, tumbled from the load and landed on the feet of this particular prince of the slalom. Not enough to break bones but still sufficient to elicit the yelp of a puppy having it balls scalded with boiling water. My apology was half-hearted and accepted with the about the same degree of grace with which it had been delivered. We had nether the time nor the inclination to indulge in unnecessary niceties. We re-stacked and when our pit-stop was over, continued the race to the finishing line in front of the domestic check-in counter.

For future reference, by the way, British airport trolleys are infinitely superior to most other foreign makes in one major detail. They are free. Try grabbing one in Germany and you are forced to insert a two Mark piece into a slot, without which it will cling, kicking and screaming for dear life, onto the one in front. You simply cannot coax it to come with you in any other way. These are the prostitutes of the trolley world. They will only do it for money. There is, of course, every reason why our trolleys should be free. They stand against the walls shamelessly copulating and reproducing themselves at a frightening rate in a most obscene orgy of excited, shiny metal. Turn away for a few seconds only and their numbers will have increased alarmingly. Do not let young children stare at these, I beg you.

I still have no idea what exactly was wrong with our pre-booked tickets but for one moment it seemed that there were no seats for us on a packed aeroplane. We had flown halfway across the world to be abandoned and dumped ignominiously on our own soil. We dropped the name of the group shamelessly. People are rarely impressed but anything is worth a try, although it is usually only worth trying on someone on the wrong side of forty. This person most definitely was. In fact she was on the wrong side of the wrong side of forty. But that does not make her a bad person. She was, in fact, the very personification of kindness and set about righting wrongs with a cheery smile.

Seats were finally found and the seven-thirty shuttle hurtled skywards and deposited its tired load of pop stars at Manchester's Ringway Airport where we had a couple of hire cars ready and waiting. Our crew were aware of our schedule and had set up the equipment in readiness at the venue that afternoon. Having squashed our baggage into the cars it was simply a matter of a fifty mile dash down the M6 to Nantwich where a sold out crowd sat completely unaware of the fragile nature of their Saturday night's entertainment. We had, by the way, kept the promoter in the same state of ignorance. He would only have worried.

At least that little piece of chicanery involved two separate days. We have from time to time accepted doubles (i.e. two separate shows in one evening) that were in two entirely different countries. One particular day springs to mind in which we boarded a twin-engined Piper Cherokee which was to fly us to Frankfurt for a huge open air concert involving ourselves, Shaking Stevens, The Hollies and The Beach Boys. If we opened the show on the stroke of 6 p.m. we could just make it back to Shrewsbury in time for a private party that night.

What the pilot neglected to tell us until we were well on our way was that the field in which we were due to land did not possess immigration facilities. It would be necessary to divert to a slightly larger one to complete these procedures before continuing. This would mean an unscheduled half an hour minimum added onto an already tight time frame. We were not happy bunnies. Some of us were also uncomfortable little bunnies with crossed legs. There are 'small craft warnings' of which one should be aware. Planes of this kind do not have lavatories. It is essential to go before you fly. Drain off all excess fluids or make sure you have an empty bottle with a neck aperture commensurate with the size of your willy and a good aim. And if you are incontinent from the other side, well, God help you. The possibilities do not bear thinking about. I have no idea what ladies do in an emergency. I suppose a bucket would be a handy vessel to have on board, but I don't recall seeing one.

As we touched down for the first stop sirens started to scream and warning lights were flashing all over the place. 'Oh, don't worry about all that. We've just got a fault in the warning system,' the pilot explained, a trifle too glibly for my liking. Well, excuse me. If I'm flying in something that is hardly bigger or more mechanically sophisticated than a motorised lawnmower, I would rather have no faults at all thank you. I wonder if Buddy Holly's pilot said 'Oh nothing to worry about. Just a bit of turbulence.'

We remained quiet and began to follow him and his co-pilot to the shed that was masquerading as a terminal. We had got a few hundred yards when we heard a frantic yell. We turned to find our drummer, Billy Adamson, pushing against the parked plane for all he was worth. 'The bloody thing's moving,' he shouted in a Glaswegian dialect that, in his current state of terror, sounded like the end product of a 'teach a chimp to recite Rabbie Burns' experiment. The pilot had forgotten to put on the brake and it was about to roll off down a slope into a ditch. A few pounds more weight and a few degrees greater incline and they would have lost an aeroplane while we would have lost a gig and its all-important financial reward.

On the return journey there were no further mishaps but the immigration delay meant that we had cut it very fine to land on our intended airfield. As the hours drew on the darkness looked ominous. Our airstrip did not have landing lights and it was quite likely that we might have to be diverted, which would throw all our arrangements into chaos. As things turned out we did make it - just. We touched down to find a lone man in a field waiting to shut the gate and go home.

The show of course ran its course with the usual smoothness, and once again the celebrants, whose birthday party we had been engaged for, never knew just how close they had come to enjoying an entertainment-free evening.

While travelling there are, of course, more than a few weird and wonderful people to be encountered. And not all of them outside the confines of the British Isles. The people who operate and frequent the social clubs of our fair land often appear to exist in some parallel universe where the points of reference are at an angle to the ones that direct our own lives.

The tales of concert secretaries posting Matt Monro's contract on the club notice board to justify where their one pound fifty entrance fee had been spent, or the compere who interrupted Johnny Ray's headlining act to announce that the pies had arrived, are well documented. We too have had our encounters of the confusing kind.

The electronic guitar tuner is possibly the single most stress reducing invention ever to lighten a plank spanker's load. Times were when the whole of the pre-show time would be spent with an ear pressed hard against the body of the instrument in a frustratingly useless attempt to get the bloody thing in some sort of reasonable tune. And all this against a background of conversation and spillage from the entertainment already under way. By 1980 a tiny oscillating meter had been devised which obviated the need for the ears to play any part whatsoever. If the guitar had

175

been previously 'set up' correctly, a couple of minutes adjusting the tuning pegs while keeping an eye on the needle and the operation was complete, silently and in a fraction of the time that was once needed.

It was time for our show to start. Three of us headed to the wings leaving John to check his instrument on the tuner. The concert secretary, not wearing the stereotypical flat cap but nonetheless a classic example of the genre, began to hustle. 'Come on mate, you're on now.'

'Okay,' I'm just tuning up.'

'For God's sake man,' the frustrated steward moaned, 'You've known about this show for three months.'

On another occasion we impressed the manager of a rival social club to the point where he simply had to get our details for a future booking. John gave him his phone number and, true to his word, several weeks later the man rang. He wanted us for his club. How much would we charge? John told him. There was an ominous silence while he digested the figure which seemed to have a couple of noughts too many. He finally regained his composure.

'But we can't afford that kind of money, man.'

'Well that's what we charge. I'm sorry.' John tried to be as kind as he could.

'But it's only a small room. We can only get two hundred in. Can you do it for less?'

'I'm sorry mate, but that's what we go out for. I've quoted as low as I can,' explained McNally apologetically. Once again there was a pause while the machinery in the man's brain ground away.

'Well, we don't really need the four of you. How much for three?'

To this day I have never forgiven John McNally for having the presence of mind to ask him which three he would prefer.

And finally on the social club front we did once have a situation where a club steward, who was waiting to lock up and go home after the show, did not quite understand the principle of the division of labours. While the road managers were breaking down the equipment after the show he encountered our drummer Billy relaxing over a newspaper in the less than spacious, not to mention luxury-denied, dressing room. He and his ferocious looking Alsatian guard dog wanted to know why Master Adamson was not assisting with the work in hand. Billy quite naturally pointed out in sentences measured carefully so that his broad Glaswegian brogue was softened to the point where an interpreter would not be required, that he was one of the band and it was the roadies who packed the gear away.

To my simple mind it would suffice as an explanation. After all, I would not expect the tea lady at the colliery canteen to muck in with a pick axe on the late late shift just because there were still a couple of tons of nutty slack to be shifted. Unfortunately it was cutting no ice with this particular follower of the doctrines of Karl Marx. If the work-shy drummer was not willing to participate in the dismantling of the equipment he must vacate the premises. Billy, very unwisely, demurred, at which point he was threatened with the angry looking mutt that was now straining at his leash and looking forward to a juicy Angus steak. The dog, as opposed to our drummer, was not a vegetarian. The drummer, as opposed to the dog, continued his reading in the van.

Odd people on terra firma are one thing. When they appear out of the blue at thirty thousand feet the experience takes on a different aspect entirely. No matter how much you fly it is still an unnatural and potentially frightening experience. The smallest problem at any distance above the ground takes on a significance of monumental proportions. Your life is in someone else's hands and you put your trust in them to keep you safe. To allay your fears they have been carefully trained in 'aero-speak', a set of cleverly constructed euphemisms designed to disguise the true meaning of words.

'In the unlikely event that we should have to land on water' one of their set pieces begins. Land on water? For goodness sakes, surely what they're really saying is 'crash into the sea'. It continues, 'your seat cushion may be used as a life raft'. A life raft? If the cushion can suddenly become a life raft why can't the plane just become a boat?

Safety is paramount and anything unusual or dramatic that happens while in the air is most unnerving. We were on a flight to Cork one time which was carrying an extended family of Irish tinkers who had been to London for a wake. The deceased, a lad called Jimmy who had apparently expired prematurely following his unfortunate collision with a moving vehicle, was also on board. Instead of a seat he was resting in a coffin somewhere deep in the cargo hold on his final journey home.

The alcohol consumed at the post-interment gathering had continued unabated through the night and into the departure lounge. By the time the undercarriage was lifted the bereaved's loved ones were already flying higher than the plane. To mix a couple of metaphors, it wasn't the straw that broke the camel's back as much as the booze from the in-flight bar supped through the straw that got the camel totally pissed.

As the seat belt warning came on for landing one of the women in the party started screaming at the top of her voice. 'Jimmy, Jimmy, I loved ya Jimmy. You were a good man. I don't want to live without you.'

Stewardesses rushed down the aisle and tried to press her back into the seat from where she was trying to extricate herself. Arms were flailing as she lashed out at what she perceived as her oppressors trying to keep her from joining her beloved Jimmy.

'Oh God, I don't want to live. Make the plane crash,' she cried.

At that point I desperately wanted to go over and thump her. I never had the pleasure of making Jimmy's acquaintance but I certainly did want to live and I was beginning to hate the bastard already. Somehow they managed to restrain the drink-sodden woman and we touched down safely. As far as I could see, it if she was typical of his family, Jimmy was well out of it. I wouldn't have been at all surprised to find he threw himself under the car.

It was on a flight back from the Middle East that we were confronted with the phantom aeroplane chanter. I had just settled down ready to watch the movie after my meal and was remonstrating with the cabin attendant yet again about the absence of white wine on not only this but also my previous three Gulf Air flights. I was about to broach the subject of possible compensation when our discussion was interrupted by an Asian woman who had run up the aisle and was shrieking her dissatisfaction about the fumes around her seat. Her wailing voice was ear piercingly loud.

'I don't want to die. The smoke will kill me and I don't want to die. It is unfair. You must do something about it. I am not a crazy lady.' I had a feeling that the last bit was a lie. This woman was definitely a few rupees short of a decent dowry.

The stewardess attempted to calm her down. It was clearly going to be a long and difficult process and I good-naturedly abandoned my criticism of the bar and its contents, or rather lack of them. When you have a complete looney causing havoc at thirty thousand feet the absence of a half decent Chardonnay seems relatively unimportant. Eventually she was coaxed to a seat and calmed by one of the crew who was then required to kneel in the aisle and hold her hand. Our road manager, who was seated near her in the smoking section explained the situation to me.

Apparently she had asked to be moved from the seat adjacent to her husband, a highly embarrassed Canadian whose stone faced expression denied all connection with his errant, and completely batty, spouse. She insisted on being moved to the rear. This was, of course, the smoking section. She objected to the smoke. It was pointed out that in the smoking section (surprise, surprise) people were allowed to smoke. They would move her forward to a non-smoking seat.

No, she did not want to be moved, but she wanted the people around her to stop smoking. At that point, had I been a Gulf Air employee, I would have cheerfully opened a hatch and slung her out without the benefit of a parachute, but highly trained cabin crews are made of sterner stuff. They are taught to remain calm in all situations. I take my hat off to them.

They managed to settle her, for a while, in a non-smoking seat where she resorted to reading from one of those religious manuals. You've seen them. The kind Americans in number one haircuts and silly robes try to foist on you as you go about your daily business in the pedestrianised shopping area of your local town. The cover, as they all do, depicted blissfully childlike scenes of sunshine, grass and flowers while the text inside no doubt promised a world of peace and love. As long as you posted off half your weekly earnings to a giggling guru raised in Delhi but now enjoying a splendid life in a luxury villa on a Florida golf course.

By now I was convinced that when God was handing out brains this woman had obviously thought he had said trains and jumped out of the way. As she read she chanted, much to the initial amusement of her fellow passengers. Amusement turned to annoyance as the chanting droned on and on and on. If there had been dogs on board they would have chewed her ankles off in the agony her high pitched whining caused. What she was chortling made rap seem almost acceptable.

She then rose from her seat, her book held high in front of her, and continued her sing-song up one aisle and down the other. A half hour later she was still aisle walking, still wailing. Her voice was a painful moan and reminiscent of one of the less successful tracks of a late sixties George Harrison album. As far as I could fathom she seemed to be attempting to break the long distance in-flight plane chanting record. And to give her her due, it looked as though she was going to succeed. Well, there's nowt so queer as folk. God bless us all, Tiny Tim.

16

But It's Oh So Nice To Come Home

What amounts to a virtual ticket to the world may, and should, be counted as a very special gift indeed. From a second hand bike in Middlesex to a jumbo jet winging its way across the globe is not something, even in these affluent and sophisticated times, which we should expect as our birthright. My birthright has turned out to be a generous one and there are just too many destinations to include in the pages of a minor opus such as this is.

I would need more than a few puny paragraphs, for instance, to even begin to convey the glory and magnificence that is Kenya. That great enigma, the African continent, proudly parades such an unimaginable vista before your eyes that 'impressive' is too ineffectual a word and the greatest sensation is the sudden realisation of your own incredible smallness in the scheme of things.

To sit in front of your five star tent, complete with flushing toilet, in the morning hours sipping a cool, freshly squeezed orange juice and nibbling at a newly baked croissant while in the near distance a giraffe meets your gaze is a special kind of heaven indeed.

The oddly-constructed creature, its mottled body tapering upwards in a grotesque approximation of a pyramid to where the most elegant and slender of necks supports an ungainly and knobbly head, stands motionless. It is a life-size replica of the carvings on display in the market places of Nairobi and Mombassa. Souvenirs that will eventually find new homes in Chelmsford or Chester, New York or Nova Scotia. Unlike the carvings it can move if it wants to but for the most part it prefers to remain in a rigid stance of tranquil contemplation. Maybe, given the space of one or two volumes one might just be able to do justice to such a land. But for now, I won't even try.

And I have left out an adventure from 1996. We had a date with a star in the summer of that year, a once beautiful creature upon whom the unforgiving years had sadly but inevitably taken their toll. Thirty years before she had been the belle of the ball and now the ball was over. But so what? She was a legend. Would you turn down a date with Lauren Bacall or refuse to dine with Katherine Hepburn? As we pulled into Southampton docks she was waiting, serenely and majestically as if time were of no consequence. Time was for mere mortals, no longer to be considered by this fabulous lady. She was above such things. She was a goddess. She was Canberra.

This once great vessel, now showing the signs of a long, hard life was about to enter a deserved and welcome state of retirement. Like us she had seen service in the Falklands, but unlike us she did not wait until the fighting was over. We returned enlightened. She returned a heroine. I was grateful to take the time to get to know her just a little before it was too late. Perhaps another time I will sit back with pen in hand and recall that two weeks floating on the warm waters of the Mediterranean when I learned that there was a form of travel where one did not need to fly quite so high or be in such an unseemly hurry to reach one's destination.

There are places I have liked better than others and some that I would prefer not to return to at all. As a general rule of thumb I try to avoid countries which have arrows through their vowels. Scandinavia is not a thrill for me. Outside the major cities such as Stockholm, Oslo or Copenhagen these countries are a bit like a eunuch's jockstrap. Once you get inside there's not a great deal of action to speak of. It is difficult to put your finger on the reason why they appear so bland, so mind-numbingly dull. The countryside is beautiful and the houses immaculately maintained. There is nothing crumbling in this land. As you motor past it reminds you in absolutely no way at all of the scruffy town you left back home in England. The central heating works and there is every chance that your dear old granny will spend her dying days in a well earned state of generously subsidised comfort. But are they happy? Not a chance.

The image of those blissfully contented blond and sun-tanned tanned Swedes taking full advantage of that free love which earned our envy in the straight laced times of our own pathetic gropings of puberty was a sham.

It did not make the loving better or bring them happiness. Sweden has one of the highest suicide rates in the world. And Norway does not fare much better. Misery is in their blood. They might not readily admit it but, believe me, they know it. Consider their most famous citizens.

Thor Heyerdahl jumped on a flimsy raft called the Kon Tiki and set off on a perilous journey across mighty oceans just to put distance between him and his homeland. Roald Amundsen's idea of a bit of light relief was to nip over to the snowy wastes of the South Pole. And Henrik Ibsen did not give the impression in his works that he was a bundle of laughs. I have sat, and slept, through Ibsen. Believe me, that man could never have written On The Buses.

And Finland? The least said the better. Time may come when I am required to go back there to perform.

I look on it as a stroke of extreme good fortune that I was able to set out on my voyages of discovery in the company of people whose moderate lifestyles fitted in with my own. In the wildest days of the new liberation, both in our lifestyles and sexual habits, bestowed on us all in the so called 'swinging sixties' I had locked in with a bunch of guys to whom boring was a state of excitement yet to be reached. And what is more they practised fidelity. Not only did they practise it, but they got it down to a fine art. A faithful rock and roll musician is a rare animal indeed. There have been more sightings of the Abominable Snowman.

The average member of a band thinks that monogamy is a kind of woodwork. But you'll never get them to own up to their Olympic standard philandering until caught with their hand in the metaphoric till or somewhere else even more unsavoury. They will swear to God that they are on the straight and narrow. And why on earth is anyone surprised? I mean, who are you going to be more afraid of? A god who you can't see or a wife who you can? God does not make you sleep on the sofa for a week. Besides, lying is a much overrated sin.

But my fellow workers spent their night times sitting in the hotel bedroom writing reams of affectionate prose to their wives and girlfriends back home in a sober script unbefuddled by booze or dubious medications. Any form of non-prescription drugs was an absolute no-no to us and even alcohol was something not to be abused too much or too often. Nuns would write to us for advice on better ways to conduct their lives. But it kept us looking pretty much okay and, more importantly, it kept us alive. The rock world is littered with talented corpses.

Dying young is a great career move but I wonder how many, given the choice, would opt for the early bath? There is a sizeable list of those that did not make it. I recall eavesdropping on an interview between a newspaperman and Ronnie Bond, the drummer with the legendary group The Troggs. Ronnie's life was sadly snuffed out ahead of time after an existence punctuated by a constant and heroic intake of alcohol. His liver finally held up a white flag of surrender and gave up under the strain. The reporter asked Mister Bond if he drank very much. The taciturn sticks man replied, 'Oh, I sometimes have a small sherry before dinner.'

Of course there are those who survive heroically against all odds. Keith Richards is a normal guy living by all accounts in the body of Superman. By all the rules of the game he should no longer be here. His face looks as though it belongs on the side of Mount Rushmore and has all the appearance of being chiselled out of the same material. With that kind of constitution it is an interesting hypothesis and a perfectly reasonable rationale that, maybe with an abstinent lifestyle and an eschewing of substance abuse, he could have ended up looking like Bonnie Langford's love child.

Mick Jagger seems to have been more moderate in his behaviour on the whole although the slim-hipped body that still would not look out of place on a tight-bummed Spanish bullfighter is propping up the face of a *shar pei* these days as he cavorts his way through his fifth decade. But even in these multi-millionaire times when the rebel consorts with the aristocracy and meets them on his own terms, Jagger is still of one the most important and enduring of the rock gods. And that is not an easy thing for a white lad from Dartford.

Rebellion, since the days of James Dean and before, has always offered a better chance of longevity. But there is no doubt that age, in the world of rock and roll, is a harder cross to bear if you are white. John Lee Hooker and B. B. King just pile on more street cred with every line in the cheek and furrow across the brow, the depths of their characters seemingly stretched and strengthened with the wizening of their faces and bodies. Age in the white man's world, on the other hand, means that your credibility rating tends to rush headlong towards the point where it is in danger of colliding with that of Val Doonican. But if you're not a rebel you're not a rebel and that's that. No use trying to fake it. Watch out Val Doonican, here I come. But I am alive and happy. I can't ask for more.

In spite of my having trotted the globe with a satisfying frequency over the years I have to hold my hand up and admit that I am a London boy at heart. I love the city with a passion that simmers gently and threatens to scald me into action if I stay away too long. I need my regular fix. It took a long time for me to realise and appreciate the delights of England's elegant and historic capital.

Back in the days of our greatest successes the clubs were the focal point for everyone's social life. Early evenings I would hang out at La Chasse, a tiny first floor drinking club in Wardour Street, just a few doors away from the famous Marquee. The Marquee was the venue where any group worth its salt built its reputation. In fact a reputation was accorded you simply because you had played there. The Searchers never played at The Marquee. We remained resolutely unsalted. It was a place for blues with maybe a touch of jazz occasionally. We were never blues and did not fit in with that image. In fact we hardly ever performed in London, apart from the theatres on one of the package tours or maybe a special concert at The Palladium.

From La Chasse I would drive on to The Cromwellian, a large four storey house in South Kensington that had been converted into private club with rooms for gaming on the upper floors. Most nights when the group was not working I would draw up in my 4.2 litre red E Type Jaguar roadster to show off my latest dent. I always had lots of dents. I never could get used to the length of the bonnet or the amount of width still out of sight beyond the graceful curve of the elegant cigar-shaped wing. Actually, it all boils down to the fact that I was, and still am, a crap driver.

I remember one particular dent acquired less than a quarter of a mile from the door of the club at the point where the Brompton Road and Knightsbridge form a T junction in front of the Brompton Oratory. I remember it especially because my opponent was a pristine white Silver Cloud Rolls Royce car. At least it was pristine until it met me. In my defence, your honour, the front of the Rolls bashed into my rear wing and the policeman who stood by the inoperative traffic lights with his hand up signalling me to halt was, in my opinion, obscured by the lamp standard. So, I still to this day do not believe it was entirely my fault. But it didn't cut any ice when it came to whose insurance was paying up. I definitely think it had more to do with the policeman holding his hand up than anything else. Another reason for remembering the incident was that the driver of the Silver Cloud was Larry Gelbart, the acclaimed writer of A Funny Thing Happened On The Way To The Forum and Mash. At least if you hit a celebrity it gives you a snippet of dinner conversation for years afterwards.

The 'Crom' was always heaving with people and atmosphere. Downstairs a band, usually The Steam Packet with Rod Stewart, Long John Baldry and Julie Driscoll on vocals, would be hammering out the latest American blues while on the ground floor Harry 'Heart', the camp barman who always accompanied his service with a toothy grin and a 'Thank you, darling heart', would be tending his domain like a mother hen. I would gulp down my molar-rotting colas at half a crown a time, I was still teetotal then, and chewed the fat with my chums. Alan Hudson, at that time the latest superstar of the Chelsea football club was my drinking buddy along with Peter Wyngarde who as Jason King, was the clothes horse star of the latest fad super agent series on television, Department S.

Jack Barry would hotfoot it down from the Marquee where he was manager as soon as he could lock up the joint. And Kenny Bell, an agent at the beginning of his empire building days back then, would sip on his vodka and tonic with the inscrutably dour look that suited his amusingly irascible, and loveable, personality. Kenny's small business was very soon to burgeon into one that controlled the careers of Roxy Music, The Jam, Jethro Tull, Rod Stewart, Culture Club and a whole bunch of others. Back then we were all just happy to be making a half-decent living out of something we enjoyed.

My clubbing days are now over and my car heads not towards a club but to the door of my favourite restaurant around which all social life is conducted. Unless of course I am taking advantage of the best theatre entertainment on offer anywhere in the world. I love the theatre. London, once the supporting player, has taken the crown from Broadway as the scene setter for what is happening in the world of the stage and, although I see more productions than most of my friends, I don't go nearly as much as I should. Most, but not all, of my theatrical pleasure has been generously provided by Bill Kenwright, the one time Coronation Street Star whose love of live theatre led him into one of the most cash-endangering professions anyone could be ill-advised to take on. He is a very brave man who I have a lot to thank for.

I enjoy the perks that fame or notoriety or simply money, even in the tiniest of degrees, can provide. I love the fact that I can get a table at The Ivy at short notice. If Joan Collins and I want the only spare table I'm sure she gets it. She certainly would if it were my restaurant. But I always know that if they can fit me in they will. And there are many who are envious of such a wonderfully superficial and pretentious power. Talk has it that the wealthy and the aristocratic no longer put their sons down at birth for a place at Eton. They now put them down for a table at The Ivy. It's all so silly, isn't it? The tat and the tinsel. But that's me, like it or lump it. Scrape away the phoney tinsel and underneath you'll find the real tinsel.

Occasionally I enjoy the delights of the city courtesy of friends who occupy a more privileged position than I do, and I am only grateful to clutch onto the coat tails of those whose sophistication and wealth outstrip mine by multiples squared. My good chums Steve and Lisa Voice entertain in the kind of manner God no doubt would if he had their kind of money. I used to be terribly overawed and nervous in the close proximity of such affluence but decided in the end that I should just go with the flow. My motto is 'when in Rome, be yourself'. Lisa lived for a decade with one of England's true icons of rock and roll music, Billy Fury, a relationship which only ended with Billy's early death. His heart, made weak by a boyhood illness, finally gave out and we lost a rare talent. Luckily Lisa found happiness again in a lasting marriage which was blessed by two children. She deserved her happiness.

As a boy my trips into the city were infrequent. We lived twelve miles out and city centres were not supposed to be for the likes of me, but gradually I gravitated in to gaze upon and marvel at the excitement and the sin that was available to me whenever I was willing to take it. These days I am happy to take the time to be a tourist in my own home town. When friends visit from abroad I am pleased to have the excuse of their convenience and pleasure to indulge myself in nostalgic wanderings that I might have missed since I was a young lad. I pretended to show them The Tower Of London and The Houses of Parliament when in fact I was showing myself.

Believe it or not there are times when I stay home. I love my house. The decoration was not the result of a designer's master plan and it did not happen overnight. It became what it is day by day over more than twenty years of providing a haven for myself. Chic probably isn't the word to apply here. Personal certainly is. This is my own comfort zone which has grown to fit me like a second skin and that skin, like the original, fits very nicely thank you.

The castle of this particular Englishman is tucked away behind a wall which is fifteen feet high and a century older than I am. And it is much more modest than that description makes it sound. The leaded windowpanes and the ageing timbers give an air of stability to both the building and my life. I have no wish to move yet, if ever. I keep my modest accruement of awards on display but in a room that the visitor does not necessarily walk through too often. I am extremely proud of them but don't want to be so crass as to shove them in people's faces. After all, awards are a little like haemorrhoids. In the end everybody gets one.

As a teenager growing up through the birth of rock and roll I would read with awe and envy of Johnny Cash whose ranch house in Tennessee was a bolt hole not only to himself but also to his friends. They would pass by and drop in for some fried chicken, a beer and some good conversation. A guitar would be taken from a corner and in that natural country manner old friends would find themselves singing and playing together in the way they did before the roll of the dice turned it into a profession.

The picking of guitar strings would be as tasty as the pickings on the leg of the chicken as they sang their songs in front of a big open fire, the logs crackling along with the beat. I was jealous. I wanted that for myself. And so I contrived to lure people out of their London cubby holes to the suburbs where I would wine and dine them and lull them into a false sense of security before closing the net. You have to provide a substantial feast to get Londoners to travel. I think it was Lady Rothermere who once opined that the new Regines in Kensington High Street would never be successful because it was so far out of London. And she was right. Most of the people I know require at least four weeks notice before they will make the trip to deepest Hillingdon. It is for them almost on a par with going on safari and therefore should not be undertaken lightly.

My cook, having placed before them dishes fit for, if not kings then certainly for discerning friends, slips off silently into the night while we, having eaten our fill, shift effortlessly into the den. Acoustic guitars have been placed conveniently to hand. I, or my most regular partner in crime Bruce Welch, will casually lift a guitar and strum a familiar intro while non-singing chums, like Daily Express showbusiness writer, David Wigg, puts his pen aside for the evening and claps along. Mr Wigg, one of the few souls of discretion in the newspaper industry, listens to the tempting morsels of dinner table gossip without any of us feeling the threat of publication. Which is just as well sometimes. Bruce, after years of pounding that poncy footwork behind Cliff Richard, has the kind of money that allows him to take things easy these days and life on the road is a fading memory of a distant past. The Shadows are no more and probably never will be again.

But once a musician, always a musician. The chance to play and to sing is an alluring prospect and twice as nice with no pressure to be good or to please anyone but yourself. It is on such occasions that Bruce and I, for a few precious moments, become the Everly Brothers. The fact that we probably sound more like the Kray Brothers is neither here nor there. It is a purely self-indulgent pastime which happens at the same time to please our friends. Or maybe our friends just lie very well. Sometimes the friends are extraordinary talents in their own right and the combinations over the years have been intriguing.

Paul Jones, at one dinner with his wife, the actress Fiona Hendley, was persuaded to run out to his car and retrieve his mouth organ. He did not want to seem presumptuous by having it in his pocket. He proceeded to play a wailing blues that altered my opinion of that particular instrument, if not forever then certainly while it was in his hands. Bruce and I, along with skiffle star Chas McDevitt chugged out a rhythm as Paul delivered his hit Pretty Flamingo. Chas took his turn and sang *Freight Train* for us, an anthem of my boyhood days when turning a hobby into a profession was nothing but a far fetched dream. Shirley Douglas who used to sing in The Chas McDevitt group added colour to the male harmonies and Henry Marsh, from the group Sailor, switched from his usual keyboards to guitar to help out.

That flamboyant wizard of the keyboards Bobby Crush, in between cursing my pleasant looking but mechanically imperfect baby grand, has spent many evenings here pounding out the ivories after dinner. He is quite relentless, although time after time we have begged him to relent. There is no one on earth who gives such good value or such good company as the ever young Master Crush. I have actually seen it written on walls that 'Bobby Crush gives good piano'.

We have had the deejay Mike Read providing backing for my old boss Cliff Bennett's still outrageously good rhythm and blues vocals while Ed Bicknell's drumming proved that he is capable of more than simply making Dire Straits and himself mega rich in his capacity as their manager. Things reached a personal pinnacle for me when Ed persuaded Mark Knopfler to grace one of our little soirées.

I had rehearsed Sultans Of Swing in readiness and was chord perfect. I even posted Bruce Welch a cassette of the track ahead of the day. But when I quietly whispered the suggestion to Mark during one of the lulls between songs he very subtly shook his head. I accepted defeat without argument. He wasn't being stubborn or pig-headed. He was simply too modest and too shy. It was enough that he was there. I managed to boob big time though by omitting to include songs that required solos. It was in the middle of *Hello Mary Lou*, when Mark's fingers leapt straight into the James Burton guitar break that I realised my gaffe, but by that time the champagne had kicked in and I was beyond repair. I had completely wasted one of the greatest guitar talents Great Britain has produced.

Peter Sarstedt, on the other hand, needs no persuasion to sing *Where Do You Go To My Lovely?* or any of the other beautiful melodies he has penned over the years. He, quite rightly, is proud of his work, is thrilled to be asked, and I in turn feel I am very privileged to be afforded a private performance in the comfort of my own home. Peter also has the most endearing habit of getting completely legless and always staves off departure till the next day. And why not indeed? We have room.

Dave Dee (without Dozy, Beaky, Mick & Tich). Mike Berry, who went on to star in Are You Being Served after his time as a pop star with Tribute To Buddy Holly. Tom McGuiness, one of Paul Jones' old cohorts in Manfred Mann. Chip Hawkes from The Tremeloes. Susie Mathis, my dearest friend who was once a Paper Doll. Songwriter Barry Mason of Delilah fame and so many others. Lyn Paul who, after years of fame with The New Seekers braved it on her own and ended up starring on the West End stage in Blood Brothers. The list is not exactly endless but it is pretty good. Lionel Blair has tapped his feet and added a vocal line or two. And, just to show there are no limits, we've even had Jess Conrad.

It is on evenings such as these that I have come to appreciate those slower times at home when, for a short while, the planes, the trains and the automobiles are left on the back burner with their engines ticking over in readiness. But not for too long. I am far from ready for retirement. Before I am whisked off to Brinsworth House to spend my dotage dribbling disgracefully out of one side of my mouth as I attempt to explain to my fellow theatricals how I absolutely killed them at Greaseborough Social Club in 1968, there is a lot more of the world I still want to see. And if I can't see new places then I am quite happy to revisit the ones whose acquaintance I have already made.

As a stranger in other people's lands I am nothing but a dilettante. Time has never allowed me to devour more than a morsel of the feast available. And maybe I am too fickle to invest such an amount of time. I enter and leave cities with all the commitment and conscience of a Casanova visiting the bedrooms of his lovers. I sneak in and I sneak out again. And when I have supped my fill I scuttle back to the reassuring haven of my roots and my comfort zones. Here I can rest and reflect and pretend that I have observed and digested much more than I really have. I am a fraud, a pretender and I am happy to allow myself that. I have enjoyed both the comings and the goings of my life. Its very nice to go travelling, but it's oh so nice to come home.

List of Illustrations

18 Jamming with Tony Sheridan in the 80s (Tony Sheridan and John McNally)
19 The Reeperbahn
20 Going by Cadillac to extend work visas, Hamburg, Jan 1963. From left: Dave Wendells, Moss Groves, Sid Phillips, Mick Burt and me
21 Me, Chubby (or is it Winnie?) and his manager Charlie
22 A singsong in the Basel hotel lounge with Susie Quatro, Kate (backing singer), Henry Marsh from Sailor and Susie's keyboard player, Reg
23 Me and Dusty at her house the night of the mysterious 'willie fiddling' incident
24 Getting friendly. Same night, same appalling clothes
25 Me and Smokey Robinson backstage at The Fox, 1964
26 With the Ronettes in their dressing room at The Fox
27 Eden Kane, John McNally and Mike Pender on Hollywood Boulevard, 1964
28 Chris Curtis, Me and John McNally on Hollywood Boulevard, 1964
29 Tired little Hectors on the way home from Australia, 1964. Me and John McNally
30 The Araneta Colosseum, Philippines, 1966
31 A big welcome at Manila Airport. Bobby Grimald, John McNally, me, and Mike Pender
32 The fateful press conference. Julie Rogers, Me, John McNally and Chris Curtis.
33 Mr Araneta, Mike Pender (seated), John McNally, me, and Barry Delaney (seated)
34 Barry Delaney in Julie Rogers' knickers
35 A week of capacity crowds at the Araneta Coliseum, Philippines
36 The Rolling Stones in those mangy kangaroo coats
37 Lunch by the Red Sea. Me, Barry Delaney, John McNally
38 Nazareth High Street. Me and Mike Pender
39 Trying not to get cheated by Tito Burns at chess
40 Ready Steady Go with John Blunt on drums
41 The 'chest from hell'
42 Our 'superior accommodation', Vitez.
43 'spammed up' for action. Back - C.S.E. crew, Under Wraps, Christina, John and Lyn from Lynx. Front - Billy, Phil (Searchers' roadie), John, me, Spencer and 'fearless leader' Richard Asbury

44   A café in Tomislavgrad - the town formerly known as 'shithole'
45   R&R in Tent City (Ploce)
46   Perks of the job. From left, Spencer James, John McNally, Lyn
      (Lynx), Billy Adamson and me
47   The forces' sweethearts. Eat your heart out Vera Lynn
48   Mummy's special soldier
49   Recording at Rockfield. Me, John McNally and Pat Moran
50   With Lonnie Donegan and Lulu at the Royal Variety Show, 1981
51   Hank Marvin, Bruce Welch and John McNally, Royal Variety Show
52   Fans in high places. Being presented to H.M. Queen Elizabeth II,
      Royal Variety Show
(below) - Touring chums in the U.S.A. 1965
53   ...with Tom Jones, Norfolk, Virginia
54   ...with Peter Asher and Brian Hyland, Norfolk, Virginia
55   The Beach Boys, Jacksonville
56   The Shangrilas, Jacksonville
57   Arthur Alexander
58   Sam The Sham, Jacksonville
59   ...with Bobby Vee, Oklahoma
60   Lesley Gore, Jacksonville
61   Billy Joe Royal
62   With Jackie De Shannon, who originally recorded *Needles & Pins*
      and wrote *When You Walk In The Room*, Heathrow, 1965
63   '86 British Invasion Tour press conference, Kennedy Airport
64   The Café La Fortuna, New York
65   Card from La Fortuna
66   USA Tour Buses
67   Our sleeping shelves
68   Whiling away the endless hours on the road
69   A singalong round the pool with Gerry Marsden, Phoenix, Arizona,
      1986
70   Relaxing in Tijuana, 1986. Me, Billy Adamson, John McNally
71   With Marie Osmond recording Solid Gold in L.A. 1986
72   On stage on a Solid Silver Sixties show
73   The finale. Pacemakers, Billy J. Kramer, Gerry and The Searchers
74   End of tour party at The Palladium, 1993. Back row: Paul Walden,
      (Flying Music), Billy Adamson, Spencer James, John McNally. Front
      row: Gerry Marsden, Billy J. Kramer, me, Derek Nicol (Flying
      Music)

75   Spencer James, John McNally, Helen Shapiro on the 1998 Solid Silver Sixties Tour
76   Backstage visitors at the Fairfield Halls, Croydon, Peter Sarstedt and Adam Faith, 1998
77   Touring, 1965 style. Searchers, Zombies, Heinz and others pull in for a 'cuppa'
78   Paul Atkinson (Zombies), Bobby Vee, me and one of Dusty Springfield's musicians, 1965
79   Programme cover for Searchers / Dionne Warwick /Isley Brothers / Zombies tour 1964
80   The famous Raffles Hotel, Singapore
81   The Hong Kong skyline
82   John McNally, my ladyfriend Lee Lowsley and me by the temples of Bangkok
83   Me, Lee Lowsley, Mary and John McNally sampling the bars of Pattaya
84   A Bangkok riverboat, powered by Chevrolet
85   A grand old lady. Canberra in Gibraltar
86   Working hard on Canberra
87   A first class lady in a first class cabin. Edwina C. Trout, survivor of The Titanic
88   John and Mike posing by my red E-type Jaguar, 1967
89   Falklands, Chinook and 'tardis'
90   Alternative transport. A Tornado
(below) - If Music Be The Food Of Love - Rock On...
91   Singing for their supper - clockwise from top left, Bruce Welch (Shadows), Ed Bicknell (Manager of Dire Straits), Susie Mathis (The Paper Dolls), Mark Knopfler, Shirley Douglas (The Chas McDevitt Skiffle Group), Chas McDevitt. Centre - Me
92   Mike Berry, Peter Sarstedt
93   from left: David Wigg (The Express), Fiona Hendley, Paul Jones, Henry Marsh (Sailor), Bruce Welch, Shirley Douglas, me.
94   from left: Dave Dee, me, Chip Hawkes (Tremeloes), Bruce Welch.
95   Lionel Blair, Helen Worth, Bobby Crush
96   Me and Mike Read
97   Me and John, partners in musical crime
98   My first day with The Searchers, August 3rd 1964, The Coventry Theatre. Mike Pender, John McNally, Chris Curtis and me

Index